GOLF

D0519392

THE FAMILY LEISURE GUIDE

A golfers guide to courses in the United Kingdom which welcome visitors, and the major leisure attractions around each course

Published in association with the National Tourist Boards of England, Scotland, Wales and Northern Ireland

This second edition published in 1992
by Charles Letts & Co Ltd,
Letts of London House,
Parkgate Road,
London SW11 4NQ

First edition published in 1990
by Robertson McCarta Ltd
122 King's Cross Road, London WC1X 9DS

Published in association with the National Tourist
Boards of England, Scotland, Wales and Northern
Ireland.

© The Pen & Ink Book Company Ltd,
Whitwell Chambers, Ferrars Road, Huntingdon,
Cambs PE18 6DH.

A CIP catalogue record for this book is available
from the British Library.

ISBN 1 85238 326 7

'Letts' is a registered trademark of Charles Letts &
Co Limited.

Research – James Tindall
Cartography – Lovell Johns Ltd., Oxford
Photographs
BTA/Britain in View
The Professional Golfers Association
Trevose Golf and Country Club
Manor House Golf Club
The Belfry
John O'Gaunt Golf Club
Windermere Golf Club
St Mellion Golf and Country Club
St Pierre Hotel Golf and Country Club
Aberdovey Golf Club
St Andrews Links
The Turnberry Hotel Golf Courses
The Edzell Golf Club
Royal Dornoch Golf Club

Design and production PEN & INK

Printed and bound in Great Britain

GUIDE TO SYMBOLS

☎ telephone	🎟 admission charged	✗ catering
i tourist information	🎟 no charge	▶18 18-hole golf course
P car parking	♿ disabled access	▶9 9-hole golf course
🚌 guided tours	♿ disabled facilities	➔A nearest 'A' road

Welcome to the new edition of GOLF – THE FAMILY LEISURE GUIDE. The first edition proved popular and useful and I hope that this new edition will enable you to increase your enjoyment of the golfing world. Once again the book has been produced in association with the four National Tourist Boards and they have checked and up-dated the 'What to see and do' sections to ensure that the information on other leisure attractions is as accurate as possible.

GOLF – THE FAMILY LEISURE GUIDE has been created to serve as a practical information source for golfing enthusiasts who like to combine the enjoyment of their favourite sport with holiday breaks around the country for the whole family.

It is not intended to be an exhaustive guide to the golf courses of the UK; there are many fine guides of this type available already.

It is intended to be a guide to golf clubs that welcome visiting players on to their course throughout the week and at weekends with few restrictions and without the need to be accompanied by a member of the club. In the first edition and in this new edition we have adhered to these selection criteria very strictly which is why you will find that some 'famous name' clubs are not included.

We are keen to extend the coverage of golf clubs that meet our criteria and as a result of the efforts of the Wales Tourist Board the coverage of clubs in Wales in the new edition is much improved.

What you can be certain of is that the courses listed in this Guide will welcome you as a visitor and by using this Guide you will be able to play a wide range of different types of courses across the whole country.

The first part of the Guide contains detailed descriptions of over 130 golf clubs organised into 48 geographical areas from Cornwall to Northern Ireland. Each golf club entry includes details on the location, course facts, green fees, restrictions on visiting players including handicap requirements, course facilities, food and drink at the club and information on any other leisure facilities the club offers. We have introduced a new cross-referencing symbol onto the golf course pages to direct you straight to the pages in the second part

of the Guide that relate to each golf course.

The second part of the guide is again organised by geographical location and contains information about major sporting, leisure and recreational facilities that can be found within approximately 15 miles of the course. Up to 50 different leisure facilities are covered ranging from historic houses and museums through racecourses and fishing locations to ballooning and hang gliding.

All the information on the golf clubs has been re-researched during Summer and Autumn 1991 and is as accurate and up-to-date as possible. The information on the green fees has been provided by the clubs and in many cases the 1992 prices had not been finalised before the guide went to press. The prices quoted are therefore the 1991 price and you should expect some increase in 1992.

We would be delighted to hear from any golf club secretaries who would like to have their club included in the next edition of the Guide.

Even when it is not specifically stated in the individual club entry it is always advisable to contact the club in advance to check on accessibility – many of the courses we have listed are popular venues for Competitions and Society Days.

Two other points worth noting from the listings are: first, that weekend green fees invariably also apply on Bank Holidays; and, second, that where weekly green fees are quoted these sometimes cover a 5-day weekday period and sometimes a full 7 days, you should check with the club which method they use.

Golfing photographs included in the Guide are of golfers enjoying a round of golf and are not necessarily shots of the club on whose pages they appear.

The information on the leisure facilities around each golf club has also been re-researched during 1991. This information is not intended to be exhaustive, merely to show the range of leisure activities available in each area. If you feel that we have missed out a major facility that should be included please let us know and we will include it in the next edition.

Many roads in the country have been re-numbered, particularly around the Oxfordshire area with the opening of the M40 extension and in view of this we have created a totally new atlas section at the end of the Guide.

The individual location maps for each golf club have not been replaced as these are designed merely to show the actual position of the club.

Finally, I would like to thank the Secretaries and Professionals of the individual golf clubs for the great assistance they have given in the creation of this new edition.

CONTENTS

CONTENTS

ENGLAND

Manor House Golf Club

The English golf clubs covered in this Guide range geographically from the Lizard Peninsula in Cornwall to Bamburgh Castle in Northumberland and from Kingsdown near Dover in Kent to Silloth on Solway in Cumbria.

In between there are representatives of every type of golf course from links to parkland including championship courses like Royal Birkdale and many friendly local courses.

Some courses such as the Belfry, the Gloucester Hotel and St. Mellion have extensive leisure facilities for visitors to enjoy whilst other clubs offer more modest but equally enjoyable facilities in their clubhouses.

Two themes link all the English golf clubs in this Guide:

- They all welcome visitors with very few restrictions
- Thanks to the motorway and A-road system in England they are all relatively easily accessible

Enjoy your golf in England, we hope that this Guide will help you to select some interesting and challenging locations.

Please let us know of any clubs which you feel deserve inclusion in future editions of this Guide. This particularly applies to the counties through which the M25 passes, especially Surrey, Buckinghamshire, Hertfordshire and Essex. There are many fine golf clubs in these counties but most of them, unfortunately, have tight restrictions on visiting players, particularly at weekends, and therefore cannot be included in this Guide.

SOUTH WEST CORNWALL

South West Cornwall with its dramatic coastal and moorland scenery, colourful fishing ports, stone-walled farmland and national parks has many fine links courses for the visitor to enjoy.

TREVOSE GOLF AND COUNTRY CLUB

Constantine Bay
Padstow
Cornwall
☎ 0841 520208

The Trevose Golf and Country Club complex is a seaside golf course with links-like fairways and views of the Atlantic Ocean. There are two golf courses, a championship 18-hole course and a 9-hole short course. The complex also includes tennis, swimming and excellent clubhouse facilities and shops as well as self-catering accommodation for rent.

THE COURSE

	Course 1 ⚑18	Course 2 ⚑9
Yds	6461	1357
Par	71	29
SSS	71	

VISITING PLAYERS

Restrictions

There are some closed events from October to May but these normally only affect Sunday mornings. Visitors should telephone the club number to check if play is affected by Society or Special Days.

Handicap requirements

A Certificate of Handicap is required by all visitors, a maximum 24 for men and 36 for women.

How to contact the club

Telephone call or letter.

GETTING THERE

Road: Off the B3276 Padstow to Newquay road, 5 miles from Padstow

COURSE FACILITIES

The Professional, Gary Alliss, can be contacted via the Pro Shop telephone number; tuition fees are £12–£15 per half hour. The Pro Shop is fully equipped and equipment can be hired for about £5 per round. Changing rooms are also available.
☎ 0841 520261 for the Pro Shop

Leisure facilities

The leisure facilities available include 3 hard tennis courts, advance booking recommended; an open air heated swimming pool, open from May to September; a snooker room; a children's games room with table tennis, pool, etc; and a ladies fashion boutique.

Self-catering cottages, bungalows and flats offer accommodation for up to 110 people in units varying from 2-beds to 6-beds; advance booking is essential.

Food and drink

A fully licensed bar and dining room overlooks the 18th green, it is open during licensing hours.

GREEN FEES

	Course 1	Course 2
Per weekday	£20– £28	£8–£12
Per weekend day	£20– £28	£8–£12
Per week	£90–£120	£35–£45

Note: Prices vary with season, June to September is the most expensive. Children are charged half the adult fees.

Methods of payment: cash/cheque with valid banker's card/Visa/Access/Mastercard

WEST CORNWALL GOLF CLUB

Lelant
Nr St. Ives
Cornwall
☎ 0736 753401

West Cornwall Golf Club has an 18-hole seaside links course overlooking St. Ives Bay. It welcomes visiting players without restriction.

THE COURSE

Yds 5854   Par 69   SSS 68

VISITING PLAYERS

Restrictions

Visiting players are welcome without restriction and need not book in advance. During the busy summer months however, it is wise to telephone the club number and check on accessibility.

Handicap requirements

Visitors must possess a Certificate of Handicap.

How to contact the club

Telephone call or letter.

GETTING THERE

Road: Off the A3074 Lelant to St. Ives road, on the north side of Lelant village

COURSE FACILITIES

The Professional can be contacted on 0736 753177 for details of tuition fees and information about other facilities which include a Pro Shop, equipment hire, a 3-hole practice course and changing rooms.

Food and drink

The Clubhouse Bar is open during normal licensing hours; it also serves snacks. The restaurant serves lunch and dinner every day.

Leisure facilities

The Clubhouse has a snooker table.

GREEN FEES

Per weekday round 🏌 £16
Per weekday 🏌 £21
Per weekend round 🏌 £21
Per weekend day 🏌 £27
Per week 🏌 £53

Methods of payment: cash/cheque with valid bankers card

MULLION GOLF CLUB

Cury
Helston
Cornwall
☎ 0326 240685

Mullion Golf Club has an 18-hole seaside links course overlooking Mounts Bay. There are very few restrictions for visitors.

THE COURSE

Yds 6022   Par 69   SSS 67

VISITING PLAYERS

Restrictions

Visitors must telephone the Professional's number to check for Competition Days or Society Days, other than this there are no restrictions.

Handicap requirements

A Certificate of Handicap is required by all visitors although there is no stated maximum.

How to contact the club

Telephone the Professional's number.

GETTING THERE

Road: Off the A3083 Helston to Lizard road, just south of Culdrose Naval Air Station, signposted

COURSE FACILITIES

The Professional, Mike Singleton, can be contacted by telephone for details of tuition fees and information about all other facilities which include a new Pro Shop, equipment hire and changing rooms.
☎ 0326 240276 for the Professional

Food and drink

The bar and restaurant serves both snacks and full meals. It is open all day every day between May and September. Opening hours are restricted to normal licensing hours during the winter.

GREEN FEES

Per weekday 🏌 £16.50
Per week 🏌 £57.50
Per weekend day 🏌 £16.50

Methods of payment: cash/cheque with valid bankers card

9

This border area is dominated by Dartmoor, a designated National Park and the largest stretch of open country remaining in southern England. Attractive market towns, remote villages and richly contrasting scenery make it an inviting area to explore.

ST MELLION GOLF AND COUNTRY CLUB

St. Mellion
Saltash
Cornwall
☎ 0579 50101

The St. Mellion Golf and Country Club has two 18-hole courses, one of which was designed by Jack Nicklaus. The complex includes a hotel, luxury lodges and extensive leisure facilities.

GETTING THERE

Road: Off the A388 Saltash to Callington road, north of St. Mellion village

THE COURSE

	Nicklaus Course ⛳18	Old Course ⛳18
Yds	6626	5927
Par	72	70
SSS	72	68

VISITING PLAYERS

Restrictions

Visitors should contact the club to book a start time, this is the only restriction.

Handicap requirements

A Certificate of Handicap is required by all visitors although there is no stated maximum.

How to contact the club

Telephone call, letter or fax.
Fax number 0579 50116

COURSE FACILITIES

The Professional, Tony Moore, can be contacted via the club telephone number for details of tuition fees and information about all other facilities which include a Pro Shop, changing rooms, equipment hire and golfing buggy hire. Tuition fees are £9 per half hour.

Food and drink

The complex includes a number of bars and restaurants. The Sports Bar and Golf Bar are two informal bars used by players immediately after, or during, their rounds; golfing dress and footwear are allowed in these bars. The Lounge Bar overlooks the 18th green of the Nicklaus course, formal dress is required.

The restaurant also overlooks the 18th green of the Nicklaus course and is open for lunch and dinner, formal dress is required. The Grill Room has a more relaxed atmosphere and serves meals from 12 noon until 10pm. The coffee shop overlooking the swimming pool is open all day and serves snacks and light refreshments.

Leisure facilities

The complex has extensive leisure facilities including all-weather tennis courts, squash courts, badminton courts, 2 snooker tables and an indoor swimming pool with sauna and solarium.

There is a 3-star 24-bedroom hotel and 30 luxury lodges; telephone the club number for prices and reservations.

GREEN FEES

Nicklaus Course per round ⛳ £50
Old Course per round ⛳ £17.50

Note: Hotel guests are eligible for 1 free round on the Old Course during each day of their stay; weekly rates for both courses are available, telephone the club number for details.

Methods of payment: cash/cheque with valid banker's card/Visa/Access/Mastercard

MANOR HOUSE GOLF CLUB

Manor House Hotel
Moretonhampstead
Devon
☎ 0647 40355

The Manor House Golf Club has a pleasant 18-hole parkland course.

GETTING THERE

Road: Off the B3212 Moretonhampstead to Two Bridges road, 2 miles south-west of Moretonhampstead

THE COURSE

Yds 6016 Par 69 SSS 69

VISITING PLAYERS

Restrictions

Visitors must telephone the club number in advance to book a start time any day of the week, this is the only restriction.

Handicap requirements

A Certificate of Handicap is required for all visitors at weekends, maximum 28 for men and 36 for women.

How to contact the club

Telephone call.

COURSE FACILITIES

Telephone the club telephone number for details of the Professional and information about other facilities available which include a Pro Shop, changing rooms, equipment and golfing buggy hire. Tuition fees are £8.75 per half hour.

Food and drink

The Clubhouse Bar is open from 11am to 11pm Mondays to Saturdays and during normal licensing hours on Sundays. The restaurant is open every day.

Leisure facilities

The Manor House Hotel is a luxurious 69-bedroom country house hotel – telephone the club number for details of prices and reservations.

The leisure facilities available at the hotel and in the club grounds include squash courts, hardcourt tennis courts, a snooker and pool room, fishing and a croquet lawn.

GREEN FEES

Per weekday round 🏌 £21.50
Per weekday 🏌 £25
Per weekend round 🏌 £25.50
Per weekend day 🏌 £31.50

Note: Children's green fees are £10 per day any day.

Methods of payment: cash/cheque with valid banker's card

TAVISTOCK GOLF CLUB

Down Road
Tavistock
Devon
☎ 0822 612049

Tavistock Golf Club has an 18-hole downland course set on the south-western edge of Dartmoor; it welcomes visitors without restrictions.

GETTING THERE

Road: On Whitcombe Down, 1 mile south-east of Tavistock town centre

THE COURSE

Yds 6250 Par 70 SSS 70

VISITING PLAYERS

Restrictions

There are no restrictions on visiting players other than the need to contact the club in advance to reserve a start time.

Handicap requirements

A Certificate of Handicap is required by all visitors although there is no stated maximum.

How to contact the club

Telephone call or letter.

COURSE FACILITIES

The Professional can be contacted by telephone for details of tuition fees and information about all other facilities which include a Pro Shop, equipment hire and changing rooms.
☎ 0822 612316 for the Professional

Food and drink

The Clubhouse Bar serves drinks and snacks and is open every day during normal licensing hours. The restaurant is also open every day and serves a full range of meals.

Leisure facilities

The Clubhouse has a snooker table.

GREEN FEES

Per weekday 🏌 £15
Per weekend day 🏌 £25

Methods of payment: cash/cheque with valid banker's card/Visa/Access/Mastercard

THURLESTONE GOLF CLUB

Thurlestone
Kingsbridge
Devon
☎ 0548 560405

Thurlestone Golf Club is an 18-hole coastal downlands course offering good golf with fine views and good club facilities.

GETTING THERE

Road: Off the A379 Plymouth to Kingsbridge road, south of Thurlestone village, on the coast

THE COURSE

Yds 6303   Par 70   SSS 70

VISITING PLAYERS

Restrictions

Visitors are not allowed on the course before 9.30am any day; Wednesday each week is Ladies Day; the course is closed to visitors when Club Competitions are underway. Telephone the club number to check.

Handicap requirements

A Certificate of Handicap is required by all visitors, a maximum 28 for men and 36 for women.

How to contact the club

Telephone call or letter.

COURSE FACILITIES

The Professional can be contacted by telephone for details of tuition fees and information about all other facilities which include a well-equipped Pro Shop, equipment hire and changing rooms.
☎ 0548 560715 for the Professional

Food and drink

The Clubhouse Bar is open during normal licensing hours. The restaurant serves lunches, snacks and teas between 10am and 5.30pm.

GREEN FEES

Per weekday round 🏌 £20
Per weekday 🏌 £20
Per weekend day 🏌 £20
Note: Children are charged half the adult fees.

Methods of payment: cash/cheque with valid banker's card

YELVERTON GOLF CLUB

Golf Links Road
Yelverton
Devon
☎ 0822 852824

Yelverton Golf Club is an 18-hole inland moorland course on the south-western edge of Dartmoor. It offers good golf in an exposed position subject to high winds. Visitors are welcome at all times.

GETTING THERE

Road: Off the A386 Plymouth to Tavistock road, 1 mile south of Yelverton village, signposted

THE COURSE

Yds 6288   Par 70   SSS 70

VISITING PLAYERS

Restrictions

There are no restrictions for visitors.

Handicap requirements

A Certificate of Handicap is required by all visitors, a maximum 28 for men and 36 for women.

How to contact the club

Telephone call or letter.

COURSE FACILITIES

The Professional can be contacted on 0822 853593; tuition fees are £10 per half hour. There is a well-equipped Pro Shop and equipment can be hired, contact the club for charges. Changing rooms are also available.

Food and Drink

The Clubhouse Bar is open from 11.30am to 2pm and 5pm to 10pm each day. The restaurant is open for lunch between 11.30am and 2pm each day but will only serve dinner by prior arrangement; snacks are available during the day.

GREEN FEES

Per weekday 🏌 £15
Per weekend day 🏌 £20
Note: Children's green fees are £6 per weekday only.

Methods of payment: cash/cheque with valid banker's card

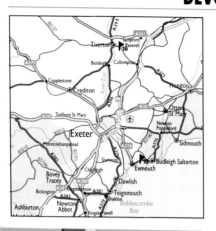

EAST DEVON GOLF CLUB

North View Road
Budleigh Salterton
Devon
☎ 03954 3370

The East Devon Golf Club has an 18-hole downland course; it welcomes visitors without restriction.

GETTING THERE

Road: Off the A376 Budleigh Salterton to Exmouth road just to the west of Budleigh Salterton town centre, on the coast

THE COURSE

Yds 6214   Par 70   SSS 70

VISITING PLAYERS

Restrictions

There are no restrictions on visiting players except that they must contact the club in advance to reserve a start time.

Handicap requirements

A Certificate of Handicap or a letter of introduction from their own club is required by all visiting players.

How to contact the club

Telephone call or letter.

COURSE FACILITIES

The Professional can be contacted by telephone for details of tuition fees and information about all other facilities which include a Pro Shop, equipment hire and changing rooms.
☎ 03954 3370 for the Professional

Food and drink

The Clubhouse Bar serves snacks and is open daily during normal licensing hours. The dining room serves lunch and tea every day.

GREEN FEES

Per weekday 🏷 £25
Per weekend day 🏷 £30

Methods of payment: cash/cheque with valid banker's card

TIVERTON GOLF CLUB

Post Hill
Tiverton
Devon
☎ 0884 252187

Tiverton Golf Club has an 18-hole parkland course. It welcomes visitors with few restrictions.

GETTING THERE

Road: Off the B3391 Tiverton to Halberton road, 3 miles east of Tiverton town centre

THE COURSE

Yds 6263   Par 73   SSS 73

VISITING PLAYERS

Restrictions

The club is popular and holds a number of Competition and Society Days during which it is closed to visiting players. Visitors must contact the club in advance to check availability and reserve a start time.

Handicap requirements

A Certificate of Handicap is required by all visiting players although there is no stated maximum.

How to contact the club

Telephone call or letter.

COURSE FACILITIES

The Professional can be contacted by telephone for details and information about all other facilities which include a Pro Shop, equipment hire and changing rooms.
☎ 0884 254836 for the Professional

Food and drink

The Clubhouse Bar serves drinks and snacks and is open every day. The restaurant is open every day for lunch and tea only.

GREEN FEES

Per weekday 🖱 £20
Per weekend day 🖱 £26

Methods of payment: cash/cheque with valid banker's card

Dorset remains a private and rural county with distinctive seaside resorts and quiet villages of thatched and limewashed cottages. The timeless quality of this area, captured so effectively in the novels and poetry of Thomas Hardy, is guaranteed to enchant.

FERNDOWN GOLF CLUB

119 Golf Links Road
Ferndown
Dorset
☎ 0202 874602

Ferndown Golf Club has 2 heathland courses, the 18-hole Old Course and the 9-hole, 18-tee, New Course. It welcomes visitors but numbers are restricted at weekends.

GETTING THERE

Road: Off the A347 Ferndown to Bournemouth road, just south of Ferndown

THE COURSE

	Old Course ▶18	New Course ▶9
Yds	6442	5604
Par	71	70
SSS	71	68

VISITING PLAYERS

Restrictions

Thursday is Ladies Day and visitors are not permitted on the courses. The number of visiting players allowed on the courses at weekends is limited and you should telephone the club number to reserve a start time for Saturdays or Sundays.

Handicap requirements

A Certificate of Handicap is required by all visitors, a maximum 28 for men and 36 for women.

How to contact the club

Telephone call.

COURSE FACILITIES

The Professional, Doug Sewell, can be contacted by telephone for details of charges and information about all other facilities which include a Pro Shop, changing rooms and equipment hire.
☎ 0202 873825 for the Professional

Food and drink

The fully licensed Clubhouse Bar is open from 11am to 9pm in the summer and from 11am to 6pm in the winter, it also serves snacks. The dining room serves lunches but will only provide dinner by prior arrangement.

GREEN FEES

	Old Course	New Course
Per weekday	£30	£15
Per weekend day	£35	£20

Methods of payment: cash/cheque with valid banker's card

15

SHERBORNE GOLF CLUB

Higher Clatcombe
Sherborne
Dorset
☎ 0935 814431

Sherborne Golf Club has an 18-hole parkland course. It welcomes visitors with few restrictions.

GETTING THERE

Road: Off the B3145 Sherborne to Wincanton road, 2 miles north of Sherborne

THE COURSE

Yds 5776   Par 70   SSS 68

VISITING PLAYERS

Restrictions

The course is closed to visiting players on Society Days. It is essential to contact the club in advance to check on accessibility and book a start time.

Handicap requirements

A Certificate of Handicap is required by all visitors although there is no stated maximum.

How to contact the club

Telephone call or letter.

COURSE FACILITIES

The Professional can be contact on 0935 812274 for details of tuition fees and information about all other facilities which include a Pro Shop, a practice area, equipment hire and changing rooms.

Food and drink

The Clubhouse Bar is open every day and serves snacks. Full lunches and tea are available every day but dinner can only be provided by prior arrangement.

GREEN FEES

Per weekday 🏌 £18
Per weekend day 🏌 £23
Methods of payment: cash/cheque with valid banker's card

ISLE OF PURBECK GOLF CLUB

Studland
Swanage
Dorset
☎ 0929 44361

The Isle of Purbeck Golf Club has an undulating moorland location with superb views over Forestry Commission land to Studland Bay and Poole Harbour. It has both an 18-hole and a 9-hole course and welcomes visitors with few restrictions.

GETTING THERE

Road: Off the B3351 Corfe Castle to Studland road, 4 miles east of Corfe Castle

THE COURSE

	Course 1 🏌18	Course 2 🏌9
Yds	6248	2022
Par	70	30
SSS	71	30

VISITING PLAYERS

Restrictions

Visitors playing on the 18-hole course must possess a Certificate of Handicap.

Handicap requirements

A Certificate of Handicap is required for the 18-hole course, although there is no stated maximum.

How to contact the club

Telephone call or letter.

COURSE FACILITIES

The Professional can be contacted via the club telephone number for details of tuition fees and information about all other facilities which include a Pro Shop, equipment hire and changing rooms.

Food and drink

The Clubhouse Bar is well-equipped, it includes a bar which is open for drinks and light refreshments all day 7 days a week from 11am onwards. The restaurant is open for lunch from 12 noon to 2pm and for tea and supper from 4pm to 6pm, meals can be served later by prior arrangement.

GREEN FEES

	Course 1	Course 2
Per weekday	£27.50	£8.50
Per weekend day	£32.50	£10.50
Per week	£165	

Note: Children's fees are approximately half price on Course 1 and £1.50 per day cheaper on Course 2.

Methods of payment: cash/cheque with valid banker's card/Access/Mastercard

Somerset and Avon, situated round the mouth of the Bristol Channel, offers visitors the facilities of major seaside towns with landscapes as diverse as the Quantock Hills and the undulating, unspoilt, little-visited countryside along the Severn Estuary to explore.

BURNHAM & BERROW GOLF CLUB

St. Christopher's Way
Burnham-on-Sea
Somerset
☎ 0278 785760

Burnham & Berrow Golf Club has a coastal location with views across Bridgewater Bay. It has 2 courses, a championship 18-hole course and a 9-hole course set in sand dunes with links fairways. It is well-equipped for visitors although there are some restrictions on the 18-hole course.

GETTING THERE

Road: Off the B3140 to the north of Burnham-on-Sea, on the coast

THE COURSE

	Course 1 ▶18	Course 2 ▶9
Yds	6327	3275
Par	71	36
SSS	72	

VISITING PLAYERS

Restrictions

There are no restrictions for visitors on the 9-hole course. Visitors are restricted to starting after certain times on the 18-hole course: after 9.45am on Mondays, Wednesdays, Thursdays and Fridays; after 11am on Tuesdays; after 2.30pm on Saturdays and after 10.30am on Sundays.

Handicap requirements

A Certificate of Handicap is required by all visitors, a maximum 22 for men and 28 for women.

How to contact the club

Telephone call or letter.

COURSE FACILITIES

The Professional can be contacted on 0278 784545 for details of tuition fees and all other facilities which include a Pro Shop, changing rooms and equipment hire.

Food and drink

The Clubhouse Bar and restaurant are open for the service of drinks, light refreshments, snacks and meals between 11am and 6pm every day; dinners can only be served by prior arrangement.

GREEN FEES

	Course 1	Course 2
Per round	£26	£8
Per weekday	£26	£8
Per weekend day	£36	£8
Per week	£150	

Note: Green fees per fortnight are £280; children are charged half the adult fee.

Methods of payment: cash/cheque with valid banker's card

17

SOMERSET/AVON

MINEHEAD AND WEST SOMERSET GOLF CLUB

The Warren
Minehead
Somerset
☎ 0643 702057

The Minehead and West Somerset Golf Club has a flat 18-hole seaside links course overlooking Bridgewater Bay. It welcomes visitors without restriction.

GETTING THERE

Road: 1 mile east of Minehead town centre, on the coast

THE COURSE

Yds 6137   Par 69   SSS 70

VISITING PLAYERS

Restrictions

Visiting players are welcome at any time. Advance booking is not required but in the summer months it is advisable to telephone the club number to check how busy the course is before setting out.

Handicap requirements

A Certificate of Handicap is not required by visiting players.

How to contact the club

Telephone call.

COURSE FACILITIES

The Professional can be contacted by telephone for details of tuition fees and information about all other facilities which include a Pro Shop, equipment hire and changing rooms.
☎ 0643 704378 for the Professional

Food and drink

The Clubhouse Bar is open every day for drinks and snacks; full lunches are also served.

GREEN FEES

Per weekday 🏌 £17.50
Per weekend day 🏌 £20.50
After 2.30 pm £12.50 all week

Methods of payment: cash/cheque with valid banker's card

WESTON-SUPER-MARE GOLF CLUB

Uphill Road North
Weston-super-Mare
Avon
☎ 0934 626968

Weston-super-Mare Golf Club has an 18-hole seaside links course overlooking Weston Bay. It welcomes visitors with few restrictions.

GETTING THERE

Road: Off the A370 Weston-super-Mare to Bridgwater road, just south of Weston-super-Mare town centre, on the coast

THE COURSE

Yds 6152   Par 70   SSS 70

VISITING PLAYERS

Restrictions

Visitors should telephone the club number to check for Competition and Society Days; other than this there are no restrictions.

Handicap requirements

A Certificate of Handicap is required by all visitors at weekends, although there is no stated maximum. Weekday visitors should supply either a Certificate of Handicap or a letter of introduction from their own club.

How to contact the club

Telephone call or letter.

COURSE FACILITIES

The Professional can be contacted by telephone for details of tuition fees and information about all other facilities which include a Pro Shop, an indoor practice net, equipment hire and changing rooms. Tuition fees are £7 per half hour.
☎ 0934 633360 for the Professional

Food and drink

The Clubhouse has 2 bars and a restaurant all of which are open all day. The restaurant serves breakfast, lunch, tea and dinner at the appropriate times of the day.

GREEN FEES

Per weekday 🏌 £20   Per week 🏌 £60
Per weekend day 🏌 £28

Methods of payment: cash/cheque with valid banker's card

Avon incorporates both the ancient and modern city of Bristol and Britain's most complete and best-preserved Georgian city, Bath, famous since Roman times for its mineral springs. Soaked in history with celebrated architecture these cities are surrounded by pleasant countryside.

BATH GOLF CLUB

Sham Castle
North Road
Bath
Avon
☎ 0225 463834

Bath Golf Club was founded in 1880 and has an 18-hole downland course on high ground overlooking the city. It welcomes visitors with few restrictions.

GETTING THERE

Road: Off the A36 Bath to Warminster road, 1 mile south-east of Bath city centre

THE COURSE

Yds 6369   Par 71   SSS 70

VISITING PLAYERS

Restrictions

Visitors should telephone the club number to check for Competition or Society Days, other than this there are no restrictions.

Handicap requirements

A Certificate of Handicap is required by all visitors although there is no stated maximum.

How to contact the club

Telephone call or letter.

COURSE FACILITIES

The Professional, Peter Hancox, can be contacted by telephone for details of tuition fees and information about all other facilities which include a Pro Shop, equipment hire and changing rooms.
☎ 0225 466953 for the Professional

Food and drink

The Clubhouse Bar is open from 11.30am to 2pm and 3.30pm to 6pm. It serves a full range of bar snacks and can remain open for evening meals to be served until 9pm, but only by prior arrangement.

GREEN FEES

Per weekday 🖰 £21
Per weekend day 🖰 £25

Methods of payment: cash/cheque with valid banker's card

AVON

BRISTOL AND CLIFTON GOLF CLUB

Beggar Bush Lane
Failand
Bristol
Avon
☎ 0272 393474

The Bristol and Clifton Golf Club has an 18-hole downland course with splendid views across the Bristol Channel. It welcomes visitors with few restrictions.

GETTING THERE

Road: Off the B3129 Leigh Woods to Failand road, 3 miles west of Clifton and 4 miles west of Bristol city centre

THE COURSE

Yds 6294   Par 70   SSS 70

VISITING PLAYERS

Restrictions

There are no restrictions on visiting players apart from Competition and Society Days. On weekdays it is advisable to contact the club in advance; at weekends it is essential to contact the club in advance and reserve a start time.

Handicap requirements

A Certificate of Handicap is required by all visitors.

How to contact the club

Telephone call or letter.

COURSE FACILITIES

The Professional, Peter Mawson, can be contacted by telephone for details of tuition fees and information about all other facilities which include a Pro Shop, equipment hire and changing rooms.
☎ 0272 393031 for the Professional

Food and drink

The Clubhouse Bar serves drinks and snacks, it is open daily during normal licensing hours. The restaurant serves lunch only.

GREEN FEES

Per weekday 🏌 £25
Per weekend day 🏌 £30

Methods of payment: cash/cheque with valid banker's card

CLEVEDON GOLF CLUB

Castle Road
Clevedon
Avon
☎ 0272 874057

Clevedon Golf Club is a well equipped 18-hole parkland course located above the cliffs overlooking the Severn Estuary.

GETTING THERE

Road: Off the B3124 Clevedon to Portishead road, north of Clevedon, on the coast

THE COURSE

Yds 5887   Par 69   SSS 69

VISITING PLAYERS

Restrictions

Visitors are not allowed on the course during Competition Days, check with the club for information about these days. Visitors are allowed on other days with certain start restrictions: not between 9am and 10am or 2pm and 3pm on Mondays; not before 9.30am on Tuesdays; not before 1.30pm on Wednesdays; not before 10am on Thursdays; not before 11am on Saturdays or Sundays; no restrictions on Fridays.

Handicap requirements

A Certificate of Handicap is required by all visiting players, a maximum 28 for men and 36 for women.

How to contact the club

Telephone call or letter.

COURSE FACILITIES

The Professional, C. Langford, can be contacted by telephone for details of charges and information about other facilities which include a Pro Shop, changing rooms and equipment hire.
☎ 0272 874704 for the Professional

Food and drink

The Clubhouse Bar is open from 11am to 2pm and 4pm to 11pm every day. The restaurant serves lunch between 11am and 2pm and dinner between 6pm and 8pm daily; snacks are available all day.

GREEN FEES

Per weekday 🏌 £20
Per weekend day 🏌 £28

Methods of payment: cash/cheque with valid banker's card

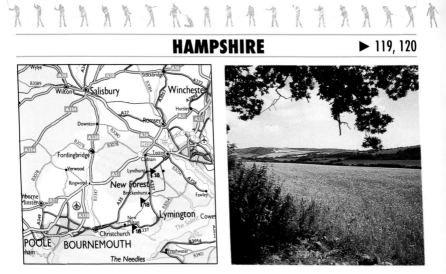

Hampshire is renowned for its New Forest, planted by William the Conqueror it is the oldest of the great forests of England. Once a hunting ground for kings it is still Crown Land but is now open to the public, it has fine facilities for walking and riding as well as excellent golf courses.

BARTON-ON-SEA GOLF CLUB

Marine Drive East
Barton-on-Sea
New Milton
Hampshire
☎ 0425 615308

Barton-on-Sea Golf Club has an 18-hole clifftop course overlooking Christchurch Bay. It is exposed and windy but has few restrictions for visitors other than they are not admitted on Tuesdays.

GETTING THERE

Road: Off the A337 Christchurch to Lymington road, just to the east of Barton-on-Sea

THE COURSE

Yds 5565   Par 67   SSS 67

VISITING PLAYERS

Restrictions
Tuesday is Ladies Day and visitors are not allowed. The only other restrictions for visitors are that start times must be after 8.30am on Mondays, Wednesdays, Thursdays and Fridays and after 11.30am at weekends.

Handicap requirements
A Certificate of Handicap is required by all visitors, there is no maximum requirement.

How to contact the club
Telephone call.

COURSE FACILITIES

The Professional can be contacted by telephone for details of fees and information about all other facilities which include a Pro Shop, equipment hire and changing rooms.
☎ 0425 611210 for the Professional

Food and drink
The Clubhouse Bar is open from 11am to 2pm and 4pm to 10pm every day. The restaurant is only open between 12 noon and 2pm for lunch and between 3pm and 5pm for tea, no evening meals are served.

GREEN FEES

Per weekday   🏌 £21.50
Per weekend day   🏌 £24.50
Methods of payment: cash/cheque with valid banker's card

21

HAMPSHIRE

BROCKENHURST MANOR GOLF CLUB

Sway Road
Brockenhurst
Hampshire
☎ 0590 23332

Brockenhurst Manor Golf Club has an 18-hole wooded parkland course on the edge of the New Forest. There are few restrictions on visiting players.

GETTING THERE

Road: Off the B3055 Brockenhurst to New Milton road, 1 mile south-west of Brockenhurst

THE COURSE

Yds 6216   Par 70   SSS 70

VISITING PLAYERS

Restrictions
Visitors are generally welcome at any time but Tuesday is Ladies Day and Thursday is used as a Societies Day so telephone the club number in advance to check availability.

Handicap requirements
A Certificate of Handicap is required by all visitors, a maximum 24 for men and 30 for women.

How to contact the club
Telephone call.

COURSE FACILITIES

The Professional can be contacted by telephone for details of tuition fees and information about all other facilities which include a Pro Shop, equipment hire and changing rooms.
☎ 0590 23092 for the Professional

Food and drink
The Clubhouse Bar is open from Mondays to Saturdays between 11am and 2.30pm and between 4.30pm and 9pm; on Sundays it is open during normal licensing hours. The dining room serves lunches and light snacks between 11am and 6pm each day.

GREEN FEES

Per weekday 🏷 £30
Per weekend day 🏷 £35

Methods of payment: cash/cheque with valid banker's card

NEW FOREST GOLF CLUB

Southampton Road
Lyndhurst
Hampshire
☎ 0703 282752

The New Forest Golf Club has an attractive 18-hole heathland course. It welcomes visiting players with few restrictions.

GETTING THERE

Road: Off the A35 Lyndhurst to Southampton road

THE COURSE

Yds 5742   Par 69   SSS 68

VISITING PLAYERS

Restrictions
Visiting players should contact the club in advance to reserve a start time. Visitors are not allowed to start before 10am on Saturdays and 1.30pm on Sundays.

Handicap requirements
A Certificate of Handicap is not required by visiting players.

How to contact the club
Telephone call or letter.

COURSE FACILITIES

The Professional can be contacted by telephone for details of charges and information about all other facilities which include a Pro Shop, a practice ground and changing rooms.
☎ 0703 282450 for the Professional

Food and drink
The Clubhouse Bar serves drinks during normal licensing hours. The dining room offers meals between 11.30am and 4pm Monday to Saturday.

GREEN FEES

Per weekday 🏷 £12
Per weekend day 🏷 £15

Methods of payment: cash/cheque with valid banker's card

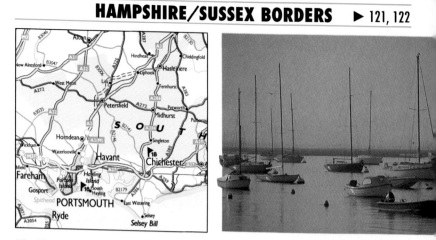

The Hampshire and Sussex border area encompasses a rich farmland plain, a large semi-enclosed area of tidal water and the heavily wooded western edge of the South Downs. Rich in history and ideal for sailing and walking there are also several fine links golf courses.

GOODWOOD GOLF CLUB

Goodwood
Chichester
West Sussex
☎ 0243 774968

Goodwood Golf Club has a superb 18-hole downland course set in the midst of the Goodwood Estate. It has few restrictions on visitors and has excellent catering facilities.

GETTING THERE

Road: Off the A286 Chichester to Midhurst road, 3 miles north-east of Chichester, on the left hand side of Racecourse Road between Goodwood House and Goodwood Racecourse

THE COURSE

Yds 6383   Par 72   SSS 70

VISITING PLAYERS

Restrictions

Visitors are not allowed on the course on Competition Days. Start times are restricted to after 8.30am on Mondays; after 12 noon on Tuesdays; after 8.30am from Wednesdays to Fridays and after 10.30am at weekends.

Handicap requirements

A Certificate of Handicap is required by all visitors, a maximum 28 for men and 36 for women.

How to contact the club

Telephone call essential.

COURSE FACILITIES

The Professional can be contacted by telephone for details of fees and information about all other facilities which include a Pro Shop, equipment hire and changing rooms. There are facilities for the disabled.
☎ 0243 774994 for the Professional

Food and drink

The Clubhouse Bar is open during normal licensing hours, it also serves snacks. The restaurant service at the club is available throughout the day.

GREEN FEES

Per weekday 🏌 £25
Per weekend day 🏌 £35
Methods of payment: cash/cheque with valid banker's card

HAYLING GOLF CLUB

Ferry Road
Hayling Island
Hampshire
☎ 0705 464446

Hayling Golf Club has an 18-hole links course with views over the Solent to the Isle of Wight. It welcomes visitors without restriction.

GETTING THERE

Road: Take the A3023 from Havant to South Hayling, then head west along the coast, it is on the south-west corner of Hayling Island

THE COURSE

Yds 6489   Par 71   SSS 71

VISITING PLAYERS

Restrictions
There are no restrictions on visitors other than the need to contact the club in advance to book a start time.

Handicap requirements
A Certificate of Handicap is required by all visiting players although there is no stated maximum.

How to contact the club
Telephone call or letter.

COURSE FACILITIES

The Professional can be contacted by telephone for details and information about all other facilities which include a Pro Shop, equipment hire and changing rooms.
☎ 0705 464491 for the Professional

Food and drink
The Clubhouse Bar is open every day during licensing hours, it also serves bar snacks. Visiting players wishing to eat a full lunch at the club should discuss their requirements when booking a start time.

GREEN FEES

Per weekday 🏷 £22
Per weekend day 🏷 £30
Methods of payment: cash/cheque with valid banker's card

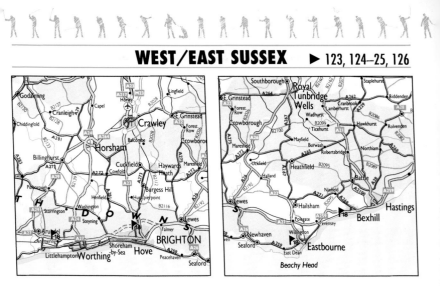

Beachy Head

The Sussex coast is backed by the rolling grassy slopes of the South Downs. Excellent riding and walking country, it is traversed by ancient paths and pretty river valleys. Amongst the many familiar coastal resorts is Brighton which retains its grandeur and special appeal.

HAM MANOR GOLF CLUB

Angmering
West Sussex
☎ 0903 783288

Ham Manor Golf Club has an 18-hole parkland course, it welcomes visitors with few restrictions.

GETTING THERE

Road: Off the A259 Worthing to Littlehampton road, just to the west of Angmering

THE COURSE

Yds 6216   Par 70   SSS 70

VISITING PLAYERS

Restrictions
Visitors must telephone the club number to obtain a reserved start time.

Handicap requirements
A Certificate of Handicap is required by all visitors although there is no maximum restriction.

How to contact the club
Telephone call or letter.

COURSE FACILITIES

The Professional, Simon Buckley, can be contacted by telephone for details of tuition fees and information about all other facilities which include a Pro Shop, equipment hire and changing rooms.
☎ 0903 783732 for the Professional

Food and drink
The Clubhouse Bar is open every day between 11am and 10.30pm, it serves snacks. The restaurant is only open for lunch.

Leisure facilities
The Clubhouse has a snooker room.

GREEN FEES

Per weekday 🛇 £25   Per week 🛇 £90
Per weekend day 🛇 £35
Methods of payment: cash only

DYKE GOLF CLUB

Dyke Road
Brighton
West Sussex
☎ 0273 857296

Dyke Golf Club has an 18-hole downland course with glorious views. It welcomes visiting players with few restrictions.

GETTING THERE

Road: Off the A2038, a branch of the A23 London to Brighton road, just before you enter the outskirts of Brighton

THE COURSE

Yds 6577   Par 72   SSS 71

VISITING PLAYERS

Restrictions

Visiting players must contact the club in advance to reserve a start time. Start times on Sundays for visitors must be after 1pm. There are no other restrictions.

Handicap requirements

A Certificate of Handicap is required by visiting players.

How to contact the club

Telephone call or letter.

COURSE FACILITIES

The Professional can be contacted by telephone for details of tuition fees and information about all other facilities which include equipment hire, a Pro Shop, a practice area and changing rooms.
☎ 0273 857230 for the Professional

Food and drink

The Clubhouse Bar is open throughout the day, every day, it serves bar snacks. The restaurant offers a full lunch and tea service daily.

Leisure facilities

The Clubhouse has a snooker table.

GREEN FEES

Per weekday round 🏌 £21
Per weekday 🏌 £31
Per weekend round 🏌 £31
Methods of payment: cash/cheque with valid banker's card

COODEN BEACH GOLF CLUB

Cooden Sea Road
Bexhill-on-Sea
East Sussex
☎ 04243 2040

Cooden Beach Golf Club has an 18-hole undulating seaside course. It welcomes visitors with few restrictions.

GETTING THERE

Road: Off the A259 Bexhill to Eastbourne road, on the coast just to the west of Bexhill, signposted

THE COURSE

Yds 6450   Par 72   SSS 71

VISITING PLAYERS

Restrictions

Visitors should contact the club in advance to book a visit at weekends and Bank Holidays, other than this there are no restrictions.

Handicap requirements

A Certificate of Handicap is required by all visiting players although there is no required maximum.

How to contact the club

Telephone call or letter.

COURSE FACILITIES

The Professional, Keith Robson, can be contacted by telephone for details of tuition fees and information about all other facilities which include a Pro Shop, equipment hire and changing rooms.
☎ 04243 3938 for the Professional

Food and drink

The Clubhouse has a fully licensed bar and a dining room serving a full range of meals. These are both open continuously between 11am and 9pm during the summer and 11am to 8pm in the winter.

Leisure facilities

The Clubhouse has a snooker room.

GREEN FEES

Per weekday 🏌 £21
Per weekend day 🏌 £26
Methods of payment: cash/cheque with valid banker's card

ROYAL EASTBOURNE GOLF CLUB

Paradise Drive
Eastbourne
East Sussex
☎ 0323 29738

Royal Eastbourne Golf Club is set in the lovely rolling Sussex Downs just outside Eastbourne. The Club has an 18-hole and a 9-hole course, it also has self-catering accommodation for visitors.

GETTING THERE

Road: Off the A22 London to Eastbourne road, ½ mile before Eastbourne town centre

THE COURSE

	Course 1 ⚑18	Course 2 ⚑9
Yds	6109	2146
Par	70	32
SSS	69	

VISITING PLAYERS

Restrictions

Apart from match days, the only restrictions on visitors are start times. On the 18-hole course start times are not before 11am on Wednesdays or 9.30am on Saturdays; there are no other restrictions. On the 9-hole course start times are not before 11am on Wednesdays or 12 noon on Sundays; there are no other restrictions.

Handicap requirements

A Certificate of Handicap is required by all visitors playing the 18-hole course.

How to contact the club

Telephone call or letter.

COURSE FACILITIES

The Professional can be contacted by telephone for details of tuition fees and information about all other facilities which include a Pro Shop, equipment hire and changing rooms.
☎ 0323 36986 for the Professional

Food and drink

The Clubhouse Bar is open during normal licensing hours and serves snacks. The restaurant serves lunch between 12 noon and 2.30pm but is only open for dinner by prior arrangement.

Leisure facilities

Self-catering cottages are available at the club for visitors to rent – telephone the club number for prices and availability.

GREEN FEES

	Course 1	Course 2
Per weekday	£24	£14
Per weekend day	£30	£17
Per week	£103	
Per fortnight	on application	

Methods of payment: cash only

27

KENT

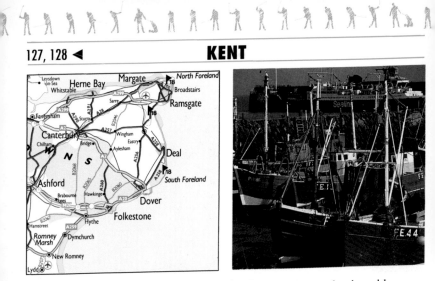

Kent, the 'garden of England', is a landscape of rich farms, orchards and hop gardens with conical oast-houses, enchanting villages and splendid mansions. By contrast the shoreline has the lonely north Kent marshes, the southern Romney marsh and the busy ports and seaside towns that cluster around the famous white cliffs of Dover.

NORTH FORELAND GOLF CLUB

Convent Road
Broadstairs
Kent
☎ 0843 62140

The North Foreland Golf Club has an 18-hole seaside downland course and a short par 3 course. It welcomes visitors although there are start time restrictions at weekends.

GETTING THERE

Road: Off the B2052 Broadstairs to Margate coast road, 1 mile north of Broadstairs

THE COURSE

Yds 6382   Par 71   SSS 70

VISITING PLAYERS

Restrictions
Visiting players are not allowed to start until after 1pm on Saturdays or Sundays. There are no other restrictions but it is advisable to contact the club in advance and book a start time, particularly during the summer.

Handicap requirements
A Certificate of Handicap is required by all visitors although there is no stated maximum.

How to contact the club
Telephone call or letter.

COURSE FACILITIES

The Professional can be contacted by telephone for details of tuition fees and information about all other facilities which include a Pro Shop, equipment hire, changing rooms and a par 3 short course, 1752 yds long. Fees for this course are £5 per weekday and £5.50 per weekend.
☎ 0843 69628 for the Professional

Food and drink
The Clubhouse Bar serves drinks and snacks every day during licensing hours. The dining room serves lunch and tea every day.

GREEN FEES

Per weekday round 🏷 £18
Per weekday 🏷 £26
Per weekend round 🏷 £26
Note: Green fees are reduced during the winter months.

Methods of payment: cash/cheque with valid banker's card

WALMER AND KINGSDOWN GOLF CLUB

The Leas
Kingsdown
Kent
☎ 0304 373256

Walmer and Kingsdown Golf Club has an 18-hole downland course perched on top of the white cliffs of Dover with fine views over St. Margaret's Bay. It welcomes visitors without restriction.

GETTING THERE

Road: On the coast, 1 mile south of Kingsdown village

THE COURSE

Yds 6451 Par 72 SSS 71

VISITING PLAYERS

Restrictions

There are no restrictions on visitors but during the summer it would be sensible to telephone the club before setting out to check on availability of start times.

Handicap requirements

A Certificate of Handicap is required.

How to contact the club

Telephone call.

COURSE FACILITIES

The Professional can be contacted via the club telephone number for details of charges and information about all other facilities which include a Pro Shop, equipment hire and changing rooms.

Food and drink

The Clubhouse Bar is open throughout the day, every day, it also serves bar snacks. Visiting players wishing more substantial meals should contact the club in advance to discuss their requirements.

GREEN FEES

Per weekday 🏌 £20
Per weekend day 🏌 £22
Methods of payment: cash/cheque with valid banker's card

ST AUGUSTINE'S GOLF CLUB

Cottington Road
Cliffsend
Ramsgate
Kent
☎ 0843 590333

St. Augustine's Golf Club has an 18-hole seaside downland course overlooking Pegwell Bay. It welcomes visitors without restriction.

GETTING THERE

Road: Off the A526 Ramsgate to Deal road, 2 miles south-west of Ramsgate

THE COURSE

Yds 5138 Par 69 SSS 65

VISITING PLAYERS

Restrictions

There are no restrictions on visiting players.

Handicap requirements

A Certificate of Handicap is required by all visitors although there is no stated maximum.

How to contact the club

Telephone call or letter.

COURSE FACILITIES

The Professional can be contacted by telephone for details of tuition fees and information about all other facilities which include a Pro Shop and changing rooms.
☎ 0843 590222 for the Professional

Food and drink

The Clubhouse Bar serves drinks and snacks throughout the day during licensing hours. Lunch and tea are also served every day in the restaurant.

GREEN FEES

Per weekday 🏌 £18.50
Per weekend day 🏌 £20.50
Methods of payment: cash/cheque with valid banker's card

Surrey has absorbed a dense commuter population whilst retaining its attractive villages and all its natural beauty. Wide commons, wooded valleys and heather-clad hills still provide thousands of acres open to the walker, rider and picnicker.

WEST SURREY GOLF CLUB

Enton Green
Godalming
Surrey
☎ 0483 421275

The West Surrey Golf Club has an 18-hole parkland course. It welcomes visiting players with few restrictions.

GETTING THERE

Road: Off the A283, 2 miles south-west of Godalming

THE COURSE

Yds 6247   Par 71   SSS 70

VISITING PLAYERS

Restrictions

Visitors must contact the club in advance to check for any special restrictions and to reserve a start time; apart from this there are no restrictions.

Handicap requirements

A Certificate of Handicap is not required by visiting players.

How to contact the club

Telephone call or letter.

COURSE FACILITIES

The Professional can be contacted by telephone for details of tuition fees and information about all other facilities which include a Pro Shop and changing rooms.
☎ 0483 417278 for the Professional

Food and drink

The Clubhouse Lounge Bar serves bar snacks and is open daily during licensing hours. The dining room provides lunches and tea every day.

Leisure facilities

The Clubhouse has a snooker table.

GREEN FEES

Per weekday 🖪 £32
Per weekend day 🖪 £39.50
Methods of payment: cash/cheque with valid banker's card

HINDHEAD GOLF CLUB

Churt Road
Hindhead
Surrey
☎ 0428 604614

Hindhead Golf Club has an 18-hole
heathland course, it has few restrictions on
visiting players.

GETTING THERE

Road: Off the A287 Hindhead to Farnham
road, 1½ miles north of Hindhead

THE COURSE

Yds 6349   Par 70   SSS 70

VISITING PLAYERS

Restrictions

Visitors must contact the club in advance of
intended arrival to check for Special Day
restrictions, there are no other restrictions.

Handicap requirements

A Certificate of Handicap is essential for all
visitors at weekends, a maximum 20 for
men and 28 for women.

How to contact the club

Telephone call essential.

COURSE FACILITIES

The Professional can be contacted on 0428
604458 for details of tuition fees and
information about all other facilities which
include a Pro Shop, equipment hire and
changing rooms.

Food and drink

The Clubhouse Bar is open from 11.30am to
2.30pm and 5pm to 10pm every day, it also
serves light snacks. The restaurant is open
for lunch each day, from 12 noon to 3pm.

GREEN FEES

Per weekday ♱ £35 (£26 after 2pm)
Per weekend day ♱ £40
Methods of payment: cash/cheque with valid
banker's card

Buckinghamshire and Hertfordshire, two of the Home Counties, are rich in history and stately homes. Beechwoods cover the Chiltern Hills in the west, ancient walkways criss-cross the area and the leafy lanes and traditional Chiltern character of the villages has not been disturbed by today's commuters or motorways.

BERKHAMSTED GOLF CLUB

The Common
Berkhamsted
Hertfordshire
☎ 0442 865832

Berkhamstead Golf Club has an 18-hole heathland course on Berkhamsted Common, part of the Chiltern Hills. The course is bunker-free but very testing. The facilities for visitors are excellent and visitors are welcome at any time.

GETTING THERE

Road: Between the A41 Hemel Hempstead to Aylesbury road and the A4146 Hemel Hempstead to Leighton Buzzard road, 1 mile north-east of Berkhamstead

THE COURSE

Yds 6605   Par 71   SSS 72

VISITING PLAYERS

Restrictions

Telephone the Professional's number before setting out to check what is happening at the club; there are no other restrictions.

Handicap requirements

A Certificate of Handicap is required for all visitors, it is not a course suitable for beginners.

How to contact the club

Telephone the Professional's number.

COURSE FACILITIES

The Professional can be contacted by telephone for details of tuition fees and information about all other facilities which include a Pro Shop, equipment hire and changing rooms.
☎ 0442 865851 for the Professional

Food and drink

The Clubhouse facilities at Berkhamsted are excellent; the bar is open at normal licensing hours; the restaurant serves lunch, tea and dinner; snacks are also available.

GREEN FEES

Per weekday 🏌 £32.50
Per weekend day 🏌 £39
Methods of payment: cash/cheque with valid banker's card

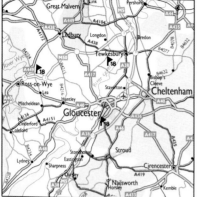

Tewkesbury Park Hotel Golf Club

Hereford and Worcester's gently picturesque landscape of old timbered houses, red-and-white Hereford cattle, hops and cider apple orchards is complemented by the fine scenery of the spectacular Wye valley, a paradise for both anglers and walkers. Gloucestershire, rich in abbeys and churches, is a great sporting county.

GLOUCESTER HOTEL AND COUNTRY CLUB

Matson Lane
Robinswood Hill
Gloucester
Gloucestershire
☎ 0452 25653

The Gloucester Hotel and Country Club has an 18-hole parkland course, a 9-hole par 3 course, a 12-bay driving range and an impressive array of other leisure facilities including one of the best dry ski slopes in Europe; it also has a 117-room luxury hotel. The club welcomes visitors without restriction and also organises special golf packages and residential golf training schools.

GETTING THERE

Road: Off the A38 Gloucester to Bristol road, 1½ miles south-west of Gloucester city centre

THE COURSE

Yds 6127   Par 70   SSS 69

VISITING PLAYERS

Restrictions

Visitors are welcome at any time but they should telephone the Club Secretary in advance to reserve a start time.
☎ 0452 411331 for the Club Secretary.

Handicap requirements

Visiting players require a Certificate of Handicap.

How to contact the hotel

Telephone call or letter.

COURSE FACILITIES

The Professional can be contacted via the main hotel telephone number for details of tuition fees and information on all other facilities which include a Pro Shop, equipment hire and changing rooms. Residential weekend or 7-day Golf Instruction Courses from Beginners to Advanced are also held.

Food and drink

The Hotel bars are open during normal licensing hours; eating facilities in the hotel range from quick snacks to the à la carte Redwell Restaurant.

Leisure facilities

The Gloucester Hotel and Country Club has many sporting and leisure facilities in addition to its golfing activities, the most important of these are a dry ski slope, swimming pool, sauna and solarium, gym, squash courts (and squash school) and tennis courts.

GREEN FEES

Per weekday round 🕐 £18.50
Per weekend day round 🕐 £24.50
Methods of payment: cash/cheque with valid banker's card/all major credit cards

33

ROSS-ON-WYE GOLF CLUB

Two Park
Gorsley
Ross-on-Wye
Herefordshire
☎ 0989 82267

Ross-on-Wye Golf Club has an 18-hole undulating parkland course. There are few restrictions on visiting players.

GETTING THERE

Road: Off the B4221 Ross-on-Wye to Newent road, adjacent to M50 jct 3

THE COURSE

Yds 6500   Par 72   SSS 73

VISITING PLAYERS

Restrictions

Tuesday is Ladies Day. Telephone the Professional's number to check for Competition or Society Days and book a start time.

Handicap requirements

The club reserves the right to ask to see a Certificate of Handicap from visitors but has no maximum handicap requirements.

How to contact the club

Telephone the Professional's number.

COURSE FACILITIES

The Professional, Adrian Clifford, can be contacted by telephone for details of tuition fees and information about all other facilities which include a Pro Shop, changing rooms and limited equipment hire.
☎ 0989 82439 for the Professional

Food and drink

The fully licensed bar overlooks the 9th and 18th greens and is open all day every day, it also sells snacks. The dining room opens at 9.30am Tuesday to Sunday and sells appropriate meals during the day; on Mondays food is limited to snacks only.

Leisure facilities

The Clubhouse has two snooker tables.

GREEN FEES

Per weekday 🏌 £25
Per weekend day 🏌 £30

Methods of payment: cash/cheque with valid banker's card

TEWKESBURY PARK HOTEL GOLF AND COUNTRY CLUB

Lincoln Green Lane
Tewkesbury
Gloucestershire
☎ 0684 295405

The Tewkesbury Park Hotel Golf and Country Club has an 18-hole parkland course and a 6-hole par 3 course; the 80-room luxury hotel also boasts many other leisure facilities. Visitors are welcome without restriction.

GETTING THERE

Road: Off the A38 Tewkesbury to Gloucester road, 1 mile south-west of Tewkesbury town centre

THE COURSE

Yds 6533   Par 73   SSS 72

VISITING PLAYERS

Restrictions

At weekends visiting players must contact the club in advance to reserve a start time. It is not essential to contact the club in advance on weekdays but it is sensible to do so, particularly during the summer.

Handicap requirements

A Certificate of Handicap is required by all visitors although there is no stated maximum.

How to contact the club

Telephone call or letter.

COURSE FACILITIES

Telephone the hotel number and ask for the Pro Shop for information on all facilities, which include equipment hire and changing rooms.

Food and drink

The hotel's bar and restaurant facilities are available to visiting players.

Leisure facilities

The club also has a swimming pool, sauna and solarium, multi-gym, squash courts, tennis courts and snooker. Residential golf packages are also available, contact the hotel for details.

GREEN FEES

Per weekday round 🏌 £22
Per weekend day round 🏌 £25

Methods of payment: cash/cheque with valid banker's card/all major credit cards

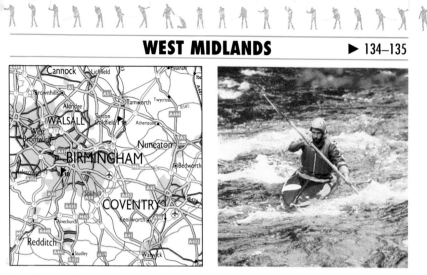

The West Midlands, once thick woodland, is now dominated by the city of Birmingham which is also the centre of Britain's inland waterways. Many attractive mediaeval market towns surround the city including Sutton Coldfield with its 2400-acre natural park and championship golf course.

EDGBASTON GOLF CLUB

Church Road
Edgbaston
Birmingham
☎ 021 454 1736

Edgbaston Golf Club has an 18-hole parkland course; it welcomes visitors without restriction.

GETTING THERE

Road: Off the B4217, which is off the A38 Birmingham to Worcester road, 1 mile south of Birmingham city centre

THE COURSE

Yds 6172   Par 69   SSS 69

VISITING PLAYERS

Restrictions

There are no restrictions on visiting players.

Handicap requirements

Visitors do not require a Certificate of Handicap.

How to contact the club

Telephone call.

COURSE FACILITIES

The Professional can be contacted via the club telephone number for details of tuition fees and information about all other facilities which include a Pro Shop, equipment hire and changing rooms.

Food and drink

The Clubhouse Bar serves drinks and snacks and is open daily during normal licensing hours; the Clubhouse also offers a full lunch service.

GREEN FEES

Per weekday 🇬 £27.50
Per weekend day 🇬 £35

Methods of payment: cash/cheque with valid banker's card

THE BELFRY

Lichfield Road
Wishaw
Warwickshire
☎ 0675 470301

The Belfry complex possesses two magnificent 18-hole parkland courses - the Brabazon and the Derby; the Brabazon is a championship course and was the venue for the Ryder Cup in 1985 and 1989 and will host the event again in 1993; it is also the headquarters of the PGA. Visiting players are welcome on both courses but need to book well in advance as the courses are very popular. 2-day residential golf breaks are also available. The Belfry has a 4-star, 220-room hotel and a wealth of leisure facilities.

GETTING THERE

Road: At the junction of the A446 Coventry to Lichfield road and the A4091 Tamworth road; there are entrances to The Belfry on both roads

THE COURSE

	Brabazon Course ⛳18	Derby Course ⛳18
Yds	6975	6127
Par	73	70
SSS	73	69

VISITING PLAYERS

Restrictions

The only restriction on visiting players is the need to reserve start times well in advance, particularly for the Brabazon.

Handicap requirements

A Certificate of Handicap is required by all visiting players who wish to play the Brabazon, maximum men's handicap is 24; there are no handicap requirements for the Derby Course.

How to contact the club

Telephone call or letter.

COURSE FACILITIES

The Professional can be contacted via the club telephone number for details of tuition fees and information about all other facilities which include a Pro Shop, equipment hire, changing rooms and a practice area.

Food and drink

The Belfry complex includes two bars in the hotel, an 'English Pub' in the grounds and a night club. Food service includes light meals and snacks which are available all day, a carvery and an award winning French restaurant (for which booking is strongly recommended).

Leisure facilities

Leisure facilities at The Belfry include a swimming pool, sauna and solarium, Turkish baths, trimnasium and squash courts.

GREEN FEES

	Brabazon Course	Derby Course
Per weekday round	£46	£20.50
Per weekend round	£51	£26

Hotel residents: 2 nights accommodation, breakfasts, dinners and 1 round on each course – £245 per person for 2 sharing a double room.

Methods of payment: cash/cheque with valid banker's card/all major credit cards

Shropshire is a beautiful and unspoilt rural county of rich arable farmland well-watered by the Severn river. Its charming black-and-white timbered villages provide a vivid contrast to the dramatic hill country with isolated valleys that lead the visitor into the wild Welsh border country.

HAWKSTONE PARK HOTEL

Weston-under-Redcastle
Shrewsbury
Shropshire
☎ 093924 611

The Hawkstone Park Hotel has two 18-hole parkland courses and also offers residential golf packages. Visiting players are welcome without restriction but are advised to contact the hotel to book start times in advance.

GETTING THERE

Road: Off the A49 Shrewsbury to Whitchurch road, 12 miles north of Shrewsbury and off the A442 12 miles from jct 6 of the M54.

THE COURSE

	Hawkstone Course 🏴18	Weston Course 🏴18
Yds	6203	5063
Par	72	66
SSS	71	66

VISITING PLAYERS

Restrictions

There are no restrictions on visiting players but they should contact the hotel in advance to reserve a start time.

Handicap requirements

Visiting players require a Certificate of Handicap to play the Hawkstone Course although none is needed to play the Weston Course.

How to contact the hotel

Telephone call or letter.

COURSE FACILITIES

The Professional can be contacted by telephone for details of tuition fees and information about all other facilities which include a Pro Shop, equipment hire and changing rooms.
☎ 093924 209 for the Professional

Food and drink

Visiting players are welcome to use the hotel's bar and restaurant facilities throughout the day.

Leisure facilities

The hotel has 59 bedrooms and offers golfing breaks throughout the year with accommodation, food, green fees and guaranteed start times. Please contact the hotel for details and tariffs.

GREEN FEES

	Hawkstone Course	Weston Course
Per weekday round	£23	£12
Per weekend round	£26	£15

Methods of payment: cash/cheque with valid banker's card/all major credit cards

37

SHROPSHIRE

HILL VALLEY GOLF AND COUNTRY CLUB

Terrick Road
Whitchurch
Shropshire
☎ 0948 3584

The Hill Valley Golf and Country Club was designed and laid out by Peter Allis and Dave Thomas and includes an 18-hole championship course, a 9-hole course and a 9-hole par 3 course. The complex also includes accommodation and other leisure facilities and welcomes visitors without restriction.

GETTING THERE

Road: Off the A49 Whitchurch to Warrington road, 1 mile north of Whitchurch

THE COURSE

	Championship Course ↑18	9-hole Course ↑9
Yds	6050	2553 x 2
Par	72	68
SSS	69	68

VISITING PLAYERS

Restrictions

Visitors should contact the club in advance to reserve a start time.

Handicap requirements

Visitors who wish to play the Championship Course must have a Certificate of Handicap although there is no stated maximum.

How to contact the club

Telephone call or letter.

COURSE FACILITIES

The Professional, Tony Minshall, can be contacted by telephone for details of tuition fees and information about all other facilities which include a Pro Shop, equipment hire and changing rooms.
☎ 0948 3032 for the Professional

Food and drink

The Clubhouse Bars are open all day every day and also serve snacks; the dining room serves breakfast, lunch and dinner every day of the week.

Leisure facilities

Leisure facilities in the complex include hard tennis courts, squash courts, a snooker room and a sauna. John Garner's European Indoor School of Golf is located in the complex and offers specialised tuition – telephone the Professional's number for details. There are 7 double bedrooms with private facilities in the Clubhouse, telephone the club number for prices and reservations.

GREEN FEES

	Championship Course	9-hole Course
Per weekday	£16	£7
Per weekend day	£21	£7

Note: Weekly rates available to resident guests only.

Methods of payment: cash/cheque with valid banker's card (by prior arrangement only)

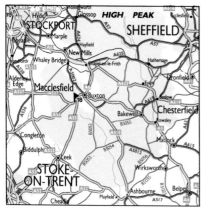

Derbyshire is well-known for its Peak District – high flat moorland, deep green valleys, rough stone crags, narrow limestone gorges and cliffs with underground quarries and caverns – a national park area and 'adventure country' for walkers, climbers and cavers.

CAVENDISH GOLF CLUB

Gadley Lane
Buxton
Derbyshire
☎ 0298 25052

The Cavendish Golf Club has an 18-hole parkland course designed by Dr McKenzie. It has few restrictions for visitors.

GETTING THERE

Road: Off the A53 Buxton to Macclesfield road, ¾ mile west of Buxton

THE COURSE

Yds 5815   Par 68   SSS 68

VISITING PLAYERS

Restrictions

Visiting players should telephone the club in advance to check on Society or Special Days, other than this there are no restrictions.

Handicap requirements

A Certificate of Handicap is required although there are no minimum handicap requirements.

How to contact the club

Telephone the Professional.

COURSE FACILITIES

The Professional, John Nolan, can be contacted by telephone for details of tuition fees and information about all other facilities which include a Pro Shop, equipment hire, changing rooms and a driving range.
☎ 0298 25052 for the Professional

Food and drink

The Clubhouse has a fully licensed bar and dining room overlooking the 18th green. These are open for drinks, snacks and meals all day in summer; opening hours in the winter are more restricted.

Leisure facilities

The Clubhouse has a snooker room.

GREEN FEES

Per weekday 🏳 £22
Per weekend day 🏳 £34

Methods of payment: cash/cheque with valid banker's card/Visa

Bedfordshire and Cambridgeshire are dominated by the River Great Ouse, a broad wandering river meandering through rolling pastureland into flatter fenland where history has been absorbed and atmospheric towns such as Cambridge and Ely have flourished.

CAMBRIDGESHIRE MOAT HOUSE HOTEL GOLF AND SPORTS CLUB

Bar Hill
Cambridge
Cambridgeshire
☎ 0954 780555

The Cambridgeshire Moat House has an 18-hole parkland course attached to the hotel. It welcomes visiting players without restriction and also offers residential golf packages.

GETTING THERE

Road: Off the A604 Cambridge to Huntingdon road, 5 miles north-west of Cambridge

THE COURSE

Yds 6734   Par 72   SSS 72

VISITING PLAYERS

Restrictions
Visiting players should telephone the club number in advance to reserve a start time, this is the only restriction.

Handicap requirements
Visiting players must have a Certificate of Handicap or a letter of introduction from their own club.

How to contact the club
Telephone call.

COURSE FACILITIES

The Professional can be contacted via the club telephone number for details of tuition fees and information about all other facilities which include a Pro Shop, equipment hire and changing rooms.

Food and drink

Visiting players are welcome to use the bar and restaurant facilities of the hotel.

Leisure facilities

The 3-star, 100-room Moat House Hotel offers special golfing packages, please contact the hotel for details. Other facilities include a health and fitness centre, indoor swimming pool, sauna and solarium, squash courts and tennis courts.

GREEN FEES

Per weekday   🎫 £19
Per weekend day   🎫 £25.50

Methods of payment: cash/cheque with valid banker's card

JOHN O'GAUNT GOLF CLUB

Sutton Park
Sandy
Bedfordshire
☎ 0767 260360

The John O'Gaunt Golf Club has two 18-hole courses, the John O'Gaunt and the Carthagena; the club has excellent facilities and very few restrictions on visitors.

GETTING THERE

Road: Off the B1042 just to the east of Potton, alongside the B1040

THE COURSE

	John O'Gaunt ▶18	Carthagena ▶18
Yds	6513	5869
Par	71	69
SSS	71	68

VISITING PLAYERS

Restrictions

Visitors should telephone the club number to check about when Match or Society Days are happening, this is the only restriction.

Handicap requirements

A Certificate of Handicap is required for visitors wishing to play the courses at weekends, but is not required mid-week.

How to contact the club

Telephone call.

COURSE FACILITIES

The Professional can be contacted by telephone for details of tuition fees and information about all other facilities which include a Pro Shop, equipment and golf buggies for hire and changing rooms.
☎ 0767 260094 for the Professional

Food and drink

The Clubhouse is a stately home built in 1859. The bar is open from 11.30am to 11pm every day; the Burgoyne Suite Dining Room can seat 120 and is open for lunch, tea and dinner every day.

GREEN FEES

Per weekday 🏌 £35
Per weekend day 🏌 £50

Note: Children's green fees are roughly half the adult fees.

Methods of payment: cash/cheque with valid banker's card

JOHN O'GAUNT GOLF CLUB
JOHN O'GAUNT COURSE

SUFFOLK

Suffolk has miles of unspoilt coastline, exquisite skyscapes, and small exclusive resorts such as Aldeburgh and Southwold that can be reached by lanes that twist amongst the rich pastureland and warm-hued villages. Sailing, bird-watching and fishing are rewarding pursuits in this area.

BURY ST EDMUNDS GOLF CLUB

Tuthill
Bury St. Edmunds
Suffolk
☎ 0284 755979

Bury St. Edmunds Golf Club has an 18-hole parkland course. It welcomes visitors although there are some start time restrictions at weekends.

GETTING THERE

Road: Off the B1106, which is off the A45 Bury St. Edmunds to Newmarket road, 2 miles north-west of Bury St. Edmunds

THE COURSE

Yds 6615   Par 72   SSS 72

VISITING PLAYERS

Restrictions

Visiting players start times must be after 10am on Saturdays and Sundays; there are no restrictions on weekdays.

Handicap requirements

At weekends all visiting players require a Certificate of Handicap although there is no stated maximum, certificates are not required by visitors during the week.

How to contact the club

Telephone call or letter.

COURSE FACILITIES

The Professional can be contacted by telephone for details of tuition fees and information about all other facilities which include a Pro Shop, equipment hire and changing rooms.
☎ 0284 755978 for the Professional

Food and drink

The Clubhouse Bar is open for drinks and snacks daily during normal licensing hours; the dining room serves a full lunch every day.

GREEN FEES

Per weekday 🎫 £12.50
Per weekend day 🎫 £16
Methods of payment: cash/cheque with valid banker's card

ALDEBURGH GOLF CLUB

Saxmundham Road
Aldeburgh
Suffolk
☎ 0728 452890

Aldeburgh Golf Club has an 18-hole and a 9-hole heath and parkland course overlooking the River Alde. It welcomes visitors without restriction.

GETTING THERE

Road: Off the A1094 Aldeburgh to Saxmundham road, 1 mile from Aldeburgh town centre

THE COURSE

	Main Course ⛳18	River Course ⛳9
Yds	6330	2114
Par	68	32
SSS	71	32

VISITING PLAYERS

Restrictions

There are no restrictions on visiting players.

Handicap requirements

A Certificate of Handicap is required for visitors playing the Main Course.

How to contact the club

Telephone call.

COURSE FACILITIES

The Professional can be contact on 0728 453309 for details of tuition fees and information about all other facilities which include a Pro Shop, equipment hire and changing rooms.

Food and drink

The Clubhouse Bar is open during normal licensing hours daily and serves snacks. The restaurant serves a full range of meals every day.

GREEN FEES

	Main Course	River Course
Per weekday	£18	£9
Per weekend day	£23	£12

Methods of payment: cash/cheque with valid banker's card

IPSWICH GOLF CLUB

Purdis Heath
Bucklesham Road
Ipswich
Suffolk
☎ 0473 728941

Ipswich Golf Club has an 18-hole and a 9-hole heathland course. It welcomes visitors with few restrictions.

GETTING THERE

Road: Off the A1156 Ipswich to Felixstowe road, 2 miles east of Ipswich town centre

THE COURSE

	Course 1 ⛳18	Course 2 ⛳9
Yds	6405	1930
Par	71	59
SSS	71	59

VISITING PLAYERS

Restrictions

Visiting players who wish to play the 18-hole course must contact the club in advance to book a start time; there are no restrictions on the 9-hole course.

Handicap requirements

Visitors playing the 18-hole course must have a Certificate of Handicap although there is no stated maximum.

How to contact the club

Telephone call or letter.

COURSE FACILITIES

The Professional can be contacted by telephone for details of tuition fees and information about all other facilities which include a Pro Shop and changing rooms.
☎ 0473 724017 for the Professional

Food and drink

The Clubhouse Bar is open every day and serves drinks and snacks; the restaurant provides a full meal service every day.

GREEN FEES

	Course 1	Course 2
Per weekday	£25.50	£7.50
Per weekend day	£31	£10

Methods of payment: cash/cheque with valid banker's card

THORPENESS GOLF CLUB HOTEL

Thorpeness
Suffolk
☎ 0728 452176

Thorpeness Golf Club Hotel has an 18-hole
moorland course; visitors are welcome
without restriction.

GETTING THERE

Road: Off the B1353 Aldringham to
Thorpeness road, just to the west of
Thorpeness

THE COURSE

Yds 6241   Par 69   SSS 71

VISITING PLAYERS

Restrictions
Telephone the club number to check on
Match or Society Days, apart from this
there are no restrictions.

Handicap requirements
A Certificate of Handicap is required by all
visitors, a maximum 28 for men and 36 for
women.

How to contact the club
Telephone call.

COURSE FACILITIES

The Professional can be contacted by
telephone for details of charges and
information about all other facilities which
include a Pro Shop, equipment and golf
buggies for hire and changing rooms.
Tuition fees are £8.50 per half hour.
☎ 0728 452524 for the Professional

Food and drink
The Clubhouse's oak panelled bar is open
during normal licensing hours. The dining
room will serve lunch, tea and dinner by
arrangement, its speciality is locally-caught
fish.

Leisure facilities
A new hotel block with 20 deluxe double
bedrooms has been built alongside the
Clubhouse. Telephone the club number for
reservations.
   The club overlooks the Meare, a 60-acre
lake that is never more than 3 feet deep and
offers facilities for sailing, rowing, canoeing
and punting.

GREEN FEES

Per round ⛳ £21   Per weekday ⛳ £31
Per weekend day ⛳ £41

Note: Children's green fees at £10 per
round or £12 per day.

Methods of payment: cash/cheque with valid
banker's card/Visa/Access/Mastercard

Norfolk, the largest of the eastern counties, is dominated by water. The reed fringed Norfolk Broads, slow-moving rivers and silent marshes are a paradise for the naturalist or sailing enthusiast. Lavender fields add their distinctive fragrance and colour to the north-western Norfolk landscape.

HUNSTANTON GOLF CLUB

Golf Course Road
Old Hunstanton
Norfolk
☎ 0485 532811

Hunstanton Golf Club has an 18-hole seaside links course overlooking the Wash. It has few restrictions for visitors.

GETTING THERE

Road: Off the A149 King's Lynn to Cromer coast road just outside the village of Old Hunstanton, 1 mile north of Hunstanton

THE COURSE

Yds 6670   Par 72   SSS 72

VISITING PLAYERS

Restrictions

Start times for visitors must be after 9.30am on weekdays and after 10.30am at weekends. The number of visiting players allowed on the course at weekends is also limited, telephone the club number to confirm.

Handicap requirements

A Certificate of Handicap is required by all visitors, a maximum 28 for men and 36 for women.

How to contact the club

Telephone call.

COURSE FACILITIES

The Professional can be contacted via the club telephone number for details of tuition fees and information about all other facilities which include a Pro Shop, equipment hire and changing rooms.

Food and drink

The Clubhouse Bar is open between 11am and 8pm during summer months and between 12 noon and 3pm in the winter, in addition to drinks and snacks it also offers a daily hot food menu.

GREEN FEES

Per weekday 🏌 £28
Per weekend day 🏌 £35

Note: Children's green fees are half the adult fees.

Methods of payment: cash/cheque with valid banker's card

45

NORFOLK

SHERINGHAM GOLF CLUB

Weybourne Road
Sheringham
Norfolk
☎ 0263 823488 (Secretary)
☎ 0263 822038 (Clubhouse)

Sheringham Golf Club has an 18-hole clifftop course overlooking the North Sea; it is famous for its gorse, its views and its finish which runs parallel to the Steam Preservation Society's railway line. It welcomes visitors with few restrictions.

GETTING THERE

Road: Off the A149 King's Lynn to Cromer coast road, ½ mile west of Sheringham village

THE COURSE

Yds 6464   Par 70   SSS 71

VISITING PLAYERS

Restrictions

There are some variable weekend restrictions and Tuesday is Ladies Day. Visiting players should telephone the club number in advance to check.

Handicap requirements

A Certificate of Handicap is required by all visitors although there is no stated maximum.

How to contact the club

Telephone call or letter.

COURSE FACILITIES

The Professional can be contacted on 0263 822980 for details of tuition fees and information about all other facilities which include a Pro Shop, equipment hire and changing rooms.

Food and drink

The Clubhouse Bar is open between 10.30am and 10pm Monday to Saturday during the summer months. On Sundays in summer and all week during the winter it is only open for restricted hours, telephone the club number to check. The restaurant serves snacks all day and lunch and dinner at the appropriate times of the day.

GREEN FEES

Per weekday 🏷 £25
Per weekend day 🏷 £30
Methods of payment: cash/cheque with valid banker's card

LINCOLNSHIRE

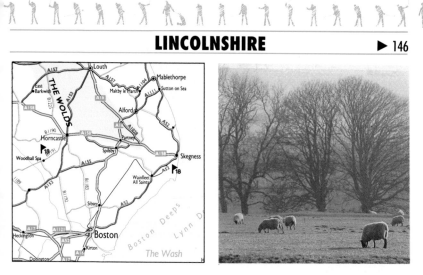

Lincolnshire, famous for its colourful bulb fields and rich agricultural fenland, also has the rolling hills, deep valleys, quiet streams and hanging beechwoods of the Wolds. Many coastal resorts and a port lie along the bracing coastal plain of marshes and sand-dunes.

SEACROFT GOLF CLUB

Drummond Road
Skegness
Lincolnshire
☎ 0754 3020

Seacroft Golf Club has an 18-hole seaside links course overlooking the North Sea. There are start time restrictions for visitors.

GETTING THERE

Road: Off the minor coast road leading south from Skegness towards the Gibraltar Point Nature Reserve

THE COURSE

Yds 6490   Par 71   SSS 71

VISITING PLAYERS

Restrictions

Visitors have restricted start times throughout the week, they must not start before 9.30am any day nor between 12 noon and 2pm; there are no other restrictions.

Handicap requirements

A Certificate of Handicap is required for all visitors, a maximum 24 for men and 36 for women.

How to contact the club

Telephone call.

COURSE FACILITIES

The Professional can be contacted via the club telephone number for details of tuition fees and information about all other facilities which include a Pro Shop and changing rooms.

Food and drink

The Clubhouse Bar is open all day every day and also serves snacks; the restaurant serves lunch, tea and dinner.

GREEN FEES

Per round 🏷 £18.50
Per weekday 🏷 £25.50
Per weekend day 🏷 £30.50
Note: Children's green fees are half the adult fees.

Methods of payment: cash/cheque with valid banker's card

LINCOLNSHIRE

WOODHALL SPA GOLF CLUB

The Broadway
Woodhall Spa
Lincolnshire
☎ 0526 52511

Woodhall Spa Golf Club has a flat 18-hole heathland course. It welcomes visitors without restriction.

GETTING THERE

Road: Off the B1191 Woodhall Spa to Horncastle road, 1 mile north-east of Woodhall Spa

THE COURSE

Yds 6866   Par 73   SSS 73

VISITING PLAYERS

Restrictions
Visiting players must contact the club in advance to reserve a start time on any day of the week.

Handicap requirements
Visitors do not require a Certificate of Handicap.

How to contact the club
Telephone call or letter.

COURSE FACILITIES

The Professional can be contacted by telephone for details of charges and information about all other facilities which include a Pro Shop, changing rooms and a practice ground.
☎ 0526 63229 for the Professional

Food and drink
The Clubhouse Bar is open daily during normal licensing hours and also serves bar snacks. The restaurant is open for lunch and dinner every day.

GREEN FEES

Per round 🎟 £21   Per weekday 🎟 £28
Per weekend round 🎟 £23
Per weekend day 🎟 £31
Methods of payment: cash/cheque with valid banker's card

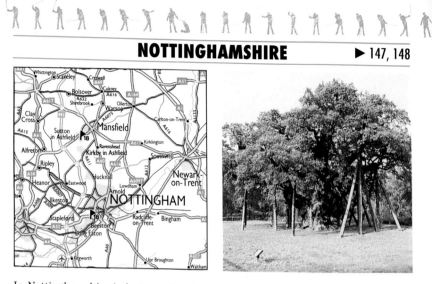

In Nottinghamshire industry and agricultural co-exist. Mixed farming, pastureland and collieries surround the ancient city of Nottingham, an historic and industrial centre. Tracts of Sherwood Forest, once a royal hunting forest and home of the legendary Robin Hood, remain providing pleasant walks.

WOLLATON PARK GOLF CLUB

Wollaton Park
Nottingham
Nottinghamshire
☎ 0602 787574

Wollaton Park Golf Club has a pleasant 18-hole parkland course in the grounds of Wollaton Hall. It welcomes visitors with few restrictions.

GETTING THERE

Road: Off the A52 Nottingham to Derby road just after it crosses the Nottingham ring road, 2½ miles west of Nottingham city centre

THE COURSE

Yds 6495   Par 71   SSS 71

VISITING PLAYERS

Restrictions

Visiting players are welcomed but it is advisable to contact the club in advance to check on any Society or Competition Days when there will be restrictions.

Handicap requirements

Visiting players do not require a Certificate of Handicap.

How to contact the club

Telephone call or letter.

COURSE FACILITIES

The Professional can be contacted via the club telephone number for details of tuition fees and information on all other facilities which include a Pro Shop, changing rooms and equipment hire.

Food and drink

The Clubhouse Bar is open during normal licensing hours and serves drinks and snacks; the restaurant serves lunch and tea.

GREEN FEES

Per weekday 🏌 £20.50
Per weekend day 🏌 £28
Methods of payment: cash/cheque with valid banker's card

NOTTINGHAMSHIRE

COXMOOR GOLF CLUB

Coxmoor Road
Sutton-in-Ashfield
Mansfield
Nottinghamshire
☎ 0623 557359

Coxmoor Golf Club has an undulating
18-hole heathland course. It has few
restrictions on visitors.

GETTING THERE

Road: Off the A611 Mansfield to Nottingham
road, 2 miles south of Mansfield

THE COURSE

Yds 6501 Par 73 SSS 72

VISITING PLAYERS

Restrictions
Tuesday is Ladies Day, there are sometimes
restrictions at weekends and visitors should
telephone the club number to check before
setting out.

Handicap requirements
A Certificate of Handicap is required by all
visiting players although there is no
maximum requirement.

How to contact the club
Telephone call or letter.

COURSE FACILITIES

The Professional, David Ridley, can be
contacted by telephone for details of tuition
fees and information about other facilities
which include a Pro Shop and changing
rooms.
☎ 0623 559906 for the Professional

Food and drink
The Clubhouse has a fully licensed bar and
restaurant and both are open from 11am to
11pm every day.

GREEN FEES

Per weekday 🏷 £22
Per weekend day 🏷 £25
Methods of payment: cash/cheque with valid
banker's card

South Yorkshire has a distinctive, rugged moorland beauty. Sheffield, its major city, lies below the moors in a natural amphitheatre of the south Pennine slopes, a fine setting with breathtaking countryside nearby.

HALLAMSHIRE GOLF CLUB

Sandygate
Sheffield
South Yorkshire
☎ 0742 302153

Hallamshire Golf Club has an 18-hole moorland course with spectacular views over the Peak District. It welcomes visiting players but has restricted start times.

GETTING THERE

Road: Off the A57 Sheffield to Manchester road, 3½ miles west of Sheffield city centre

THE COURSE

Yds 6396   Par 71   SSS 71

VISITING PLAYERS

Restrictions

During the week visitors may not start before 9.30am nor between 12 noon and 1.30pm. In order to play the course at weekends a visitor must notify the course in advance and agree a start time.

Handicap requirements

A Certificate of Handicap is required by all visitors but with no set maximum handicap.

How to contact the club

Telephone call or letter.

COURSE FACILITIES

The Professional can be contacted by telephone for details of charges and information about all other facilities which include a Pro Shop, equipment hire and changing rooms. Tuition fees are £6 per half hour.
☎ 0742 305222 for the Professional

Food and drink

The Clubhouse Bar is open during normal licensing hours and also serves snacks; the restaurant is open only for lunch, between 12 noon and 2pm.

GREEN FEES

Per weekday 🏌 £27
Per weekend day 🏌 £33
Methods of payment: cash only

51

MANCHESTER

Manchester, a key industrial and commercial centre and once a major inland port, is sited close to the wooded valleys and moors of the Pennines. A lively modern city with some exciting redevelopment programmes underway, it is home to the Hallé orchestra and several notable museums.

STOCKPORT GOLF CLUB

Offerton Road
Stockport
Cheshire
☎ 061 427 2001

Stockport Golf Club has an 18-hole parkland course and welcomes visitors without restriction.

GETTING THERE

Road: Off the A627 Romiley to Hazel Grove road, just south of jct with the A626 Stockport to Marple road

THE COURSE

Yds 6290   Par 71   SSS 71

VISITING PLAYERS

Restrictions

Tuesday is Ladies Day and there are often Society Days on Wednesdays and Thursdays, telephone the Professional's number to check on accessibility. Other than these there are no restrictions on visiting players.

Handicap requirements

Visiting players do not require a Certificate of Handicap.

How to contact the club

Telephone call or letter.

COURSE FACILITIES

The Professional can be contacted by telephone for details of tuition fees and information on all other facilities which include a Pro Shop and changing rooms.
☎ 061 427 2421 for the Professional

Food and drink

The Clubhouse Bar is open during normal licensing hours and serves snacks; the restaurant offers lunch and tea every day.

GREEN FEES

Per weekday 🏌 £20
Per weekend day 🏌 £30

Methods of payment: cash/cheque with valid banker's card

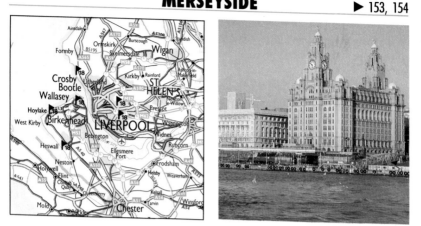

Merseyside offers both the attractions of the city of Liverpool; renowned for its spirit, humour and patronage of the arts as well as the scenery and resorts of the Wirral peninsula, miles of beaches, dunes, parks and sporting facilities, the Merseyside playground.

WEST LANCASHIRE GOLF CLUB

Hall Road West
Blundellsands
Liverpool
Merseyside
☎ 051 924 1076

West Lancashire Golf Club was founded in 1873 and has a challenging 18-hole links course overlooking the Mersey Estuary. It welcomes visitors with few restrictions.

GETTING THERE

Road: Off the A565 Liverpool to Southport road on the coast just north of Crosby

THE COURSE

Yds 6286   Par 72   SSS 73

VISITING PLAYERS

Restrictions

Tuesday is Ladies Day. On competition days visitors may not start before 3pm. Please telephone the club number to check. Other than these there are no restrictions on visitors.

Handicap requirements

Visiting players require a Certificate of Handicap.

How to contact the club

Telephone call or letter.

COURSE FACILITIES

The Professional, David Lloyd, can be contacted by telephone for details of tuition fees and information about all other facilities which include a Pro Shop, equipment hire and changing rooms.
☎ 051 924 5662 for the Professional

Food and drink

The Clubhouse Bar has three licensed bars: Gentlemen, Ladies and Mixed – which also serve bar snacks and are open all day, every day. The restaurant is open for lunch and dinner.

Leisure facilities

The Clubhouse has a snooker room (gentlemen only).

GREEN FEES

Per weekday round 🏌 £20
Per weekday 🏌 £30
Per weekend round 🏌 £35

Methods of payment: cash/cheque with valid banker's card

MERSEYSIDE

HEWSWALL GOLF CLUB

Cottage Lane
Gayton
Heswall
Wirral
☎ 051 342 1237

Heswall Golf Club has a pleasant 18-hole parkland course overlooking the Dee Estuary and the mountains of North Wales. It has very few restrictions for visitors.

GETTING THERE

Road: Off the A540 Chester to West Kirby road just to the south of Heswall

THE COURSE

Yds 6472   Par 72   SSS 72

VISITING PLAYERS

Restrictions

Visitors are welcome at any time but they should telephone the club number to check for Competition or Society Days.

Handicap requirements

A Certificate of Handicap is required by all visitors, a maximum 28 for men and 36 for women.

How to contact the club

Telephone call.

COURSE FACILITIES

The Professional may be contacted by telephone for details of charges and information on all other facilities which include a Pro Shop, equipment hire, changing rooms and a very large practice green.
☎ 051 342 7431 for the Professional

Food and drink

The Clubhouse Bar is open all day every day and serves bar snacks; full meals can only be provided by prior arrangement.

Leisure facilities

The Clubhouse has a snooker room with 2 tables.

GREEN FEES

Per weekday 🏌 £20
Per weekend day 🏌 £25

Methods of payment: cash/cheque with valid banker's card

ROYAL LIVERPOOL GOLF CLUB

Meols Drive
Hoylake
Wirral
☎ 051 632 3101 (Clubhouse)
☎ 051 632 6757 (Starter)

The Royal Liverpool Golf Club has a classic 18-hole championship links course and has staged 10 British Open Championships. It has few restrictions on visitors but, because of its popularity, it is essential that visiting players contact the club well in advance of their intended visit to check on availability and reserve start times.

GETTING THERE

Road: Off the A553 Moreton to Hoylake road just outside Hoylake; on the Wirral Peninsula

THE COURSE

Yds 6804   Par 72   SSS 74

VISITING PLAYERS

Restrictions

Telephone the starter to check on availability and reserve start times.

Handicap requirements

A Certificate of Handicap or a letter of introduction from your club is essential, although there is no maximum handicap.

How to contact the club

Telephone call, letter or fax.
Fax number 051 632 6737

COURSE FACILITIES

The Professional can be contacted by telephone for details of tuition fees and information about all other facilities which include limited equipment hire, a Pro Shop and changing rooms.
☎ 051 632 5868 for the Professional

Food and drink

The Clubhouse Bars are open all day between the beginning of May and the end of September, at other times of the year opening times are more restricted. The bars serve hot bar snacks between 12 noon and 2.15pm every day and soup and sandwiches throughout the afternoon.

GREEN FEES

Per weekday round 🏌 £32
Per 2 rounds (weekdays) 🏌 £45
Per weekend round 🏌 £45

Methods of payment: cash/cheque with valid banker's card

CHILDWALL GOLF CLUB

Naylors Road
Gateacre
Liverpool
☎ 051 487 0654

Childwall Golf Club has an 18-hole parkland course on the outskirts of Liverpool. It is a very popular and busy course which welcomes visitors without restriction.

GETTING THERE

Road: Off the B5178 Liverpool to Widnes road, 7 miles east of Liverpool city centre and 1 mile east of Childwall

THE COURSE

Yds 6425   Par 72   SSS 71

VISITING PLAYERS

Restrictions

There are no restrictions on visitors but the course is very popular, particularly with Societies, and it is sensible to contact the club in advance to check on accessibility.

Handicap requirements

Visiting players do not require a Certificate of Handicap.

How to contact the club

Telephone call or letter.

COURSE FACILITIES

The club has a Professional who can be contacted by telephone for details of tuition fees and information about all other facilities which include a Pro Shop, changing rooms and equipment hire.

Food and drink

The Clubhouse Bar is well-equipped and serves snacks, it is open during normal licensing hours. The restaurant provides lunch, tea and dinner.

GREEN FEES

Per weekday 🏷 £17
Per weekend day 🏷 £25

Methods of payment: cash/cheque with valid banker's card

WEST DERBY GOLF CLUB

Yewtree Lane
West Derby
Liverpool
Merseyside
☎ 051 254 1034

West Derby Golf Club has an 18-hole parkland course with tree lined fairways. It welcomes visitors but holds many competitions which restrict accessibility.

GETTING THERE

Road: 2½ miles from the M57, in central Liverpool

THE COURSE

Yds 6332   Par 72   SSS 70

VISITING PLAYERS

Restrictions

Visiting players must telephone the club number in advance to check on Competition and Society Days, other than this there are no restrictions.

Handicap requirements

A Certificate of Handicap is required by all visitors but there is no stated maximum.

How to contact the club

Telephone call or letter.

COURSE FACILITIES

The Professional can be contacted by telephone for details of tuition fees and information about all other facilities which include a Pro Shop and changing rooms.
☎ 051 220 5478 for the Professional

Food and drink

The Clubhouse Bar is open during normal licensing hours and serves bar snacks and sandwiches.

GREEN FEES

Per weekday 🏷 £18.50
Per weekend day 🏷 £25

Methods of payment: cash/cheque with valid banker's card

MERSEYSIDE

WALLASEY GOLF CLUB

Bayswater Road
Wallasey
Merseyside
☎ 051 691 1024

Wallasey Golf Club has an 18-hole seaside links course overlooking Liverpool Bay. Frank B.G. Stableford was a member of the club from 1914 until his death in 1959 and devised the 'Stableford System' for competitions, it was first used at Wallasey in 1932. The club welcomes visitors but there are restrictions on start times.

GETTING THERE

Road: Off the A554 Wallasey to New Brighton road just north of Wallasey town centre, on the Wirral Peninsula

THE COURSE

Yds 6607   Par 72   SSS 73

VISITING PLAYERS

Restrictions

During weekdays visiting players must tee-off after 9.30am, on Wednesdays they cannot tee-off between 12 noon and 2pm. At weekends visitors should telephone the Professional to reserve a start time.
☎ 051 638 3888 for the Professional

Handicap requirements

Visiting players require a Certificate of Handicap.

How to contact the club

Telephone call or letter.

COURSE FACILITIES

The Professional can be contacted by telephone for details of tuition fees and information about all other facilities which include a Pro Shop, equipment hire and changing rooms.
☎ 051 638 3888 for the Professional

Food and drink

The Clubhouse Bar serves drinks and snacks from 11.30am to 2.30pm and 4.30pm to 11pm every day. The restaurant is open for lunch only between 12 noon and 2.30pm every day.

GREEN FEES

Per weekday 🏌 £20.50
Per weekend day 🏌 £24.50
Methods of payment: cash/cheque with valid banker's card

LANCASHIRE

Lancashire's 60 miles of sandy coastline, plus the excellent entertainment facilities that have been developed, make it the resort area for the north of England. A rich contrast is provided by the rugged fells and tiny valleys that lead up to the Pennines in the east.

THE CHORLEY GOLF CLUB

Hall O' Th' Hill
Heath Charnock
Chorley
Lancashire
☎ 0257 480263

The Chorley Golf Club has an 18-hole rolling moorland course with views across the Pennines and the Lancashire coast. It welcomes visitors with few restrictions.

GETTING THERE

Road: Off the A673, 2 miles south of Chorley

THE COURSE

Yds 6277 Par 71 SSS 70

VISITING PLAYERS

Restrictions

There are no restrictions for visiting players; contact the club in advance to confirm availability.

Handicap requirements

A Certificate of Handicap is required for all visitors but there is no maximum handicap requirement.

How to contact the club

Letter preferred.

COURSE FACILITIES

The Professional, Paul Wesselingh, can be contacted via the club telephone number for details of tuition fees and information on all other facilities which include a Pro Shop, equipment hire and changing rooms.

Food and drink

The Clubhouse lounge bar is open 7 days a week during normal licensing hours. The restaurant serves meals every day.

Leisure facilities

The Clubhouse has a games room and a snooker room.

GREEN FEES

Per weekday 🏷 £20
Per weekend day 🏷 £30
Methods of payment: cash/cheque with valid banker's card

57

LANCASHIRE

FLEETWOOD GOLF CLUB

Princes Way
Fleetwood
Lancashire
☎ 0253 873661

Fleetwood Golf Club has a windy 18-hole seaside links course overlooking the Irish Sea. It welcomes visitors with few restrictions.

GETTING THERE

Road: On the coast just to the west of Fleetwood town centre

THE COURSE

Yds 6628   Par 72   SSS 72

VISITING PLAYERS

Restrictions

There are no formal restrictions on visitors but check with the club about Society Days and Competition Days.

Handicap requirements

A Certificate of Handicap is required by all visitors but there is no maximum requirement.

How to contact the club

Telephone call or letter.

COURSE FACILITIES

The Professional, Clive T. Burgess, can be contacted via the club telephone number for details of charges and information on all other facilities which include limited equipment hire, a Pro Shop and changing rooms. Tuition fees are £7 per half hour.

Food and drink

The Clubhouse Bar and dining room overlook the 18th green; the bar is open from 11.30am to 2pm and from 4pm to 11pm every day and serves snacks. The dining room serves lunch and dinner daily.

Leisure facilities

The Clubhouse has a snooker room.

GREEN FEES

Per weekday 🏷 £20
Per weekend day and Bank
Holidays 🏷 £25
Methods of payment: cash/cheque with valid banker's card

ORMSKIRK GOLF CLUB

Cranes Lane
Lathom
Ormskirk
Lancashire
☎ 0695 572112

Ormskirk Golf Club has an 18-hole parkland course. It welcomes visiting players.

GETTING THERE

Road: Off the A577 Ormskirk to Skelmersdale road, 2 miles east of Ormskirk town centre

THE COURSE

Yds 6333   Par 70   SSS 70

VISITING PLAYERS

Restrictions

There are no restrictions on visiting players but it is advisable to contact the club in advance to reserve a start time.

Handicap requirements

Visitors do not require a Certificate of Handicap.

How to contact the club

Telephone call or letter.

COURSE FACILITIES

The Professional can be contacted on 0695 572074 for details of tuition fees and information on all other facilities which include changing rooms and a Pro Shop.

Food and drink

The Clubhouse catering facilities include a bar which also serves snacks and a restaurant that offers a full range of meals throughout the day.

GREEN FEES

Per weekday excluding Wednesdays 🏷 £30
Per weekend day and Wednesdays 🏷 £35
Methods of payment: cash/cheque with valid banker's card

LANCASHIRE

PENWORTHAM GOLF CLUB

Blundell Lane
Penwortham
Preston
Lancashire
☎ 0772 742345

Penwortham Golf Club has an 18-hole tree-lined parkland course, it welcomes visitors although there are start time restrictions on Saturdays.

GETTING THERE

Road: Off the A59 Southport to Liverpool road, 1½ miles west of Preston

THE COURSE

Yds 5915   Par 69   SSS 68

VISITING PLAYERS

Restrictions
Saturdays are Competition Days and visiting players cannot tee-off between 10am in the mornings and 2pm in the afternoons, other than this there are no restrictions.

Handicap requirements
Visiting players are not required to have a Certificate of Handicap.

How to contact the club
Telephone call or letter.

COURSE FACILITIES

The Professional, J. Wright, can be contacted via the club telephone number for details of tuition fees and information on all other facilities which include a Pro Shop and changing rooms.

Food and drink
The Clubhouse has a fully licensed bar and the restaurant serves lunches and dinner.

Leisure facilities
The Clubhouse has a snooker table.

GREEN FEES

Per weekday   £20
Per weekend day   £25

Methods of payment: cash/cheque with valid banker's card

HESKETH GOLF CLUB

Cockle Dick's Lane
Cambridge Road
Southport
Lancashire
☎ 0704 536897

Hesketh Golf Club was founded in 1885 and has an 18-hole links course. It welcomes visitors.

GETTING THERE

Road: Off the A585 Southport to Preston road, 1 mile north of Southport town centre, on the coast

THE COURSE

Yds 6478   Par 71   SSS 72

VISITING PLAYERS

Restrictions
Visiting players must contact the club in advance to reserve a start time.

Handicap requirements
All visiting players must have a Certificate of Handicap although there is no stated maximum.

How to contact the club
Telephone call or letter.

COURSE FACILITIES

The Professional can be contacted by telephone for details of fees and information on all other facilities which include a Pro Shop, changing rooms and a practice ground.
☎ 0704 580050 for the Professional

Food and drink
The Clubhouse has 2 bars open daily during normal licensing hours, both also serve bar snacks. The dining room serves lunch and dinner every day by arrangement.

GREEN FEES

Per weekday round   £20.50
Per weekday   £30.75
Per weekend round   £35.75

Methods of payment: cash/cheque with valid banker's card

LANCASHIRE

THE ROYAL BIRKDALE GOLF CLUB

Waterloo Road
Birkdale
Southport
Lancashire
☎ 0704 67920

The Royal Birkdale Golf Club has a championship 18-hole links course and is one of the venues for the British Open Championship. It welcomes visiting players but it is a very popular course and there are restrictions on start times.

GETTING THERE

Road: Off the A565 Southport to Liverpool road, 1½ miles south of Southport town centre

THE COURSE

Yds 6703   Par 72   SSS 73

VISITING PLAYERS

Restrictions
Visitors are welcome but they must contact the club well in advance to check accessibility and reserve a start time; there are restrictions on visitors throughout the week.

Handicap requirements
Visiting players must have a Certificate of handicap, a maximum 24 for men and 36 for women.

How to contact the club
Telephone call or letter.

COURSE FACILITIES

The Professional can be contacted by telephone for details of tuition fees and information about all other facilities which include a Pro Shop, equipment hire and changing rooms.
☎ 0704 68857 for the Professional

Food and drink
The Royal Birkdale Clubhouse has a bar that is open during normal licensing hours and also serves bar snacks. More substantial meals can be provided, arrangements must be made with the club when you contact them to reserve a start time.

GREEN FEES

Per round 🏌 £46 Per weekday 🏌 £67
Per weekend round 🏌 £67

Methods of payment: cash/cheque with valid banker's card

SHAW HILL HOTEL GOLF AND COUNTRY CLUB

Preston Road
Whittle-le-Woods
Chorley
Lancashire
☎ 0257 269221

Shaw Hill is a well-equipped hotel and country club with a scenic 18-hole parkland course. It welcomes visitors without restriction and offers green fee reductions for hotel residents.

GETTING THERE

Road: Off the A6 Chorley to Preston Road, 1 mile north of Chorley

THE COURSE

Yds 6311   Par 72   SSS 71

VISITING PLAYERS

Restrictions
There are no restrictions for visiting players.

Handicap requirements
A Certificate of Handicap is required by all visiting players, a maximum 28 for men and 36 for women.

How to contact the club
Telephone call or letter.

COURSE FACILITIES

The Professional, David Clarke, can be contacted by telephone for details of tuition fees and information on all other facilities which include a Pro Shop, equipment hire and changing rooms.
☎ 0257 279222 for the Professional

Food and drink
The hotel has a fully licensed bar, which also serves hot and cold snacks, and a restaurant open to both residents and visitors during normal licensing hours.

Leisure facilities
The hotel offers first class accommodation, please telephone the main club number for information on prices and reservations. The leisure club offers a wide range of facilities which include a sauna and solarium.

GREEN FEES

Per round 🏌 £20 Per weekday 🏌 £30
Per weekend day 🏌 £40

Methods of payment: cash/cheque with valid banker's card/Visa/Access/Mastercard/American Express/Diners

YORKSHIRE

▶ 157, 158

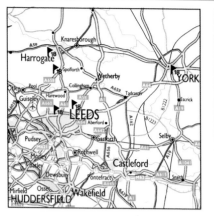

Yorkshire's huge moorland expanses of grass, heather and peat seem untouched by the passage of time. Elsewhere the castles, cathedrals, great houses and industrial architecture document the area's turbulent history highlighting the key role it played in Britain's Industrial Revolution.

OAKDALE GOLF CLUB

Kent Road
Harrogate
North Yorkshire
☎ 0423 567162

Oakdale Golf Club has an 18-hole parkland course, and welcomes visitors without restriction.

GETTING THERE

Road: Off the A61 Harrogate to Ripon road, 1 mile north of Harrogate town centre

THE COURSE

Yds 6456   Par 71   SSS 71

VISITING PLAYERS

Restrictions

Visiting players are welcome without restriction other than the need to contact the club in advance to book a start time.

Handicap requirements

Visitors need either a Certificate of Handicap or a letter of introduction from their own club.

How to contact the club

Telephone call or letter.

COURSE FACILITIES

The Professional can be contacted by telephone for details of tuition fees and information about all other facilities which include a Pro Shop, changing rooms and a practice ground.
☎ 0423 560510 for the Professional

Food and drink

The Clubhouse Bar serves drinks and snacks and is open daily during normal licensing hours. The dining room serves appropriate meals throughout the day.

GREEN FEES

Per weekday 🏌 £25
Per weekend round 🏌 £23
Methods of payment: cash/cheque with valid banker's card

MOORTOWN GOLF CLUB

Harrogate Road
Alwoodley
Leeds
☎ 0532 686521

Moortown Golf Club has an 18-hole heathland course. It welcomes visitors but it is essential that the visiting player confirms the arrangements in advance with the club secretary.

GETTING THERE

Road: Off the A61 Leeds to Harrogate road, 5 miles north of Leeds city centre

THE COURSE

Yds 6544 Par 71 SSS 72

VISITING PLAYERS

Restrictions

Visiting players are not subject to any specific restrictions but must make and confirm their arrangements in advance with the Club Secretary or the Professional.

Handicap requirements

A Certificate of Handicap is required by all visiting players.

How to contact the club

Telephone call or letter.

COURSE FACILITIES

The Professional can be contacted by telephone for details of tuition fees and information on all other facilities which include a Pro Shop, changing rooms and a large practice area.
☎ 0532 683636 for the Professional

Food and drink

Visiting players should discuss their catering arrangements and make reservations for the dining room with the Catering Manager before starting play.

GREEN FEES

Per round ♿ £30   Per weekday ♿ £35
Per weekend day ♿ £40
Methods of payment: cash/cheque with valid banker's card

SAND MOOR GOLF CLUB

Alwoodley Lane
Leeds
West Yorkshire
☎ 0532 685180

Sand Moor Golf Club has an 18-hole heathland course situated alongside Eccup Reservoir. It welcomes visitors with few restrictions.

GETTING THERE

Road: Off the A61 Leeds to Harrogate road, 5 miles north of Leeds city centre

THE COURSE

Yds 6429 Par 71 SSS 71

VISITING PLAYERS

Restrictions

Visiting players are welcome but are advised to contact the club in advance to check accessibility and reserve a start time.

Handicap requirements

All visiting players must have a Certificate of Handicap (no stated maximum) or a letter of introduction from their own club.

How to contact the club

Telephone call or letter.

COURSE FACILITIES

The Professional can be contacted by telephone for details of charges and information about all other facilities which include a Pro Shop and changing rooms.
☎ 0532 683925 for the Professional

Food and drink

The Clubhouse Bar serves drinks and snacks and is open during normal licensing hours; full lunches are also served throughout the week.

GREEN FEES

Per weekday ♿ £30
Per weekend round ♿ £30
Methods of payment: cash/cheque with valid banker's card

PANNAL GOLF CLUB

Follifoot Road
Pannal
Harrogate
North Yorkshire
☎ 0423 872628

Pannal Golf Club has a fine championship 18-hole moorland course. It welcomes visitors but is very popular and hosts many competitions, particularly at weekends; it is essential to contact the club in advance to check accessibility and reserve a start time.

GETTING THERE

Road: Off the A61 Harrogate to Leeds road at Pannal village, 2 miles south of Harrogate

THE COURSE

Yds 6559 Par 72 SSS 72

VISITING PLAYERS

Restrictions
Because of its popularity, visiting players must contact the club in advance to reserve a start time.

Handicap requirements
Visitors do not require a Certificate of Handicap.

How to contact the club
Telephone call or letter.

COURSE FACILITIES

The Professional can be contacted by telephone for details of tuition fees and information about all other facilities which include a Pro Shop, changing rooms and equipment hire.
☎ 0423 872620 for the Professional

Food and drink
The Clubhouse Bar serves drinks and snacks and is open during normal licensing hours. The restaurant serves lunches throughout the week.

GREEN FEES

Per weekday 🏌 £26
Per weekend round 🏌 £31
Methods of payment: cash/cheque with valid banker's card

FULFORD GOLF CLUB

Heslington Lane
York
North Yorkshire
☎ 0904 413579

Fulford Golf Club has a flat 18-hole parkland course. It welcomes visiting players but it is very popular and hosts a number of nationally-known competitions; it is essential to contact the club in advance to check on accessibility and reserve a start time.

GETTING THERE

Road: Off the A19 York to Selby road, 2 miles south of York city centre in Heslington village

THE COURSE

Yds 6809 Par 72 SSS 72

VISITING PLAYERS

Restrictions
Visiting players must contact the Club Secretary in advance to check on restrictions and reserve a start time.

Handicap requirements
All visitors must have a Certificate of Handicap (no stated maximum) or proof of membership of a recognised golf club.

How to contact the club
Telephone call or letter.

COURSE FACILITIES

The Professional can be contacted via the club telephone number for details of fees and information on all other facilities which include a Pro Shop, changing rooms and equipment hire.

Food and drink
The Clubhouse Bar is open during normal licensing hours, it also serves bar snacks. If you require more substantial food you should discuss your catering needs with the Club Secretary when you contact him to check accessibility and reserve a start time.

GREEN FEES

Per weekday 🏌 £25
Per weekend day 🏌 £30
Methods of payment: cash/cheque with valid banker's card

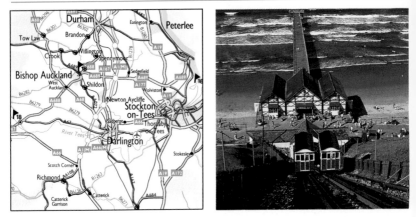

Durham and Cleveland incorporate the spectacular rugged scenery of the west Durham moors, the dramatic cliffs of the coast and the inland escarpments, outstanding beauty spots and majestic cathedrals with the most densely populated part of the country, the coastal area between the Tees and the Tyne estuary.

BARNARD CASTLE GOLF CLUB

Barnard Castle
Durham
☎ 0833 38355

Barnard Castle Golf Club has an 18-hole moorland course overlooking the River Tees. It welcomes visitors without restriction.

GETTING THERE

Road: Off the B6278, 1 mile north of Barnard Castle town centre

THE COURSE

Yds 5838   Par 71   SSS 68

VISITING PLAYERS

Restrictions

There are no restrictions on visiting players.

Handicap requirements

Visitors do not require a Certificate of Handicap.

How to contact the club

Telephone call.

COURSE FACILITIES

The Professional can be contacted by telephone for details of tuition fees and information about all other facilities which include a Pro Shop, changing rooms and equipment hire.
☎ 0833 37237 for the Professional

Food and drink

The Clubhouse Bar serves drinks and snacks and is open daily during normal licensing hours. If you require a full lunch you should contact the club in advance to discuss arrangements.

GREEN FEES

Per weekday 🍴 £12
Per weekend day 🍴 £18
Methods of payment: cash/cheque with valid banker's card

BISHOP AUCKLAND GOLF CLUB

High Plains
Durham Road
Bishop Auckland
Durham
☎ 0388 602198

Bishop Auckland Golf Club has a large acreage 18-hole parkland course. There are few restrictions for visitors.

GETTING THERE

Off the A689 Bishop Auckland to Rushyford road, 1 mile east of Bishop Auckland

THE COURSE

Yds 6420   Par 72   SSS 71

VISITING PLAYERS

Restrictions

Tuesday is Ladies Day and the club holds most of its competitions at weekends, when the course can get very busy. Telephone the Professional before setting out to check availability, other than this there are no restrictions.

Handicap requirements

Visiting players require a Certificate of Handicap or a letter of introduction from their golf club.

How to contact the club

Telephone call.

COURSE FACILITIES

The Professional can be contacted by telephone for details of tuition fees and information on all other facilities which include a Pro Shop, equipment hire and changing rooms.
☎ 0388 661618 for the Professional

Food and drink

The Clubhouse Bar is open for drinks and snacks from 12 noon to 2pm and 4pm to 10.30pm every day except Sundays when it closes at 8.30pm; full lunches and dinners are also served.

GREEN FEES

Per weekday 🎫 £19
Per weekend round 🎫 £19

Methods of payment: cash/cheque with valid banker's card

SEATON CAREW GOLF CLUB

Tees Road
Seaton Carew
Hartlepool
Cleveland
☎ 0429 266249

Seaton Carew Golf Club was founded in 1874 and is one of the oldest golf clubs in the world. It has two 18-hole seaside links courses (the two courses have 14 shared holes) and welcomes visitors with few restrictions.

GETTING THERE

Road: Off the A178 Hartlepool to Middlesbrough road, on the south side of Seaton Carew

THE COURSE

	Old Course 🏴18	Brabazon Course 🏴18
Yds	6604	6849
Par	72	73
SSS	72	72

VISITING PLAYERS

Restrictions

Visiting players are welcome without restriction but they should telephone the club in advance as it hosts many Society and Competition Days.

Handicap requirements

There is no requirement for visitors to have a Certificate of Handicap.

How to contact the club

Telephone call or letter.

COURSE FACILITIES

The Professional, W. Hector, may be contacted via the club telephone number for details of charges and information on all other facilities which include a Pro Shop, equipment hire and changing rooms.

Food and drink

The Clubhouse has a lounge bar and Blue Room Bar serving drinks during the day, and a separate ladies lounge. The restaurant serves meals throughout the day, including dinner.

Leisure facilities

The Clubhouse has a snooker room.

GREEN FEES

Per weekday 🎫 £19
Per weekend day and Bank Holidays 🎫 £26
Per week 🎫 £85
Visiting ladies per day 🎫 £19
Juniors per day 🎫 £12

Methods of payment: cash/cheque with valid banker's card

SOUTH CUMBRIA

South Cumbria contains the Lake District, an area of ouestanding beauty, fertile valleys, picturesque lakes, lofty fells, high and lonely places, noisy mountain streams, a dream landscape for the walker, hiker, sailing enthusiast, naturalist and the inspiration for many famous writers.

WINDERMERE GOLF CLUB

Cleabarrow
Bowness-on-Windermere
Cumbria
☎ 05394 43123

Windermere Golf Club has an 18-hole moorland course with spectacular views over the Lake District. It welcomes visitors with few restrictions.

GETTING THERE

Road: Off the B5284, 1 mile east of Bowness-on-Windermere

THE COURSE

Yds 5006   Par 67   SSS 65

VISITING PLAYERS

Restrictions

Visiting players start times must be between 10am and 12 noon or 2pm and 4.30pm, other than this there are no restrictions.

Handicap requirements

All visitors must have a Certificate of Handicap although there is no maximum handicap limit.

How to contact the club

Telephone call or letter.

COURSE FACILITIES

The Professional, Stephen Rooke, can be contacted by telephone for details of tuition fees and information about all other facilities which include a Pro Shop, equipment hire, changing rooms and a large practice area.
☎ 05394 43550 for the Professional

Food and drink

The well-equipped Clubhouse has a bar serving drinks and snacks between 11am and 11pm every day; the dining room is open for lunch between 12 noon and 2pm and for dinner between 6.30pm and 9pm every day.

Leisure facilities

The Clubhouse has a games room with snooker and pool tables.

GREEN FEES

Per weekday 🏷 £17
Per weekend day 🏷 £23
Methods of payment: cash only

66

SEASCALE GOLF CLUB

The Banks
Seascale
Cumbria
☎ 09467 28202

Seascale Golf Club has an 18-hole seaside links course. Visitors are welcome without restriction.

GETTING THERE

Road: Off the B5343 to the north of Seascale village, on the coast

THE COURSE

Yds 6419   Par 71   SSS 71

VISITING PLAYERS

Restrictions

There are no restrictions but visiting players should telephone the club number to check on course availability.

Handicap requirements

Visiting players do not require a Certificate of Handicap.

How to contact the club

Telephone call or letter.

COURSE FACILITIES

Facilities at the course include equipment hire, a Pro Shop and changing rooms.

Food and drink

The Clubhouse is open between 8am and 11pm every day and snack food is available throughout these hours; the bar is open from 12 noon to 11pm on Monday to Saturday and normal Sunday licensing hours.

GREEN FEES

Per weekday 🛒 £18
Per weekend day 🛒 £22

Methods of payment: cash/cheque with valid banker's card

ULVERSTON GOLF CLUB

Bardsea Park
Ulverston
Cumbria
☎ 0229 52824

Ulverston Golf Club has an 18-hole parkland course. The club welcomes visitors with few restrictions.

GETTING THERE

Road: Off the A5087 Ulverston to Barrow-in-Furness coast road just north of Bardsea village

THE COURSE

Yds 6122   Par 71   SSS 69

VISITING PLAYERS

Restrictions

Visiting players are welcome at all times, but members have priority on the first tee before 9.30am every day and all day on Tuesdays (Ladies Day) and Saturdays (Men's Competition Day).

Handicap requirements

A Certificate of Handicap is required by all visiting players, maximum 28 for men and 36 for women.

How to contact the club

Telephone call or letter.

COURSE FACILITIES

The Professional, M.R. Smith, can be contacted by telephone for details of tuition fees and information on all other facilities which include a Pro Shop, equipment hire and changing rooms.
☎ 0229 52806 for the Professional

Food and drink

The Clubhouse Bar and restaurant are open during normal licensing hours; snacks are available during the day.

GREEN FEES

Per weekday 🛒 £17
Per weekend day 🛒 £20

Methods of payment: cash/cheque with valid banker's card

NORTH CUMBRIA

North Cumbria around Carlisle, the ancient capital of north-west England, is rich in historical associations and remains including fragments of Hadrian's Wall. There are superb sands at Silloth and glorious views both inland and across the Solway Firth.

BRAMPTON GOLF CLUB

Taulin Tarn
Brampton
Cumbria
☎ 06977 2255

Brampton Golf Club has a very scenic 18-hole mixed parkland and fellside course. It welcomes visitors without restriction.

GETTING THERE

Road: Off the B6413 Brampton to Castle Carrock road, 2 miles south-east of Brampton

THE COURSE

Yds 6420   Par 72   SSS 71

VISITING PLAYERS

Restrictions

There are no restrictions for visitors, although it is advisable to telephone the club number before setting out to confirm the availability of start times.

Handicap requirements

Visiting players do not require a Certificate of Handicap.

How to contact the club

Telephone call or letter.

COURSE FACILITIES

The Professional, Stephen Harrison, may be contacted by telephone for details of tuition fees and information on all other facilities which include a Pro Shop, equipment hire and changing rooms.
☎ 06977 2000 for the Professional

Food and drink

The Clubhouse Bar is open every day from 11am to 2pm and 5pm to 11pm. The restaurant is also open daily and serves everything from sandwiches to 5-course lunches and dinners.

Leisure facilities

The Clubhouse has a games room with a snooker table and other indoor games.

GREEN FEES

Per weekday 🏌 £12
Per weekend day 🏌 £16
Per week 🏌 £40

Methods of payment: cash/cheque with valid banker's card

STONEYHOLME MUNICIPAL GOLF CLUB

St Aidans Road
Carlisle
Cumbria
☎ 0228 34856

Stoneyholme Golf Club is a council-owned 18-hole parkland course bounded by the River Eden. It welcomes visitors without restriction.

GETTING THERE

Road: Off the A69 Carlisle to Brampton road, 2 miles east of Carlisle

THE COURSE

Yds 5773 Par 68 SSS 68

VISITING PLAYERS

Restrictions

There are no restrictions on visiting players but pre-booking of start times is recommended, particularly at weekends.

Handicap requirements

Visiting players do not require a Certificate of Handicap.

How to contact the club

Telephone call.

COURSE FACILITIES

The Professional can be contacted via the club telephone number for details of tuition fees and information on all other facilities which include a Pro Shop, changing rooms, equipment hire and a practice ground.

Food and drink

The Clubhouse Bar serves drinks and snacks and is open during normal licensing hours. The restaurant serves lunch and tea daily.

SILLOTH ON SOLWAY GOLF CLUB

Silloth
Cumbria
☎ 06973 31304

Silloth on Solway Golf Club has a wonderful 18-hole links course overlooking the Solway Firth, with views over Scotland and the Lake District. It welcomes visiting players without restriction.

GETTING THERE

Road: On the B5300 coast road north from Maryport just west of Silloth village, on the coast

THE COURSE

Yds 6343 Par 72 SSS 70

VISITING PLAYERS

Restrictions

There are no restrictions on visitors although it is advisable to telephone the club in advance to reserve a start time.

Handicap requirements

Visiting players do not require a Certificate of Handicap.

How to contact the club

Telephone call or letter.

COURSE FACILITIES

The Professional can be contacted via the club telephone number for details of tuition fees and information about other facilities which include a Pro Shop, equipment hire and changing rooms.

Food and drink

The Clubhouse Bar is open daily during licensing hours and serves bar snacks. The restaurant is open every day for lunch, tea and dinner.

GREEN FEES

Per weekday round 🏷 £4.95
Per weekend round 🏷 £5.50
Methods of payment: cash only

GREEN FEES

Per weekday 🏷 £18
Per weekend day 🏷 £23
Methods of payment: cash/cheque with valid banker's card

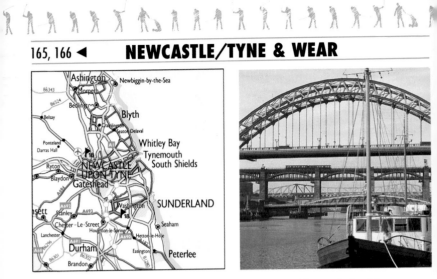

Newcastle and Tyne and Wear's skyline is characterised by symbols of the industries that once dominated this area. Newcastle is fashioning its future, incorporating the elements that have made it the great city it is with ambitious rebuilding schemes.

CITY OF NEWCASTLE GOLF CLUB

Three Mile Bridge
Gosforth
Newcastle upon Tyne
☎ 091 285 1775

The City of Newcastle Golf Club has a flat, 18-hole parkland course. It welcomes visitors without restrictions.

GETTING THERE

Road: Off the A1 Newcastle to Edinburgh road, 3 miles north of Newcastle city centre

THE COURSE

Yds 6508   Par 72   SSS 71

VISITING PLAYERS

Restrictions
There are no restrictions for visiting players except the need to check in advance for Competition Days.

Handicap requirements
Visiting players do not require a Certificate of Handicap.

How to contact the club
Telephone call or letter.

COURSE FACILITIES

The Professional can be contacted by telephone for details of tuition fees and information about all other facilities which include a Pro Shop and changing rooms.
☎ 091 285 5481 for the Professional

Food and drink
The Clubhouse Bar serves drinks and snacks and is open daily during normal licensing hours. The restaurant serves lunch and tea throughout the week.

GREEN FEES

Per weekday 🏌 £14.50
Per weekend day 🏌 £18.50
Methods of payment: cash/cheque with valid banker's card

WEARSIDE GOLF CLUB

Coxgreen
Sunderland
Tyne & Wear
☎ 091 534 4269

Wearside Golf Club has an 18-hole parkland
course alongside the south bank of the
River Wear. It welcomes visitors with few
restrictions.

GETTING THERE

Road: Off the A183 Sunderland to Chester-
le-Street road, 3½ miles west of Sunderland

THE COURSE

Yds 6373   Par 71   SSS 70

VISITING PLAYERS

Restrictions
There are no specific restrictions for visiting
players but there are numerous weekend
competitions on the course which restrict
accessibility. Visitors should telephone the
club number in advance to check
availability.

Handicap requirements
Visitors require a Certificate of Handicap
(no stated maximum) or proof of golf club
membership.

How to contact the club
Telephone call.

COURSE FACILITIES

The Professional, Steve Wynn, can be
contacted via the club telephone number for
details of the tuition fees and information
about all other facilities which include a Pro
Shop, changing rooms, a 4-hole par 3 course
and large practice fields.

Food and drink
The Clubhouse Bar serves drinks and bar
meals and is open every day throughout the
day except for between 2pm and 4pm; the
restaurant serves lunch and dinner.

GREEN FEES

Per weekday 🎫 £15
Per weekend day 🎫 £20

Methods of payment: cash/cheque with valid
banker's card

NORTHUMBERLAND

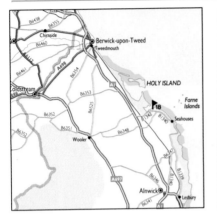

Northumberland is beautiful, remote and unspoilt with a superb coastline of rocky cliffs, sand-dunes, fisherman's villages, harbour towns and imposing cliff castles. An outstanding attraction is the wildlife sanctuary on the Farne Islands.

BAMBURGH CASTLE GOLF CLUB

Bamburgh
Northumberland
☎ 06684 378

Bamburgh Castle Golf Club has a delightful 18-hole seaside links course overlooking the North Sea and offers breathtaking views over Holy Island and the Farne Islands. It welcomes visiting players except on Bank Holidays.

GETTING THERE

Road: From the A1 Alnwick to Berwick-on-Tweed road, take the B1342. On the coast, to the north-east of Bamburgh village

THE COURSE

Yds 5468 Par 68 SSS 67

VISITING PLAYERS

Restrictions
Visitors are not allowed on the course on Bank Holidays; there are some additional restrictions during the month of August. Visiting players should contact the club in advance to check on accessibility and to reserve a start time.

Handicap requirements
Visiting players require a Certificate of Handicap.

How to contact the club
Telephone call or letter.

COURSE FACILITIES

Facilities at the course include changing rooms and a practice ground.

Food and drink
The Clubhouse Bar serves drinks and snacks and is open during normal licensing hours. The restaurant serves lunch, tea and dinner daily.

GREEN FEES

Per weekday 🏦 £20
Per weekend day 🏦 £25

Methods of payment: cash only

The Edzell Golf Club

Scotland is not only the home of golf it is also a country that understands that golf is a sport for all people and a sport that should be open and accessible to members and visitors alike.

Because of this many major Scottish championship courses meet the essential criteria for welcoming visiting players that are needed in order to be included in the Guide. The Scottish golf clubs and courses in this section include detailed listings on courses that host the British Open Championship including St Andrews, Turnberry and Carnoustie.

Also included in the listings are some of the oldest golfing societies and golf clubs in the World including the oldest, The Royal Burgess Golfing Society of Edinburgh, which was established in 1735.

Golf in Scotland is often played in the middle of spectacular scenery, both mountain and seashore, and the Scottish clubs in the listing are representative of all the best of Scottish golf on many different types of course.

Visiting the Highland courses will involve most people in considerable travelling – but a golfing holiday in the Highlands would be well worth the effort although you must remember that play on the more Northern courses will be affected by the winter weather and you should contact the clubs in advance to check conditions.

Please let us know of other Scottish golf clubs which meet out selection criteria and which you feel should be included in future editions of this Guide.

LOTHIAN

Lothian is a richly productive corner, agriculture and fishing thrive alongside an industrial overlay. Edinburgh's elegance is renowned and the eastern part of Lothian has been called 'The Holy Land of Golf', its golfing tradition going back to the 16th century.

DUNBAR GOLF CLUB

East Links
Dunbar
East Lothian
☎ 0368 62317

Dunbar Golf Club dates from 1856 and has a fine old 18-hole seaside links course. It welcomes visitors without restriction although advance booking is required.

GETTING THERE

Road: Off the A1087, ½ mile east of Dunbar town centre

THE COURSE

Yds 6426   Par 71   SSS 71

VISITING PLAYERS

Restrictions
There are no restrictions on visiting players apart from the need to contact the club in advance.

Handicap requirements
Visitors do not require a Certificate of Handicap.

How to contact the club
Telephone call or letter.

COURSE FACILITIES

The Professional can be contacted via the club telephone number for details of tuition fees and information about all other facilities which include a Pro Shop and changing rooms.

Food and drink
The Clubhouse Bar serves drinks and snacks during normal licensing hours; more substantial meals can be made available by prior arrangement.

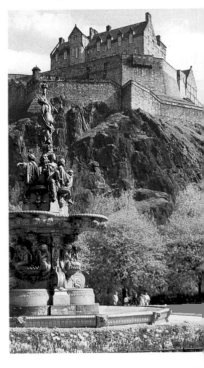

GREEN FEES

Per weekday 🏌 £18
Per weekend day 🏌 £30

Methods of payment: cash/cheque with valid banker's card

THE ROYAL BURGESS GOLFING SOCIETY OF EDINBURGH

181 Whitehouse Road
Edinburgh
Lothian
☎ 031 339 2075

The Royal Burgess is the oldest instituted Golfing Society in the world, it was established in 1735. It has an 18-hole parkland course and welcomes visiting players without restriction.

GETTING THERE

Road: Off the A90 Edinburgh to Queensferry Road, 5 miles west of Edinburgh city centre

THE COURSE

Yds 6494 Par 71 SSS 71

VISITING PLAYERS

Restrictions
There are no restrictions on visitors.

Handicap requirements
A Certificate of Handicap is not required by visiting players.

How to contact the club
Telephone call or letter.

COURSE FACILITIES

The Professional, G.S. Yuille, can be contacted by telephone for details of tuition fees and information about all other facilities which include a Pro Shop, equipment hire and men's changing rooms. Tuition fees are £10 per half hour and £17 per hour.
☎ 031 339 6474 for the Professional

Food and drink
The Royal Burgess Clubhouse is open from 12 noon to 10pm in summer and from 12 noon to 7pm in winter. It contains a fully licensed bar which serves snacks and is open during normal licensing hours, and a dining room overlooking the 18th green which serves lunch.

GREEN FEES

Per weekday 🏌 £31
Per weekday round 🏌 £23
Per weekend day 🏌 £35
Methods of payment: cash/cheque with valid banker's card

LONGNIDDRY GOLF CLUB

Links Road
Longniddry
East Lothian
☎ 0875 52141

Longniddry Golf Club has an 18-hole mixed seaside links and parkland course overlooking the Firth of Forth. It welcomes visiting players; the only major restriction being the need to telephone the club number to obtain a start time.

GETTING THERE

Road: Off the A198 Edinburgh to North Berwick road, just to the west of Longniddry village

THE COURSE

Yds 6210 Par 68 SSS 70

VISITING PLAYERS

Restrictions
Visiting players are not allowed on the course during local holidays or on Competition Days. Visitors need to contact the starter in advance on the club telephone number to reserve a start time.

Handicap requirements
A Certificate of Handicap is not needed by visitors.

How to contact the club
Telephone call or letter.

COURSE FACILITIES

The Professional can be contacted via the club telephone number for details of tuition fees and information about all other facilities which include a Pro Shop, putting green, a practice ground, equipment hire and changing rooms. Tuition fees are £8.50 per half hour.

Food and drink
The Clubhouse Bar is open between 11am and 11pm every day, it also serves snacks. The restaurant opens every day at 12.30pm for lunch and again at 5.30pm for dinner.

GREEN FEES

Per round 🏌 £18 Per weekday 🏌 £27
Per weekend day 🏌 £30
Methods of payment: cash/cheque with valid banker's card

LOTHIAN

GULLANE GOLF CLUB

West Links Road
Gullane
East Lothian
☎ 0620 842255

Gullane Golf Club was formed in 1882 and has three 18-hole courses, Course 1 is of championship standard. It welcomes visitors to play on all 3 courses every day of the week although there are start time restrictions on Course 1.

GETTING THERE

Road: Off the A198 Edinburgh to North Berwick road, 18 miles east of Edinburgh at the entrance to Gullane village

THE COURSE

	Course 1 ⛳18	Course 2 ⛳18	Course 2 ⛳18
Yds	6466	6244	5166
Par	71	70	65
SSS	71	70	65

VISITING PLAYERS

Restrictions

Visiting players are welcome to play Courses 2 and 3 every day of the week with start times between 8am and 4pm. Visiting players are more restricted on Course 1; on weekdays start times must be either between 10.30am and 12 noon or between 2.30pm and 4pm; at weekends visitors start times are restricted to 10 minutes in the mornings (10.50–11) and 10 minutes in the afternoon (2.50–3). All visitors should pre-book a start time with the club.

Handicap requirements

A Certificate of Handicap is required by visiting players wishing to play courses 1 and 2.

How to contact the club

Telephone call or letter.

COURSE FACILITIES

The Professional, J. Hume, can be contacted via the club telephone number for details of tuition fees and information about all other facilities which include a Pro Shop, equipment hire and changing rooms.

Food and drink

The Clubhouse Bars are open during normal licensing hours throughout the week, they also serve snacks. The restaurant is open for lunch between 12 noon and 2pm every day and can also serve dinner by prior arrangement. Please note that a jacket and tie are required throughout the Clubhouse except when drinking in the "Dirty Bar".

GREEN FEES

	Course 1	Course 2	Course 3
Per weekday round	£31	£14	£10
Per weekday	£46	£21	£14
Per weekend round	£41	£17	£12
Per weekend day	n/a	£29	£17

Methods of payment: cash/cheque with valid banker's card

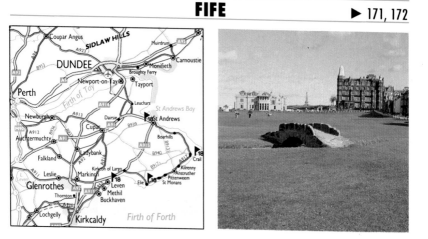

Fife's varied aspects include a picturesque coastline, Loch Leven famed amongst anglers and a rich agricultural landscape scattered with historic buildings, but perhaps its greatest fame is as the home of golf which has been played in St Andrews for over 500 years.

CRAIL GOLFING SOCIETY

Balcomie Clubhouse
Crail
Fife
☎ 0333 50686

The Crail Golfing Society is the seventh oldest golf club in the world, it was founded in 1786. The society plays on the 18-hole mixed links and parkland Balcomie course, it welcomes visiting players throughout the week with only start time restrictions.

GETTING THERE

Road: Take the A918 from St Andrews or the A917 from Kirkton of Largo to Crail road; in the centre of Crail take a minor road north-east for 2 miles to Balcomie, the course is on Fife Ness overlooking the North Sea

THE COURSE

Yds 5720   Par 69   SSS 68

VISITING PLAYERS

Restrictions

Visiting players start times must be between 10am and 12 noon in the morning or between 2.30pm and 4.30pm in the afternoon every day of the week. Visiting players must telephone 0333 50278 in advance to book a start time.

Handicap requirements

A Certificate of Handicap is not required by visiting players.

How to contact the club

Telephone call or letter.

COURSE FACILITIES

The Professional can be contacted by telephone for details of tuition fees and information about all other facilities which include a Pro Shop, a practice ground, equipment hire and changing rooms. Tuition fees are £12 per session.
☎ 0333 50960 for the Professional

Food and drink

The Clubhouse is open all day every day until 11pm, it also serves snacks. The dining room is open every day from lunchtime until 9pm and serves a wide range of high quality meals.

GREEN FEES

Per weekday round 🐚 £13.50
Per weekday 🐚 £19.50
Per weekend round 🐚 £16.50
Per weekend day 🐚 £24.50

Methods of payment: cash/cheque with valid banker's card

THE GOLF HOUSE CLUB

Elie
Fife
☎ 0333 330301

The Golf House Club has an 18-hole links course overlooking the Firth of Forth. It welcomes visitors with few restrictions but is very popular in the summer and often has to hold ballots for start times.

GETTING THERE

Road: Off the A917 St. Andrew to Kirton of Largo coast road, just west of Elie village

THE COURSE

Yds 6250   Par 70   SSS 70

VISITING PLAYERS

Restrictions

Visiting players must start after 10am in the morning or after 1.30pm in the afternoon every day of the week. A ballot for visiting players operates on all Bank Holiday weekends and throughout July and August. There are no other restrictions on visitors.

Handicap requirements

A Certificate of Handicap is not required by visiting players.

How to contact the club

Telephone call or letter.

COURSE FACILITIES

The Professional can be contacted by telephone for details of tuition fees and information about all other facilities which include a Pro Shop, equipment hire and changing rooms.
☎ 0333 330955 for the Professional

Food and drink

The Clubhouse Bar is open during normal licensing hours, it also serves snacks. The restaurant is open for lunch and high tea.

GREEN FEES

Per weekday round 🏷 £16
Per weekday 🏷 £24
Per weekend day 🏷 £30
Per week 🏷 £80

Methods of payment: cash/cheque with valid banker's card

LEVEN THISTLE GOLF CLUB

3 Balfour Street
Leven
Fife
☎ 0333 26397

Leven Thistle Golf Club has an 18-hole links course overlooking Largo Bay and the Firth of Forth. It welcomes visitors without restriction every day of the week except Saturdays.

GETTING THERE

Road: Off the A915 St Andrews to Kirkcaldy road, just to the east of Leven town centre

THE COURSE

Yds 6434   Par 71   SSS 71

VISITING PLAYERS

Restrictions

Visiting players may play the course anytime from Sunday to Friday without restriction. The course is closed to members on Saturdays only.

Handicap requirements

A Certificate of Handicap is not required by visiting players.

How to contact the club

Telephone call or letter.

COURSE FACILITIES

The Professional can be contacted via the club telephone number for details of tuition fees and information about all other facilities which include a Pro Shop, equipment hire and men's changing rooms.

Food and drink

The Clubhouse Bars are open during normal licensing hours, they also serve snacks. The restaurant serves lunch, tea and dinner throughout the week.

GREEN FEES

Per weekday round 🏷 £13.50
Per weekday 🏷 £18.50
Per Sunday round 🏷 £18.50
Per Sunday 🏷 £25

Methods of payment: cash/cheque with valid banker's card

ST ANDREWS LINKS

St. Andrews
Fife
☎ 0334 75757

The St. Andrews Links Management Committee looks after golf at St Andrews and adminsters four 18-hole courses around the town. There are few restrictions on visitors but those wishing to play the famous Old Course will probably need to reserve a start time at least 6 months in advance. The Old Course operates a daily ballot system for visitors who arrive without a reservation, but to guarantee a round visiting players must book well in advance. The Old Course is allocated only to golfers playing at least one other course.

GETTING THERE

Road: All the St. Andrews Links courses are easy to find by road from the centre of St. Andrews

VISITING PLAYERS

Restrictions

The Old Course is closed on Sundays. In order to guarantee a start time on the Old Course reservations should be made at least 3 months before you want to play. Telephone in advance to reserve start times on the other 3 courses.

Handicap requirements

A Certificate of Handicap or letter of introduction from your club is required for all visitors wishing to play the Old Course. There are no restrictions on the other 3 courses.

How to contact the Links Management Committee

Telephone call or letter.

COURSE FACILITIES

There are large practice areas and a driving range on the New Course. Other facilities available include golf trolley hire for £1 per round and free fully-equipped changing rooms at the Eden Course.

Food and drink

There are no catering facilities provided by the St. Andrews Links Management Committee but St. Andrews is surrounded by golf-orientated hotels offering bar and restaurant facilities to residents and non-residents.

THE COURSE

	Old Course ▶18	New Course ▶18	Jubilee Course ▶18	Eden Course ▶18
Yds	6566	6604	6805	6315
Par	72	71	72	70
SSS	72	72	73	70

GREEN FEES

	Old Course	New Course	Jubilee Course	Eden Course
Per round	£31	£13	£13	£11

Note: 3-day and 1-week tickets are available for the New, Jubilee and Eden Courses at a cost of £36 for 3 days and £72 for 1-week.

Note: There are no reductions for children on the Old Course but on the other three courses under 16s are charged half the adult fees.

Methods of payment: cash/cheque with valid banker's card

CLYDE COAST

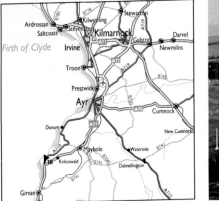

The Clyde coast has sheltered sandy bays between rocky promontories. The warm currents of the Gulf Stream contribute to its mild climate and make it a natural playground with many attractive resorts and fishing villages.

THE TURNBERRY HOTEL GOLF COURSES

Turnberry
Ayrshire
☎ 0655 31000 ext 376

The Turnberry Hotel Golf Course Complex possesses two magnificent 18-hole championship links courses, The Ailsa (which has twice been the venue of the British Open) and the Arran. The 5-star hotel offers special rate green fees to residents and the courses also welcome day visitors. The courses are very popular and visiting players must make a written request for a start time well before their planned visit.

GETTING THERE

Road: Off the A719, to Turnberry coast road, just north of Turnberry village

THE COURSE

	Ailsa course ⚑18	Arran course ⚑18
Yds	6408	6249
Par	69	69
SSS	72	72

VISITING PLAYERS

Restrictions

Start times must be reserved well in advance by written request to 'Golf Reservations' at the hotel address. For visitors intending to stay in the hotel, once your hotel reservation is confirmed the hotel will arrange start times for you.

Handicap requirements

A Certificate of Handicap is required by all visiting players, a maximum 24 for men and 36 for women.

How to contact the club

By letter only.

COURSE FACILITIES

The Professional, R.S. Jamieson, can be contacted by telephone for details of tuition fees and information about all other facilities which include a Pro Shop, equipment hire, changing rooms and caddy hire for £15 per round.
☎ 0655 31000 ext 378 or 380 for the Professional

Food and drink

The Clubhouse Bar is open between 10.30am and 10pm from April to November and between 10.30am and 7pm from December to March.

The bars and restaurants in the hotel offer a range of service at the standards of quality you would expect from a 5-star hotel.

Leisure facilities

The hotel has 115 bedrooms and offers a wide range of leisure facilities to residents. It is equipped to provide for the comfort of disabled visitors.

GREEN FEES

	Ailsa	Arran
Day visitors		
Per round	£56	£25.50
Hotel residents		
Per round	£30.50	

Methods of payment: cash/cheque with valid banker's card/all major credit cards

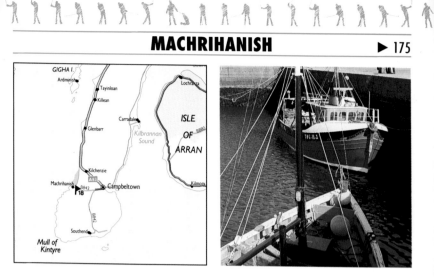

Machrihanish on the Mull of Kintyre is part of a network of islands and peninsulas where stretches of sea and lochs are overlooked by imposing mountains, an ideal area for fishing, sailing, walking, climbing or, indeed, golf.

MACHRIHANISH GOLF CLUB

Machrihanish
Campbeltown
Argyllshire
☎ 058681 213

Machrihanish Golf Club has a magnificent 18-hole Championship Links Course overlooking the Atlantic, there is also a 9-hole, 2395 yard links course. The club welcomes visitors with few restrictions.

GETTING THERE

Road: Off the B843, 5 miles west of Campbeltown on the Kintyre Peninsula

Air: Loganair offer fly/golf packages from Glasgow Airport to Machrihanish Airfield

THE COURSE

Yds 6228   Par 70   SSS 70

VISITING PLAYERS

Restrictions

The Championship Course is closed to visitors during occasional competitions and tournaments in the summer. It is advisable to contact the club in advance to reserve a start time. There are no other restrictions on visitors.

Handicap requirements

A Certificate of Handicap is not required by visiting players.

How to contact the club

Advance telephone call or letter.

COURSE FACILITIES

The Professional can be contacted by telephone for details of tuition fees and information about all other facilities which include a Pro Shop, practice ground, equipment hire and changing rooms.
☎ 058681 277 for the Professional

Food and drink

The Clubhouse Bar is fully licensed, it is open during normal licensing hours and also serves snacks. The restaurant is open every day and serves lunch and high tea.

Leisure facilities

A number of hotels around the Machrihanish and Campbeltown area have arrangements with the club to provide accommodation/golf packages. Please telephone the club number for information.

GREEN FEES

Per weekday round 🏌 £12
Per weekday 🏌 £15
Per weekend day 🏌 £16
Per week 🏌 £60

Methods of payment: cash/cheque with valid banker's card

Oban, in northern Argyll, is the port for the Western Isles. Great sea lochs and more than a thousand miles of jagged coastline backed by wild highland peaks give this area its breathtaking scenic majesty.

GLENCRUITTEN GOLF CLUB

Glencruitten Road
Oban
Argyllshire
☎ 0631 62868 and 64115 (Starter)

Glencruitten Golf Club has an 18-hole parkland course in the hills overlooking Oban. It welcomes visitors with few restrictions.

GETTING THERE

Road: Off the A85, 1 mile east of Oban town centre

THE COURSE

Yds 4452   Par 61   SSS 63

VISITING PLAYERS

Restrictions

The club holds some competitions on weekends and on Thursdays, there are restrictions on visitors when these events are underway. Please contact the club to check availability; there are no other restrictions on visiting players.

Handicap requirements

A Certificate of Handicap is not required by visitors.

How to contact the club

Telephone call or letter.

COURSE FACILITIES

The Starter can be contacted on 0631 64115 for details of fees and information about all other facilities which include a shop, a practice ground, equipment hire and changing rooms.

Food and drink

The Clubhouse Bar is open during normal licensing hours, it also serves snacks. The restaurant serves lunch, tea and dinner every day.

GREEN FEES

Per weekday round 🏌 £9
Per weekday 🏌 £11
Per weekend round 🏌 £10.50
Per weekend day 🏌 £12.50
Methods of payment: cash/cheque with valid banker's card

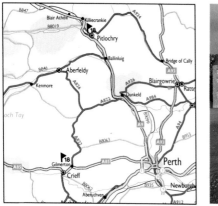

Perthshire is varied and beautiful with lochs and glens, mountains and moors, hills and woods, rich farmland, discrete villages, charming small towns and many reminders of its ancient past.

CRIEFF GOLF CLUB

Perth Road
Crieff
Perthshire
☎ 0764 2909

Crieff Golf Club has an 18-hole and a 9-hole parkland course. It welcomes visitors to both courses.

GETTING THERE

Road: Off the A85 Crieff to Perth road, ½ mile east of Crieff town centre

THE COURSE

	Ferntower Course ⴲ18	Dornock Course ⴲ9
Yds	6402	2386
Par	71	64
		(2 rounds)
SSS	71	63
		(2 rounds)

VISITING PLAYERS

Restrictions

Visiting players are welcome to play either course with start times between 9am and 11am in the morning or between 2pm and 4pm in the afternoon any day of the week. Visiting players must contact the club in advance to book a start time.

Handicap requirements

A Certificate of Handicap is required by all visiting players.

How to contact the club

Telephone call or letter.

COURSE FACILITIES

The Professionals, David Murchie and J.M. Stark, can be contacted via the club telephone number for details of tuition fees and information about all other facilities which include a Pro Shop, changing rooms and limited practice facilities.

Food and drink

The Clubhouse has a mixed lounge and a dining room. The bars serve drinks and snacks. The dining room serves full meals during the day but advance booking is advised.
☎ 0764 2397 for advance booking

GREEN FEES

	Ferntower Course	Dornock Course
Per weekday round	£15	£11
		(2 rounds)
Per weekday	£25	n/a
Per weekend round	£17	£13
		(2 rounds)

Methods of payment: cash/cheque with valid banker's card

PERTHSHIRE

PITLOCHRY GOLF COURSE

Pitlochry
Perthshire
☎ 0796 2114

Pitlochry Golf Course is an 18-hole heathland course set in the attractive Pitlochry Estate. It welcomes visitors without restriction although the location obviously curtails activity in the winter months.

GETTING THERE

Road: ½ mile north of Pitlochry heading towards the A9 and Killiecrankie

THE COURSE

Yds 5811   Par 69   SSS 68

VISITING PLAYERS

Restrictions

Visiting players should contact the club in advance to check conditions and book a visit.

Handicap requirements

A Certificate of Handicap is not required by visiting players.

How to contact the club

Telephone call or letter.

COURSE FACILITIES

The Professional can be contacted by telephone for details of tuition fees and information about all other facilities which include a Pro Shop, equipment hire and changing rooms.
☎ 0796 2792 for the Professional

Food and drink

The Clubhouse Bar is fully licensed, it serves snacks and is open during normal licensing hours in the summer. Main meals can also be served by prior arrangement. During the winter months the Clubhouse facilities and opening times are very restricted.

GREEN FEES

Summer (April to October)
Per weekday ☝ £12
Per weekend round ☝ £9
Per weekend day ☝ £15
Winter (November to March)
Per day ☝ £10

Note: A restricted course is played during the winter.

Methods of payment: cash/cheque with valid banker's card

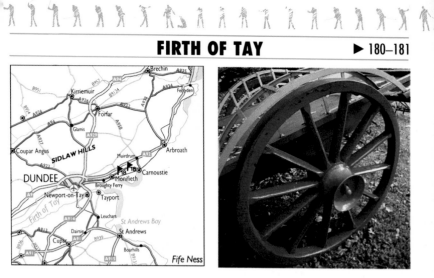

FIRTH OF TAY

The Firth of Tay is bounded by the Sidlaw Hills, gentle walking country leading down to the fishing villages, ports and resorts along the Firth. Carnoustie, a resort with good beaches and fine coastal walks is well known for its fine golf courses.

CARNOUSTIE GOLF LINKS

Starters Box
Links Parade
Carnoustie
Angus
☎ 0241 53789

Carnoustie Golf Links adminsters three 18-hole seaside links courses including the British Open hosting Championship Course. Visiting players are welcome to play all 3 courses with few restrictions but advance booking of start times is essential and a ballot system operates for the Championship Course.

GETTING THERE

Road: Off the A930 Dundee to Carnoustie road south-west of Carnoustie

VISITING PLAYERS

Restrictions

Visiting players are not allowed on the Championship Course during competitions and tournaments. Visitors are welcome to play the courses at all other times but they are very popular so advance booking is essential. The starters use a ballot system to allocate start times.

Handicap requirements

A Certificate of Handicap is required by visiting players although there is no stated maximum.

How to contact the club

Telephone call or letter.

COURSE FACILITIES

There is no Professional or Pro Shop. There are changing rooms and equipment is available for hire.

Food and drink

The Links has no facilities of its own but by prior arrangement facilities can be made available with the local golf clubs who use the Links' courses.

GREEN FEES

	Championship Course	Burnside Course	Buddon Links
Per round	£31	£12	£7
Per day	£54	£20	£10
Per 3-days	on application		
Per week			

Note: The 3-day and weekly tickets allow play on all courses.

Methods of payment: cash/cheque with valid banker's card/all major credit cards

THE COURSE

	Championship Course 🏁18	Burnside Course 🏁18	Buddon Links 🏁18
Yds	6936	6020	5196
Par	72	68	66
SSS	74	69	66

MONIFIETH

The Links
Monifieth
Dundee
Angus
☎ 0382 532767

The Monifieth Golf Links Committee of
Management adminsters two 18-hole seaside
links courses, Apart from start times
there are very few restrictions on visitors.

GETTING THERE

Road: Off the A930 Dundee to Carnoustie
road, 7 miles east of Dundee

THE COURSE

	Medal Course ⛳18	Ashludie Course ⛳18
Yds	6651	5123
Par	71	64
SSS	72	64

VISITING PLAYERS

Restrictions

Weekend start times are the only
restrictions for visitors. On Saturdays
visitors must start after 2pm and on
Sundays after 10am. It is advisable to ring
the Starter to reserve a start time.
☎ 0382 532767 for the Starter

Handicap requirements

There are no handicap restrictions for
individual visitors.

How to contact the club

Telephone call.

COURSE FACILITIES

The Professional can be contacted via the
club telephone number for information
about all facilities which include a Pro
Shop, a practice area, a putting green,
equipment hire and changing rooms.
☎ 0382 532945 for the Professional

Food and drink

There are 4 Golf Clubs affiliated to the
Monifieth Golf Links courses. A full range
of bar and catering facilities is available at
their Clubhouses. Visitors should telephone
in advance to arrange access to these
facilities.
☎ 0382 78117 for the Links Secretary

GREEN FEES

	Medal Course	Ashludie Course
Per day (weekdays/ Saturdays)	£22.50	£12
Per day (Sunday)	£25.50	£14

Methods of payment: cash/cheque with valid
banker's card

SCOTSCRAIG GOLF CLUB

Golf Road
Tayport
Fife
☎ 0382 552515

Scotscraig Golf Club is one of the oldest
golf clubs in the world, it was founded in
1817. It has an 18-hole links course and
welcomes visitors with few restrictions.

GETTING THERE

Road: Off the B945, just south of Tayport

THE COURSE

Yds 6496   Par 71   SSS 71

VISITING PLAYERS

Restrictions

Visitors wishing to play the course at
weekends must book start times in advance
by telephoning the club number. Visitors
are only allowed to start the course between
10-11am and 2.30-3.30pm on weekends.

Handicap requirements

A Certificate of Handicap is not required.

How to contact the club

Telephone call or letter.

COURSE FACILITIES

There is a Pro Shop with limited stock,
trolleys are available for hire and there are
changing room facilities.

Food and drink

The Clubhouse has a mixed lounge and a
separate men's bar which are open every day
from 11am onwards until the Clubhouse
closes. Bar snacks are also available. Lunch or
high tea can be provided, but only by prior
arrangement.

GREEN FEES

Per weekday 🏷 £24
Per weekend day 🏷 £30
Per week 🏷 £50

Methods of payment: cash/cheque with valid
banker's card

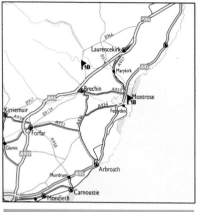

THE EDZELL GOLF CLUB

High Street
Edzell
Angus
☎ 03564 7283

The Edzell Golf Club has an 18-hole heathland course in the Scottish Highlands.

GETTING THERE

Road: Off the B966 just south of Edzell

THE COURSE

Yds 6299   Par 71   SSS 70

VISITING PLAYERS

Restrictions

The course is closed to visitors when open tournaments are underway. Visitors should contact the club in advance for start times.

Handicap requirements

A Certificate of Handicap is required.

How to contact the club

Telephone call or letter.

COURSE FACILITIES

The Professional can be contacted on 03564 462 for details of tuition fees and information about all other facilities which include a Pro Shop, a practice area, a putting green, equipment hire and changing rooms. Tuition fees are £10 per half hour.

Food and drink

The Clubhouse Bar is open daily between 11am to 11pm. The restaurant serves lunch and dinner every day.

GREEN FEES

Per weekday 🏌 £21
Per weekend day 🏌 £27
Per week 🏌 £70

Methods of payment: cash/cheque with valid banker's card

MONTROSE LINKS TRUST

Traill Drive
Montrose
Angus
☎ 0674 72932

The Montrose Links Trust administers two 18-hole links courses. Visitors are welcome to play the courses with few restrictions.

GETTING THERE

Road: Off the A92 Dundee to Aberdeen road, just north-east of Montrose town centre, on the coast

THE COURSE

	Medal Course ⛳	Broomfield Course ⛳
Yds	6443	4815
Par	71	66
SSS	71	63

VISITING PLAYERS

Restrictions

Visitors are welcome to play the Broomfield Course without restrictions. The Medal Course is closed to visitors all day on Saturday, they may not start until after 10am on Sundays; there are no restrictions on weekdays. Visiting players should contact the Trust telephone number in advance to secure start times.

Handicap requirements

A Certificate of Handicap is not required.

How to contact the club

Telephone call or letter.

COURSE FACILITIES

The Professional can be contacted on 0674 72634 for details of tuition fees and information about all other facilities which include a Pro Shop and equipment hire. Contact the secretary via the Trust telephone number to arrange changing room facilities

Food and drink

The 3 clubs which use the courses have their own Clubhouses, contact the secretary via the Trust telephone number in advance of your visit to arrange access.

GREEN FEES

	Medal Course	Broomfield Course
Per weekday	£16	£9
Per weekend day	£21	£11.50
Per week	£40	£30

Methods of payment: cash/cheque with valid banker's card

CRUDEN BAY

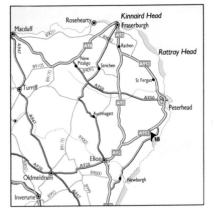

Cruden Bay is a resort with good beaches and a championship golf course. To the north there are red-sandstone cliffs, attractive fishing villages in cliffside settings and busy seaports thriving after the development of the North Sea oilfields.

CRUDEN BAY GOLF CLUB

Cruden Bay
Peterhead
Aberdeenshire
☎ 0779 812285

The Cruden Bay Golf Club has an 18-hole and a 9-hole seaside links course. The 18-hole course is regarded by many as one of the top courses in Britain. It welcomes visiting players but has some start time restrictions at weekends.

Handicap requirements

A Certificate of Handicap is required by all visitors at weekends only, a maximum 28 for men and 36 for women.

How to contact the club

Telephone call or letter.

GETTING THERE

Road: Off the A975 Aberdeen to Peterhead coast road just south of Cruden Bay

THE COURSE

	Main Course ⛳18	St Olaf Course ⛳18
Yds	6370	4710
Par	70	64
SSS	71	62

VISITING PLAYERS

Restrictions

On the Main Course on Competition Days visitors are not allowed to start before 3.30pm; apart from this the only restriction on visiting players during weekdays is that they are not allowed to start between 4.30pm and 6.30pm on Wednesdays. At weekends specific start times are reserved for visitors, contact the club to reserve one of these start times. The St. Olaf course has no restrictions on visitors.

COURSE FACILITIES

The Professional can be contacted via the club telephone number for details of tuition fees and information about all other facilities which include a Pro Shop, equipment hire and changing rooms.

Food and drink

The Clubhouse Bar serves drinks and snacks, it is open from 11am to 11pm every day. The restaurant is open daily between 12 noon and 9pm, it serves a range of meals.

GREEN FEES

	Main Course	St Olaf Course
Per weekday	£16.50	£9
Per weekend day	£22.50	£12
Per week	£67	n/a

Methods of payment: cash/cheque with valid banker's card

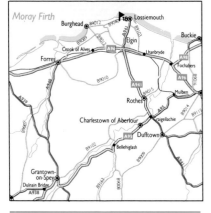

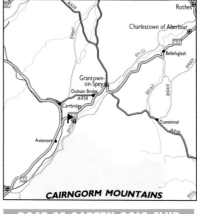

MORAY GOLF CLUB

Stotfield Road
Lossiemouth
Moray
☎ 034381 2018

The Moray Golf Club overlooks the Moray
Firth and has two 18-hole links courses.

GETTING THERE

Road: Off the A941 Elgin to Lossiemouth
road, east of Lossiemouth town centre

THE COURSE

	Old Course ⏴18	New Course ⏴18
Yds	6643	6005
Par	71	69
SSS	72	69

VISITING PLAYERS

Restrictions

Visitors are welcome without restriction on
both courses and should contact the club in
advance to book start times.

Handicap requirements

A Certificate of Handicap may be asked for.

How to contact the club

Telephone call or letter.

COURSE FACILITIES

The Professional can be contacted for
information about all facilities.
☎ 034381 330 for the Professional

Food and drink

The Clubhouse Bar is open every day from
11am to 2pm and again from 5pm to 11pm.
The restaurant is open every day for lunch.

GREEN FEES

	Old Course	New Course
Per weekday	£18	£12
Per weekend day	£25	£18
Per week	£60	£45

Methods of payment: cash/cheque with valid
banker's card/all major credit cards

BOAT OF GARTEN GOLF CLUB

Boat of Garten
Nr Inverness
☎ 047983 282

Boat of Garten Golf Club has an 18-hole
birch-tree lined course overlooking the
Cairngorms and the River Spey. It welcomes
visitors without restriction.

GETTING THERE

Road: Off the B970 Aviemore to Grantown-
on-Spey road, 27 miles south-east of
Inverness and east of Boat of Garten village

THE COURSE

Yds 5765   Par 69   SSS 68

VISITING PLAYERS

Restrictions

There are no restrictions on visiting players
although it is important to contact the club
in advance to check accessibility.

Handicap requirements

A Certificate of Handicap is required.

How to contact the club

Telephone call or letter.

COURSE FACILITIES

Facilities include a Pro Shop, equipment
hire and changing rooms.

Food and drink

The Clubhouse Bar is open every
day during the summer. The restaurant
serves lunch and high tea. Telephone the
club number to find out about available
facilities at other times of the year.

GREEN FEES

Per weekday ⏴ £12
Per weekend day ⏴ £15
Methods of payment: cash only

DORNOCH

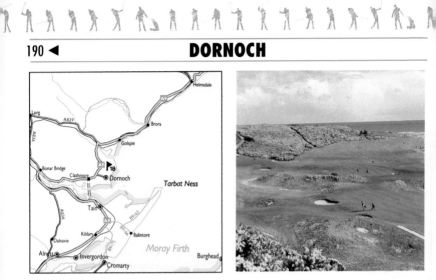

Dornoch is a resort with good views over Dornoch Firth, golden sands, good fishing, a famous golf course and safe bathing along a rocky coast that has some wild and magnificent scenery. Inland lies the great Caithness plateau, wild, remote and unspoilt.

ROYAL DORNOCH GOLF CLUB

Golf Road
Dornoch
Sutherland
☎ 0862 810219

The Royal Dornoch Golf Club has two 18-hole links courses including a challenging Championship Course. Visitors are welcome to play both courses with few restrictions.

GETTING THERE

Road: Off the A9, 50 miles north of Inverness, on the coast at the end of the A949, east of Dornoch

THE COURSE

	Championship Course 🏴18	Struie Course 🏴18
Yds	6581	5250
Par	72	70
SSS	72	

VISITING PLAYERS

Restrictions

The Championship Course hosts a number of tournaments and is closed to visiting players whilst these are underway, please check accessibility with the club. There are no other restrictions on visiting players although they must contact the club in advance of their visit.

Handicap requirements

A Certificate of Handicap is required by all visiting players; a maximum 24 for men and 35 for women.

How to contact the club

Telephone call or letter.

COURSE FACILITIES

The Professional can be contacted via the club telephone number for details of tuition fees and information about all other facilities which include a Pro Shop, equipment hire and changing rooms.

Food and drink

The Clubhouse Bar is open during normal licensing hours, it also serves snacks. The restaurant serves a variety of meals and is open daily from 12 noon with last orders at 7pm. These times may vary with weather conditions during the winter months.

GREEN FEES

	Championship Course	Struie Course
Per weekday	£45	£10
Per weekend day	£55	£10
Per week	£100	£30

Methods of payment: cash/cheque with valid banker's card

WALES

The Welsh golf clubs covered in this section of the Guide demonstrate some of the best of Welsh golf and hospitality for visiting players.

They include the impressive St. Pierre complex outside Chepstow in Gwent with its championship parkland course and wealth of other leisure activities and the splendidly isolated championship links course at Aberdovey in Gwynedd.

There are many other fine golf clubs in Wales and we would welcome your suggestions concerning clubs to be included in future editions of this Guide. Most particularly we would like to include more clubs in South and West Wales and we would be delighted to hear from golf club secretaries who feel that their club meets our selection criteria and want to be included.

Gwent stretches from the wooded and beautiful Wye valley, Wales' river frontier with England, to the dramatic Welsh Hills in the west, it is quiet pastoral countryside with several historic, fortified border towns and excellent salmon fishing in the waters of the Usk.

ST PIERRE HOTEL, GOLF AND COUNTRY CLUB

St. Pierre Park
Chepstow
Gwent
☎ 0291 625261

The St. Pierre complex is located near the coast with views over the Severn Estuary. It has two 18-hole courses, the championship Old Course is a parkland course which has hosted major professional tournaments, and the Mathern Course is a pleasant, meadowland course.

GETTING THERE

Road: Off the A48 Chepstow to Newport road, 2 miles south-west of Chepstow

THE COURSE

	Old Course 🏴18	Mathern Course 🏴18
Yds	6748	5713
Par	71	68
SSS	73	68

VISITING PLAYERS

Restrictions

There are no restrictions for visitors other than the need to obtain a start time which must be booked with the Professional. Visitors who are staying in the hotel and visiting societies can book their start times with their reservations; all other visitors can book their start time up to 7 days in advance, subject to availability.

Handicap requirements

A Certificate of Handicap is required by all visiting players, a maximum 28 for men and 36 for women.

How to contact the club

Contact the Professional to book a start time, telephone preferred.

COURSE FACILITIES

The Professional can be contacted via the club telephone number to book start times and obtain information about other facilities available which include a Pro Shop, changing rooms and equipment hire.

Food and drink

All the catering facilities of the hotel are opened to visitors. Visitors are required to be dressed in smart casual clothes in the bars and restaurants. The bars are open during normal licensing hours, they serve sandwiches and light snacks; it is recommended that these should be ordered before commencing play. The Park Cavery overlooks the 18th green of the Mathern Course, it serves lunch and dinner; reservations are strongly recommended as it is very popular, as is the new a la carte restaurant, The Gun Room, which is perfect for all special occasions. The Poolside Grill serve light meals throughout the day.

The leisure complex includes an indoor swimming pool, sauna, solarium, jacuzzi, and facilities for squash, badminton, tennis, snooker and la croquet lawn. The St Pierre Hotel is a 3-star, 150-bedroom hotel.

GREEN FEES

	Old Course	Mathern Course
Per weekday round	£35	£20
Per weekend or Bank Holiday round	£45	£25

One round per course: Per weekday 🏴 £50
Per weekend day or Bank Holiday 🏴 £55
Note: There are no reduced fees for children and no weekly rates.

Methods of payment: cash/cheque with valid banker's card/American Express/Diners Club/Visa/Access/Mastercard

NEWPORT GOLF CLUB

Great Oak
Rogerstone
Newport
Gwent
☎ 0633 892643

Newport Golf Club has an 18-hole parkland course at the foot of the Welsh Valleys. It welcomes visitors with few restrictions.

GETTING THERE

Road: Off the B4591 Newport to Risca road, M4 jct 27, 3½ miles from Newport

THE COURSE

Yds 6431   Par 72   SSS 71

VISITING PLAYERS

Restrictions

Tuesday is Ladies Day; visitors should telephone the club number to check for any temporary restrictions.

Handicap requirements

A Certificate of Handicap is required by all visitors although there is no stated maximum.

How to contact the club

Telephone call.

COURSE FACILITIES

The Professional can be contacted via the club telephone number for details of charges and information about other facilities available which include a Pro Shop, changing rooms and equipment hire.

Food and drink

The Clubhouse Bar is open from 11.30am to 2pm and 4pm to 10.30pm every day. The dining room serve lunch between 11.30 and 2pm; tea and dinner between 5.30 and 9.30pm every day; coffee and light snacks are also available every day between 8.30am and 8.30pm.

GREEN FEES

Per weekday ⛳ £49
Per weekend day ⛳ £50

Methods of payment: cash/cheque with valid banker's card

LLANWERN GOLF CLUB

Tennyson Avenue, Newport, Llanwern, Gwent
☎ 0633 412029

Llanwern Golf Club is the biggest club in Wales, it has two parkland courses, an 18-hole and a 9-hole, and welcomes visitors without restriction.

GETTING THERE

At Llanwern village, one mile south of M4 jct 24.

THE COURSE

	New Course ⛳18	Old Course ⛳9
Yds	6115	5237*
Par	70	67
SSS	69	67

* 2 rounds; different fees

VISITING PLAYERS

Restrictions

There are no restrictions on visiting players other than the need to be smartly casual in their dress.

Handicap requirements

Visiting players must possess a handicap certificate although there is no stated maximum.

How to contact the club

Telephone call or letter.

COURSE FACILITIES

The Professional, Stephen Price, can be contacted on 0633 413233 for details of tuition fees and information on the club facilities which include a Pro Shop, practice area and changing rooms; the club does not offer equipment hire.

Food and drink

The clubhouse bar is open during normal licensing hours. The restaurant serves lunch between 12 noon and 2.00pm and dinner between 6.00pm and 9.30pm.

Leisure facilities

The clubhouse has a snooker room.

GREEN FEES

Per weekday: Old Course ⛳ £15; New Course ⛳ £20
Per weekend day: Old Course ⛳ £15; New Course ⛳ £25

Methods of payment: cash/cheque with valid banker's card

93

THE ROLLS OF MONMOUTH GOLF CLUB

The Hendre, Monmouth, Gwent
☎ 0600 715353

The Rolls of Monmouth Golf Club has a beautiful 18-hole parkland course set in a private hilly wooded estate; the course features streams and lakes and the views of the surrounding hills are spectacular. It welcomes visiting players with very little restriction.

GETTING THERE

On the B4233 Monmouth to Abergavenny Road 3½ miles west of Monmouth.

THE COURSE

Yds 6723 **Par** 72 **SSS** 72

VISITING PLAYERS

Restrictions

Visiting players cannot start before 9.30am on Sundays, this is the only restriction.

Handicap requirements

Visiting players do not need to have a handicap certificate.

How to contact the club

Telephone call

COURSE FACILITIES

The Professional can be contacted on the club number for details of tuition fees and information on the club facilities which include a Pro Shop, equipment hire, practice net, practice area and changing rooms.

Food and drink

The clubhouse bar is open from 11.00am to 11.00pm on weekdays and Saturdays and from 12 noon to 3.00pm and 7.00pm to 10.30pm on Sundays. The restaurant serves breakfast between 8.00am and 11.00am, lunch between 12 noon and 3.00pm and dinner between 5.00pm and 9.00pm.

GREEN FEES

Per weekday 🏷 £25
Per weekend day 🏷 £30

Methods of payment: cash/cheque with valid banker's card/Access/Visa

GWYNEDD/DYFED ▶ 193. 194–195, 196

Gwynedd and Dyfed, sweeping moorlands rising to higher mountain masses back the coastal cliffs, coves and fine beaches, provide a landscape ideally suited to the walker, pony trekker, fisherman and naturalist.

ABERDOVEY GOLF CLUB

Aberdovey
Gwynedd
☎ 0654 767493

Aberdovey Golf Club has an 18-hole championship links course sited at the mouth of the River Dovey, sandwiched between the Cambrian Mountains and Cardigan Bay.

GETTING THERE

Road: Off the A493 Aberdovey to Tywyn road, ½ mile west of Aberdovey

THE COURSE

Yds 6445   Par 71   SSS 71

VISITING PLAYERS

Restrictions
Visitors are welcome every day of the week but start times are restricted to either between 10am and 12.30pm or after 2pm each day.

Handicap requirements
A Certificate of Handicap is required by all visitors, a maximum 28 for men and 36 for women.

How to contact the club
Telephone call or letter.

COURSE FACILITIES

The Professional can be contacted by telephone for details of tuition fees and information about all other facilities which include a Pro Shop, equipment hire and changing rooms.
☎ 0654 767602 for the Professional

Food and drink
The bar in the main lounge of the Clubhouse and the dining room are both open from 11am to 8pm for the service of drinks, light snacks and full meals.

Leisure facilities
The Clubhouse has a snooker room.

GREEN FEES

Per round 🏌 £17   Per weekday 🏌 £27
Per weekend day 🏌 £27

Note: Children's green fees are £10 per day, any day.

Methods of payment: cash/cheque with valid banker's card

95

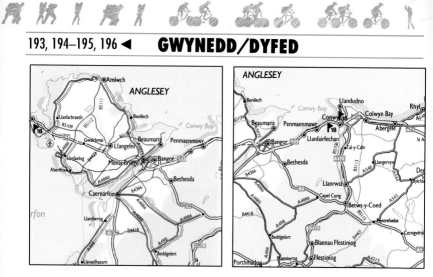

Anglesey and north Gwynedd include amongst their aspects the grandeur of the Snowdon mountain range, the long sandy beaches of the northern coast and the delights of the island of Anglesey where there are charming stone villages and four excellent trout lakes.

CONWAY (CAERNARFONSHIRE) GOLF CLUB

The Morfa
Conwy
Gwynedd
☎ 0492 593400

Conway (Caernarfonshire) Golf Club has an 18-hole coastal links course. It is established on sand-dunes between the Snowdonia Mountains and Conwy Bay and is an exposed and windy course. It

GETTING THERE

Road: Off the A55 Conwy to Bangor road, ½ mile north-west of Conwy

THE COURSE

Yds 6458   Par 72   SSS 71

VISITING PLAYERS

Restrictions

Visitors are welcome every day of the week. Start times must be after 10am and not between 11.45am and 2.30pm.

Handicap requirements

A Certificate of Handicap is required by all visitors, maximum 28 for men, 36 for ladies.

How to contact the club

There is no need to contact the club before arrival.

COURSE FACILITIES

The Professional can be contacted on 0492 593225 for details of fees and information about all other facilities which include a Pro Shop and changing rooms.
rooms.

Food and drink

The Clubhouse Bar is open on Sundays from 12 noon to 2pm and 7pm to 10.30pm; and for the rest of the week from 11.30am to 11pm. Snacks are available throughout the week. The restaurant is open throughout the week from 12 noon to 2pm and 5pm to 9.30pm; except on Mondays open lunch only between 11.30am and 2pm and it is closed all day on Tuesdays.

GREEN FEES

Per weekday 🏌 £16
Per weekend day or Bank Holiday 🏌 £21
Methods of payment: cash/cheque with valid banker's card

Trearddur Bay
Holyhead
Anglesey
Gwynedd
☎ 0407 763279

Holyhead Golf Club has an 18-hole seaside moorland course overlooking the Irish Sea. It welcomes visitors without restriction.

GETTING THERE

Road: Off the B4545, 1 mile south of Holyhead town centre, on the coast

THE COURSE

Yds 6050   Par 71   SSS 70

VISITING PLAYERS

Restrictions

Visiting players should contact the club in advance to confirm a start time; there are no other restrictions.

Handicap requirements

Visitors require a Certificate of Handicap or a letter of introduction from their own club.

How to contact the club

Telephone call or letter.

COURSE FACILITIES

The Professional can be contacted via the club telephone number for details of charges and information about all other facilities which include a Pro Shop and changing rooms.

Food and drink

The Clubhouse has a bar and a dining room which offer a complete range of food from full meals to bar snacks every day.

GREEN FEES

Per weekday 🏷 £14.50
Per weekend day 🏷 £16.50

Methods of payment: cash/cheque with valid banker's card

---

72 Bryniau Road
West Shore
Llandudno
Gwynedd
☎ 0492 875325

The North Wales Golf Club has an 18-hole seaside links course overlooking Conwy Bay. It welcomes visitors with few restrictions.

GETTING THERE

Road: Off the A546, ½ mile west of Llandudno town centre, on the coast

THE COURSE

Yds 5888   Par 71   SSS 68

VISITING PLAYERS

Restrictions

Visiting players are not allowed to start before 9.45am any day. Visitors must contact the club in advance to reserve a start time.

Handicap requirements

A Certificate of Handicap is required by all visiting players although no maximum is quoted.

How to contact the club

Telephone call or letter.

COURSE FACILITIES

The Professional can be contacted by telephone for details and information about all other facilities which include a Pro Shop, equipment hire and changing rooms.
☎ 0492 876878 for the Professional

Food and drink

The Clubhouse Bar is open during licensing hours every day, it also serves snacks. The restaurant serves lunch, tea and dinner every day.

Leisure facilities

The Clubhouse has a snooker table.

GREEN FEES

Per weekday 🏷 £15.50
Per weekend day 🏷 £20.50

Methods of payment: cash/cheque with valid banker's card

ROYAL ST. DAVID'S GOLF CLUB

Harlech, Gwynedd
☎ 0766 780361

Royal St. David's Golf Club has an 18-hole championship links course set on the edge of the sea with spectacular views over Snowdonia, the Lleyn Peninsular and Harlech Castle, it welcomes visiting golfers without restriction but is very popular and visitors wishing to play the course must contact the club in advance to reserve a start time.

GETTING THERE

On the coast off the A496 Harlech to Blaenau Ffestiniog road just north of Harlech.

THE COURSE

Yds 6427 Par 69 SSS 71

VISITING PLAYERS

Restrictions

Visiting players must obtain a confirmed start time in advance from the club secretary or professional, this is the only restriction.

Handicap requirements

Visiting players must have a handicap certificate with a maximum of 28 for men and 36 for ladies..

How to contact the club

Telephone call or letter.

COURSE FACILITIES

The Professional, John Barnett, can be contacted on 0766 780857 for details of tuition fees and information on the club facilities which include a Pro Shop, practice area and changing rooms. The club does not offer equipment hire.

Food and drink

During the summer the clubhouse bar is open during full licensing hours, in the Winter [November–March] opening is more restricted. The restaurant serves food through the day but a visiting player should contact the club to confirm details.

GREEN FEES

Per weekday 🗓 £20
Per weekend day 🗓 £25

Methods of payment: cash/cheque with valid banker's card

ASHBURNHAM GOLF CLUB

Cliffe Terrace, Burry Port, Dyfed
☎ 05546 2269

The Ashburnham Golf Club has an 18-hole championship links course overlooking Carmarthen Bay, it welcomes visitors with very few restrictions.

GETTING THERE

Off the B4311 Burry Port to Pembrey Road just outside Burry Port.

THE COURSE

Yds 6916 Par 72 SSS 73

VISITING PLAYERS

Restrictions

Visiting players start times are restricted on competition days, contact the club for details on these, this is the only restriction.

Handicap requirements

Visiting players need to have a handicap certificate.

How to contact the club

Telephone call or letter.

COURSE FACILITIES

The Professional can be contacted on 05546 3846 for details of tuition fees and information on the club facilities which include a Pro Shop, equipment hire, practice area and changing rooms.

Food and drink

The clubhouse bar is open from 12 noon to 11.00pm daily. The restaurant serves lunch and dinner.

Leisure facilities

The clubhouse has a pool table.

GREEN FEES

Per weekday 🗓 £22
Per weekend day 🗓 £28

Methods of payment: cash/cheque with valid banker's card/Access/Visa

BORTH AND YNYSLAS GOLF CLUB

Borth, Dyfed
☎ 0970 871202

The Borth and Ynyslas Golf Club is the oldest golf club in Wales. It has an 18-hole links course overlooking Cardigan Bay and can be very testing in windy conditions with prevailing south-westerly winds. The club is opening a new clubhouse in Spring 1992 and welcomes visiting golfers without restriction.

GETTING THERE

On the coast just north of Borth village, Borth is signposted off the A487 Aberystwyth to Machynlleth road.

THE COURSE

Yds 6116 Par 70 SSS 70

VISITING PLAYERS

Restrictions

Visiting players must be members of a recognised golf club and demonstrate a basic knowledge of the game, these are the only restrictions.

Handicap requirements

Visiting players do not need to have a handicap certificate.

How to contact the club

Telephone call or letter.

COURSE FACILITIES

The Professional can be contacted on 0970 871557 for details of tuition fees and information on the club facilities which include a Pro Shop, equipment hire, practice area and changing rooms.

Food and drink

The clubhouse bar is open daily during licensing hours. The restaurant serves food but opening times and arrangements will change when the new clubhouse opens and you should contact the club for the latest information.

GREEN FEES

Per weekday 🏌 £12
Per weekend day 🏌 £15
Five day ticket 🏌 £45

Please contact the club to check on special terms that are available for bona fide tourists.

Methods of payment: cash/cheque with valid banker's card/Access/Visa

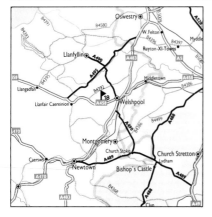

Powys, an area of outstanding natural beauty, with rugged moutain scenery that contrasts with beautiful valleys and sparkling lakes. An area sleeped in history, including castles, caves, mines, churches and monuments.

WELSHPOOL GOLF CLUB

Red Bank, Welshpool, Powys
☎ 0938 552215

Welshpool Golf Club has a beautiful and very hilly 18-hole parkland course with spectacular views, it welcomes visiting players without restriction.

GETTING THERE

Off the A458 Welshpool to Llanfair Caereinion road 3 miles west of Welshpool.

THE COURSE

Yds 5708   Par 70   SSS 69

VISITING PLAYERS

Restrictions

Visiting players must be members of a recognised golf club, this is the only restriction.

Handicap requirements

Visiting players must have a handicap certificate with a maximum of 28.

How to contact the club

Telephone call or letter.

COURSE FACILITIES

The Secretary can be contacted on the club number for information on the club facilities which include equipment hire and changing rooms. The club does not have a Professional or a Pro Shop.

Food and drink

The clubhouse bar is open from 8.00am to 10.30pm every day and serves snacks and meals throughout the day.

Leisure facilities

The clubhouse has a pool table.

GREEN FEES

Per weekday 🖰 £8
Per weekend day 🖰 £15
Methods of payment: cash/cheque with valid banker's card

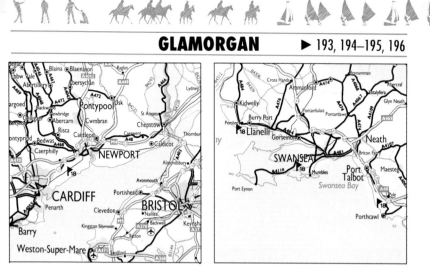

Glamorgan, whose beautiful hills and vales are dominated by the Brecon Beacons to the north, stretches east to the Black Mountains, and south towards the idyllic Gower Peninsular, where the rolling dunes meet shores washed by the Atlantic Ocean.

PETERSTONE GOLF CLUB AND LEISURE COMPLEX

Peterstone Wentlooge, Cardiff, South Glamorgan
☎ 0633 680009

The Peterstone Golf Club and Leisure Complex offers two links-type courses, an 18-hole and a 9-hole. The complex also offers the golfer a 40-bay driving range, an indoor golf range, floodlit greens and video lessons. Other leisure facilities include fishing and a gymnasium and there are 16 bedrooms.

GETTING THERE

Between Marshfield and Peterstone Wentlooge south of the A48 Newport to Cardiff road at the Marshfield turn.

THE COURSE

	Peterstone Course ⛳18	Scrivens Course ⛳9
Yds	6481	3081
Par	71	36
SSS	71	

VISITING PLAYERS

Restrictions

There are no restrictions on visiting players other than the need to be smartly casual in their dress.

Handicap requirements

Visiting players must possess a handicap certificate to play the Peterstone Course, a maximum of 28 for men although there is no stated maximum for ladies.

How to contact the club

Telephone call followed by confirming letter.

COURSE FACILITIES

The Professional, Mike Bendall, can be contacted on the club number for details of tuition fees and information on the club facilities which include a Pro Shop, equipment hire, practice area and changing rooms.

Food and drink

The clubhouse bar is open from 11.00am to 1.00am daily. The restaurant serves breakfast between 7.00am and 10.00am, lunch between 11.30am and 3.30pm and dinner between 5.30pm and 11.00pm.

Leisure facilities

The clubhouse has a games room and gymnasium and an accommodation block of 16 bedrooms. Please contact the club for information and tariff.

GREEN FEES

Per weekday: Peterstone Course 🎫 £16; Scrivens Course 🎫 £5
Per weekend day: Peterstone Course 🎫 £25; New Course 🎫 £7.50

Methods of payment: cash/cheque with valid banker's card/Access/Visa/American Express/Diners' Club

101

ROYAL PORTHCAWL GOLF CLUB

Rest Bay, Porthcawl, Mid Glamorgan
☎ 0656 782251

Royal Porthcawl Golf Club has an 18-hole championship links course overlooking the Bristol Channel and Swansea Bay. It welcomes visitors without restriction but is very popular and visiting players must contact the club in advance and obtain a confirmed start time.

GETTING THERE

On the coast to the north of Porthcawl, 3 miles south of the M4 jct 37.

THE COURSE

Yds 6691   Par 72   SSS 74

VISITING PLAYERS

Restrictions

Visiting players must obtain a confirmed start time in advance from the club secretary or professional, this is the only restriction.

Handicap requirements

Visiting players must have a handicap certificate with a maximum of 28 for men.

How to contact the club

Telephone call or letter.

COURSE FACILITIES

The Professional, Graham Poor, can be contacted on 0656 786984 for details of tuition fees and information on the club facilities which include a Pro Shop, equipment hire, practice area and changing rooms.

Food and drink

The clubhouse bar is open from 8.00am daily. The restaurant normally only serves lunch, between 12 noon and 2.00pm, although dinner can be organised by prior booking.

GREEN FEES

Per weekday 🏷 £30
Per weekend day 🏷 £45

Methods of payment: cash/cheque with valid banker's card

FAIRWOOD PARK GOLF CLUB

Blackhills Lane, Upper Killay, Swansea, West Glamorgan
☎ 0792 297849

Fairwood Park Golf Club has an 18-hole championship parkland course on the edge of the beautiful Gower Peninsular. The club welcomes visitors without restriction.

GETTING THERE

Off the A4118 Swansea to Port Eynon road at Upper Killay, 3 miles south west of Swansea.

THE COURSE

Yds 6606   Par 72   SSS 72

VISITING PLAYERS

Restrictions

Visiting players must be a member of a recognised golf club, this is the only restriction.

Handicap requirements

Visiting players do not need to have a handicap certificate.

How to contact the club

Telephone call or letter.

COURSE FACILITIES

The Professional, Mark Evans, can be contacted on 0792 299194 for details of tuition fees and information on club facilities which include a Pro Shop, practice area and changing rooms. The club does not offer equipment hire.

Food and drink

The clubhouse bar is open from 11.00am to 11.00pm daily. The restaurant serves meals appropriate to the time of the day continuously between 8.00am and 9.00pm.

Leisure facilities

The clubhouse has a games room offering snooker, pool and darts.

GREEN FEES

Per weekday 🏷 £18
Per weekend day 🏷 £23

Methods of payment: cash/cheque with valid banker's card

NORTHERN IRELAND

Any visiting player would find a golfing holiday in Northern Ireland very rewarding, it is marvellous natural golfing country and has superb championship links courses, meadowland courses and parkland courses. In total there are 80 golf clubs in Northern Ireland including nearly 30 with 18-hole courses that welcome visitors with very few restrictions.

Most visitors to Northern Ireland from Great Britain and international visitors deciding to play golf on a course in Northern Ireland will be arranging a longer holiday involving a ferry trip or air flight rather than just pursuing the desire to play a particular course. For this reason the information on golfing in the province is presented in a slightly different form.

Belfast is the capital of Northern Ireland and the easiest access point by sea or air, there are 11 golf clubs within 5 miles of the city centre. Northern Ireland is only 5500 square miles in area — about the size of Yorkshire or Connecticut – making all golf clubs within an easy drive of each other.

This section is only a sampler of the 80 golf courses in Northern Ireland. There are many excellent 18-hole courses with some minor restrictions on visitors and many fine 9-hole courses. The Northern Ireland Tourist Board publishes an Information Bulletin entitled *GOLF – where to play*, which provides detailed information on all the courses in Northern Ireland.

GETTING TO NORTHERN IRELAND

Northern Ireland is easy to get to by air and by sea from many parts of the rest of the UK.

BY AIR

Northern Ireland has three commercial airports with passenger services from the rest of the UK.

Belfast International (Aldergrove) receives regular services from:
- London (Heathrow)
- London (Luton)
- Birmingham International
- East Midlands
- Glasgow
- Leeds/Bradford
- Manchester
- Newcastle

Belfast City receives regular services from:

Birmingham	Leeds/Bradford
Blackpool	Liverpool
Bristol	Manchester
Cardiff	Newcastle
Edinburgh	Southampton
Exeter	
Glasgow	
Isle of Man	

Londonderry receives regular services from:
- Glasgow
- Manchester

BY SEA

Northern Ireland has two ferry ports receiving regular daily sailings from UK ports.

Belfast from:
- Liverpool
- Douglas (Isle of Man), summer only
- Stranraer (SeaCat)

Larne from:
- Stranraer
- Cairnryan

PLAYING

As with golf clubs in the rest of the UK it is always sensible to contact the clubs in advance to check for Competitions or Society Days and to ensure that there are no local or temporary restrictions in place.

Green fees in Northern Ireland are usually very reasonable.

The following is a summary of the main golf clubs in Northern Ireland featuring 18-hole courses that welcome visiting players to the club without restriction every day of the week.

BELFAST AREA ▶ 197, 198–199

BALMORAL GOLF CLUB

518 Lisburn Road
Balmoral
Belfast
☎ 0232 381514

An 18-hole parkland course located 3 miles south-west of Belfast city centre.

Yds 6238   Par 69   SSS 70

The club has a Professional, a Pro Shop, changing rooms and equipment hire; the Clubhouse serves drinks, bar snacks and full meals.

GREEN FEES

Per weekday (excl. Wednesdays) £10
Wednesdays £12
Per weekend day £15

DUNMURRY GOLF COURSE

91 Dunmurry Lane
Dunmurry
Belfast
☎ 0232 610834
An 18-hole, parkland course located 4 miles south-west of Belfast city centre.

Yds 5832   Par 69   SSS 68

The club has a Pro Shop, changing rooms and a practice area and the Clubhouse serves drinks, bar snacks and full meals.

GREEN FEES

Per weekday 🏷 £11
Per weekend day 🏷 £15

FORTWILLIAM GOLF CLUB

Downview Avenue
Belfast
☎ 0232 370770
An 18-hole, parkland course located 3 miles north of Belfast city centre.

Yds 5771   Par 70   SSS 68

The club has a Professional, a Pro Shop, a changing room and a practice area. The Clubhouse has a bar and snooker room and serves full meals.

GREEN FEES

Per weekday 🏷 £12
Per weekend day 🏷 £17

KNOCK GOLF CLUB

Summerfield
Dundonald
Belfast
☎ 0232 483251
An 18-hole, parkland course located 4 miles east of Belfast city centre.

Yds 6392   Par 70   SSS 71

The club has a Professional, a Pro Shop, equipment hire, changing rooms and a practice area. The Clubhouse has a bar and snooker room and serves full meals Monday to Saturday and Sunday lunchtime.
☎ 0232 483825 for the Professional

GREEN FEES

Per weekday 🏷 £12
Per weekend day 🏷 £16

KNOCKBRACKEN GOLF & COUNTRY CLUB

24 Ballymaconaghy Road
Newtownbreda
Belfast
☎ 0232 792108
An 18-hole, undulating parkland course located 4½ miles south-east of Belfast city centre.

Yds 5312   Par 67   SSS 68

The club requires all visiting players to have a Certificate of Handicap. It has a Professional, a Pro Shop, equipment hire, changing rooms and two driving ranges. The Clubhouse has a bar and dining room open 7 days a week. It also has 2 dry ski slopes, 2 bowling alleys, 19 snooker tables and video games.

GREEN FEES

Per weekday 🏷 £8
Per weekend day 🏷 £10

COUNTY ANTRIM

COUNTY ARMAGH ▶ 200

COUNTY ARMAGH GOLF CLUB

4 Newry Road
Armagh
☎ 0861 525861
An 18-hole, parkland course located in the grounds of Armagh Palace.

Yds 6120 **Par** 69 **SSS** 69

The club has a Professional, a Pro Shop, changing rooms and a practice area; the Clubhouse has a bar and snooker room and serves full meals.

GREEN FEES

Per weekday ⌂ £9
Per weekend day ⌂ £12

BALLYCLARE GOLF CLUB

25 Springvale Road
Ballyclare
☎ 096 03 22696
An 18-hole, parkland course located 2 miles north of Ballyclare town centre.

Yds 5699 **Par** 72 **SSS** 71

The Clubhouse has a bar and serves full meals; the club also offers snooker and bowls.

GREEN FEES

Per weekday ⌂ £10
Per weekend day ⌂ £15

CRAIGAVON GOLF CENTRE

Turmoyra Lane
Lurgan
☎ 0762 326606
An 18-hole, parkland course located 2 miles north of Lurgan town centre.

Yds 6496 **Par** 72 **SSS** 72

The club has a Professional, a Pro Shop, equipment hire, changing rooms, a 9-hole par 3 course, a 12-hole pitch & putt course, a putting green and a floodlit driving range.

GREEN FEES

Per weekday ⌂ £6
Per weekend day ⌂ £8

ROYAL PORTRUSH GOLF CLUB

Bushmills Road
Portrush
☎ 0265 822311
Three seaside links courses, two 18-hole and one 9-hole, located ½ mile east of Portrush town centre.

	Dunluce ⌂18	Valley ⌂18	Skerries ⌂9
Yds	6680	6278	1187
Par	72	68	
SSS	73	70	

Visiting players must contact the club in advance to check accessibility, particularly for the championship Dunluce course. The club has a Professional, a Pro Shop, equipment hire, changing rooms, a practice area and a pitch & putt course. The Clubhouse has a bar and a snooker room; bar snacks are available but full meals must be booked in advance.

GREEN FEES

	Dunluce ⌂18	Valley ⌂18
Per weekday	£25	£12
Per weekend day	£30	£16

COUNTY DOWN ▶ 197

BANGOR GOLF CLUB

Broadway
Bangor
☎ 0247 270922
An 18-hole, undulating parkland course.

Yds 6490 **Par** 71 **SSS** 70

The club has a Professional, a Pro Shop and changing rooms; the Clubhouse serves drinks, bar snacks and full meals.

GREEN FEES

Per weekday ⌂ £14
Per weekend day ⌂ £20

DOWNPATRICK GOLF CLUB

43 Saul Road
Downpatrick
☎ 0396 612152
An 18-hole, undulating parkland course 1 mile north-east of Downpatrick town centre.

Yds 5834   Par 69   SSS 69

The Clubhouse has a bar which serves bar snacks; full meals can only be served by prior arrangement. The club also offers snooker, billiards and bowls.

GREEN FEES

Per weekday 🏌 £12
Per weekend day 🏌 £15

COUNTY LONDONDERRY

CITY OF DERRY GOLF CLUB

49 Victoria Road
Londonderry
☎ 0504 46369
An 18-hole and a 9-hole parkland course located 2½ miles south of Londonderry town centre.

	⛳18	⛳9
Yds	6406	4708
Par	71	63
SSS	71	63

Visiting players should contact the club in advance to check accessibility on the 18-hole course. The club has a Professional, a Pro Shop and changing rooms; the Clubhouse serves drinks, snacks and full meals.

GREEN FEES

⛳18 Per weekday 🏌 £11
⛳18 Per weekend day 🏌 £13
⛳9 Per round 🏌 £5

MOYOLA PARK GOLF CLUB

Shanemullagh
Castledawson
Magherafelt
☎ 0648 68468
A parkland course located 3 miles north-east of Magherafelt town centre.

Yds 6517   Par 71   SSS 71

The club has a Professional, a Pro Shop, equipment hire and changing rooms; the Clubhouse serves drinks, bar snacks and full meals.

GREEN FEES

Per weekday 🏌 £11
Per weekend day 🏌 £14

COUNTY TYRONE

STRABANE GOLF CLUB

33 Ballycolman Road
Strabane
☎ 0504 382271
An 18-hole parkland course located 1 mile south of Strabane town centre.

Yds 5969   Par 69   SSS 69

The club has changing rooms and a practice area, it also offers snooker and indoor bowls. The Clubhouse Bar serves snacks but full meals can only be supplied by prior arrangement.

GREEN FEES

Per weekday 🏌 £6
Per weekend day 🏌 £10

The most famous club in Northern Ireland, not included in this Guide, as it imposes restrictions on visitors, is the Royal County Down Golf Club in Newcastle. This club has 2 superb championship links courses and is well worth playing; contact the club on 039 67 23314 for details. Its restrictions include access to the Clubhouse facilities being available only to visitors invited to play by the club.

WHAT·TO·DO·AND·SEE

SOUTH WEST CORNWALL

i 28 Killigrew Street, Falmouth, Cornwall
☎ 0326 312300
i The Guildhall, Street-an-Pol, St. Ives,
Cornwall
☎ 0736 796297

AERIAL SPORTS

Parachuting and Paragliding

Cornwall Paragliding Club
Residential courses, paragliding, multi-
activity breaks.
Lester Cruse, Carnkie Farm House, Carnkie,
Redruth
☎ 0209 218962

ADVENTURE

Caving, Potholing and Rock Climbing

Adventureline
Exploring old tin mines.
North Trefula Farm, Redruth
☎ 0209 820847

Compass West International School of Rock
Climbing
Rock climbing including sea cliffs.
Sennen, nr Lands End
☎ 073 6871447

Multi-activity Centres

Adventure Sports
Hang gliding, waterskiing, sailing, surf
skiing, speed sailing, snorkelling, surfing,
parascending and sand yachting.
Carnkie Farm House, Carnkie, Redruth
☎ 0209 218962

Cornish Activity Holidays
Dinghy sailing, canoe expeditions, sea
fishing, riding, marine life study.
2 Treworval Cottages, Treworval Farm,
Constantine, nr Falmouth
☎ 0326 250737

Cornwall Activity Centre
Surfing, sailing, surf skiing, canoeing,
sailboarding, catamaran sailing, water
sledging, pony trekking, rock climbing, hill
walking and camping.
Mylor Yacht Harbour, Falmouth
☎ 0326 76191

EQUESTRIAN

Riding and Pony Trekking

Wheal Buller Riding School
Butler Hill, Redruth
☎ 0209 211852

LOCAL FEATURES

Arts and Crafts

Barbara Hepworth Museum and Sculpture
Garden
Home of the late Dame Barbara Hepworth
from 1949–1975, her sculptures are inside
the museum and in a sub-tropical garden.
St Ives
☎ 0736 796226

Factory Visits

Goonhilly Satellite Earth Station
High tech satellite technology, neolithic
burial sites, nature reserve, impressive
visitor centre.
Goonhilly Downs
P 🏛

Poldark Mine and Heritage Complex
Extensive workings of an 18th century tin
mine.
Wendron, nr Helston
☎ 0326 573173
On the B3297, 2 miles north of Helston

Festivals and Fairs

April
Trevithick Day

May
Helston Flora Day

July
Stithians Show

Gardens

Glendurgan Gardens
National Trust garden beside the Helford
River.
Mawnan Smith, nr Falmouth
On the road to Helford Passage, 4 miles
south-west of Falmouth
🏛

Trebah Gardens
Garden and beach.
Mawnan Smith

Historic Buildings

Godolphin House
A Tudor house with colonnaded front. Civil
War exhibition.
5 miles north-west of Helston, nr Godolphin
Cross
🏛

Pendennis Castle
Henry VIII's reply to the Pope's crusade
against him was to fortify his coast. Built
high on a promontory, Pendennis was
besieged for 5 months by the Parliamentary
Army under Fairfax.
1 mile south-east of Falmouth
🏛 ♿

SOUTH WEST CORNWALL

WHAT TO DO AND SEE

Museums

Shire Horse Farm and Carriage Museum
Working shire horse farm with a large
carriage collection.
Treskillard, nr Redruth

Natural History

Seal Sanctuary
Haven for seals washed up around the coast.
Gweek, nr Helston
☎ 032622 361

Tamar Otter Park and Wild Wood
Park devoted to the conservation of otters
and other wildlife.
North Petherwin, nr Launceston
♿

Argal and College Water Park
Rainbow trout fishery. Boat fishing only
from 1 June to 15 Sept and from boat and
bank at other times.
Bob Evans (Ranger), Little Argal Farm,
Budock, nr Penryn
☎ 0326 72544

Walking

The Cornish Coastal Path
i Guide books are available from the
Tourist Information Centre.
   Adventureline offer guided walks

OUTDOOR LEISURE/SPORTS

Birdwatching and Wildlife

Polgreen Farm
Birdwatching holidays with an experienced
ornithologist.
St. Mawgan-in-Pydar, nr Newquay
☎ 0637 860700

Cornwall Birdwatching and Preservation
Society
2 hides for members' use around Stithians.
☎ 0326 74865

Angling on Stithians
Season and day permits:
G Maddern, Golden Lion Inn, Menherion,
Redruth.
☎ 0209 860332

WATERSPORTS

Diving

Cornish Diving and Watersports
Bar Road, Falmouth
☎ 0326 311265

Sailing

The Catamaran Clinic
Laser sailing centre and traditional yacht
school.
Mylor Yacht Harbour, Falmouth
☎ 0326 76191

Windsurfing

Skewjack Windsurfing School
Sennen, Penzance
☎ 0736 871287

i Civic Centre, Royal Parade, Plymouth, Devon
☎ 0752 674303
i Town Hall Buildings, Bedford Square, Tavistock, Devon
☎ 0822 612938

ADVENTURE

Multi-activity Centres

Cornish Activities
Trewardale, Blisland, nr Bodmin
☎ 020 882 226

EQUESTRIAN

Riding and Pony Trekking

Lydford House Riding Stables
Lydford House Hotel, Lydford
Okehampton, Devon
☎ 082 282347

Shilstone Rocks Stud and Trekking Centre
Widecombe-in-the-Moor, Newton Abbot
☎ 03642 281

HEALTH

Leisure Centres

Central Park Leisure Pools
Heated indoor leisure pool.
Plymouth
☎ 0752 264894

LOCAL FEATURES

Festivals and Fairs

July
Cutty Sark Tall Ships Race, Plymouth

Guided Tours

Armada Guides
Elburton
☎ 0752 772355

Guides South West
☎ 0752 667790

Historic Buildings

Antony House
Queen Anne House, unaltered with panelled rooms and fine furniture. National Trust.
Torpoint
☎ 0752 812191
North of the A374
🏛

Bowden House
Tudor mansion with Queen Anne facade, the oldest house in Totnes, it houses the British Photographic Museum.
Totnes, Devon
☎ 0803 863664
➔A A381
P 🏛 🚌 ✕ ♿ ♿

Buckland Abbey
Originally a Cistercian monastery, then the home of Sir Francis Drake. National Trust.
Nr Yelverton, Devon
☎ 0822 853607
➔A A386
P 🏛 ✕ ♿

Cotehele House
Fine mediaeval home with armour, furniture and tapestries. Memorial watermill and Cotehele Quay Museum. National Trust.
Calstock
☎ 0579 50434
8 miles south-west of Tavistock
🏛 ✕ ♿ ♿

Mount Edgcumbe House and Country Park
The only Grade I listed house in Devon and Cornwall, a restored Tudor mansion, set in a park stretching along 10 spectacular miles of coastline.
Torpoint, nr Plymouth
☎ 0752 822236
➔A A374
🏛 ✕

Pencarrow House and Gardens
Georgian House, privately owned, with a superb collection of paintings and fine French and oriental furniture.
Bodmin, Cornwall
☎ 020 884 369
1 mile south-east of Falmouth
🏛

Museums

City of Plymouth Museum and Art Gallery
Fine paintings and porcelain, treasures of the region on display.
Drake Circus, Plymouth
☎ 0752 668000
➔A A386

WHAT TO DO AND SEE

Natural History

Dartmoor Wildlife Park
Including falconry centre.
Sparkwell, nr Plymouth
☎ 075 537 209
Off the A38, 3 miles from Plymouth,
signposted
P 🏠

Miniature Pony Centre
Ponies and other farm animals.
Moretonhampstead, Devon
☎ 0647 432400
Off the B3212
P 🏠 ♿ ♿

National Shire Horse Centre
Parades of shire horses, falconry displays, an
adventure playground, carriage rides.
Yealmpton, Plymouth
☎ 0752 880268
➜A A379
P 🏠 ♿

Pennywell Farm Centre
Nr Rattery, Buckfastleigh, South Devon
☎ 0364 42023
Off the A38
P 🏠 ✕ ♿

Zoos

Paignton Zoo
A large zoo with over 1300 animals.
Totnes Road, Paignton
☎ 0803 527936
P 🏠 ✕ ♿ ♿

OUTDOOR LEISURE/SPORTS

Cycling

Battery Cycle Works
52 Embankment Road, Plymouth
☎ 0752 665553

Plymouth Mountain Bike Company
Queen Anne's Battery, Plymouth
☎ 0752 268328

Fishing

Newhouse Fishery
Newhouse Farm, Moreleigh, nr Totnes
☎ 0548 82426

Plymouth Angling Boatmans Association
Reef, wreck and shark fishing
Gordon House, Fore Street, Witheridge, nr
Tiverton, Devon

Skiing

Ski Plymouth
The south west's largest dry ski slope.
Alpine Park, Marsh Mills, Plymouth
☎ 0752 600220

Walking

The following centres arrange guided walks:

Dartmoor Expedition Centre
Rowden, Widecombe-in-the-Moor
☎ 03642 249

Dartmoor National Park
Parke, Haytor Road, Bovey Tracey
☎ 0626 832093

Overcombe Hotel
Yelverton
☎ 0822 853501

WATERSPORTS

Diving

Fort Bovisand Underwater Centre
Plymouth
☎ 0752 408021

Sailing

Newton Ferrars Sailing School
☎ 0752 872375

Plymouth Sailing School
☎ 0752 667170

DEVON

i Fore Street, Budleigh Salterton, Devon
☎ 0395 445275
i The Den, Sea Front, Teignmouth, Devon
☎ 0626 779769
i Phoenix Lane, Tiverton, Devon
☎ 0884 255827

EQUESTRIAN

Riding and Pony Trekking

Elliotts Hill Riding Centre
Buckland-in-the-Moor
☎ 0364 53058
Signposted from Buckland-in-the-Moor church

Smallacombe Farm Riding Stables
Islington
☎ 03646 265
½ mile from Ilsington, signed Trumpeter

HEALTH

Leisure Centres

Dyrons Leisure Centre
Pool with fun slide, sauna, sunbeds, squash and tennis.
Highweek Road, Newton Abbot
☎ 0626 60426
Close to the town centre. Access from the A383 and the A382

LOCAL FEATURES

Arts and Crafts

Dartington Cider Press Centre
Craft shops and visitor centre in attractive landscaped site.
Shinners Bridge, Dartington
☎ 0803 864171
→A A384
P &

The Devon Guild of Craftsmen
Museum and demonstrations with a continuous series of changing craft exhibitions.
Riverside Mill, Bovey Tracey
☎ 0626 832223
On the A382, 2 miles north of the Drumbridges jct on the A38
P ✕ &

Gardens

Bicton Park
60 acres of gardens including an Italian garden laid out in 1735.
East Budleigh, Budleigh Salterton
☎ 0395 68465
P ✕

Historic Buildings

A La Ronde
Unique 16-sided house built in 1795; parkland walks, sea and estuary views.
Summer Lane, Exmouth
☎ 0395 265514
→A A376
P 🚌 ✕ &

111

DEVON

Bradley Manor
A small 15th century mediaeval manor house and chapel set in woodland and meadows. National Trust.
Newton Abbot
☎ 0626 4513
On the A381, on the outskirts of town

Buckfast Abbey
The abbey, founded nearly a thousand years ago, was rebuilt earlier this century by the present community. Today it is a living Benedictine monastery well-known for its beekeeping, stained glass and tonic wine.
Buckfastleigh
☎ 0364 42519
→A A38
P 🚌 ♿

Castle Drogo
A 20th century granite 'castle' designed by Sir Edwin Lutyens. Gardens. National Trust.
Drewsteignton
☎ 0647 433306
4 miles south of the A30 via Crockernwell
P ♿

Compton Castle
A fortified manor house, the home of Sir Humphrey Gilbert, coloniser of Newfoundland and half-brother to Sir Walter Raleigh. National Trust.
Marldon, nr Paignton
☎ 0803 872112
→A A381
P

Ugbrooke House and Park
Ancestral home of the Lords Clifford of Chudleigh with fine furniture and paintings and a park landscaped by Capability Brown.
Chudleigh
☎ 0626 852179
→A A38
P 🚌 ✕ ♿

Natural History

Buckfast Butterfly Farm and Otter Sanctuary
Tropical butterflies and moths, otter pools and underwater viewing.
Buckfast Steam and Leisure Park, Buckfastleigh
☎ 0364 42916
→A A38/A384
P 🚌 ✕ ♿

Miniature Pony Centre
A large collection of rare miniature ponies, and an adventure playground.
Wormhill Farm, nr Bovey Tracey
☎ 0647 432400
On the B3212, 3 miles west of Moretonhampstead
P 🚌 ✕ ♿

Rare Breeds Farm
Farm trails, river walks and rare breeds of farm animals.
Parke, nr Bovey Tracey
☎ 0626 833909
Off the B3387
P ✕ ♿

Zoos

Paignton Zoo
Over 1300 animals, a botanical garden and an adventure playground.
Totnes Road, Paignton
☎ 0803 527936
P ♿

Birdwatching and Wildlife

Dawlish Warren Nature Reserve
500 acres of mixed dune, saltmarsh and sandy shores, an important wildfowl habitat. Guided walks are available.
i The Tourist Information Centre can provide details of all-inclusive accompanied weekend breaks offered through the year.

Shaldon Wildlife Trust
A collection of rare and endangered small mammals, exotic birds and reptiles, and a breeding centre.
Ness Drive, Shaldon
☎ 0626 872234
Off the A379 Torquay to Teignmouth road
🚌 ✕ ♿

Walking

Becky Falls Estate
A popular spot where the water tumbles 70 feet through lovely woodland to join the River Bovey; picnic areas and nature trails.
Manaton, nr Bovey Tracey
☎ 064722 259
On the B3344 Bovey Tracey to Manaton road
P

The National Park Authority
Guided walks are offered throughout the summer, they give an excellent introduction to Dartmoor.
Parke, Haytor Road, Bovey Tracey
☎ 0626 832093
i The Tourist Information Centre can provide detailed literature on short town trails or longer walks along the coast or over the moor. Regular theme walks and activities are also organised on Hakney Marshes, Coombe Valley, Dawlish Warren and the Decoy Park.

DORSET

i Westover Road, Bournemouth, Dorset
☎ 0202 789789
i Hound Street, Sherborne, Dorset
☎ 0935 815341
i The White House, Shore Road,
  Swanage, Dorset
☎ 0929 422885

EQUESTRIAN

Riding and Pony Trekking

Fir Tree Farm Riding Centre
Fir Tree Farm, Ogdens, Fordingbridge
☎ 0425 654744

The Glebe Riding Stables
Glebe Farm, Corfe Castle
☎ 0929 480280

HEALTH

Leisure Centres

Ferndown Sports and Recreation Centre
Badminton, basketball, circuit-training, a
fitness centre, five-a-side, keep-fit, netball,
racketball, a rock climbing wall, roller
skating, squash, swimming, table tennis,
trampolining and tennis are available.
Cherry Grove, Ferndown
☎ 0202 877468

Littledown Centre
Aerobics, badminton, basketball, bowls,
circuit-training, a fitness and health suite,
five-a-side football, netball, racketball,
squash, swimming, table tennis and tennis
are available.
Chaseside, Bournemouth
☎ 0202 417600

LOCAL FEATURES

Aquariums

Natural World
Exotic fish, sharks and piranhas.
The Quay, Poole
☎ 0202 686712
P 🍴 ✕ ♿

Public Aquariums
Extensive displays of marine and freshwater
animals.
Pier Approach, Bournemouth
☎ 0202 295393

Art Galleries

Russell-Cotes Art Gallery and Museum
Paintings, ceramics and oriental material in
a witty building. The Bournemouth Art
Gallery displays a fine collection of
Victorian and Edwardian paintings.
Russell-Cotes Road, East Cliff,
Bournemouth
☎ 0202 551009
✕ ♿

Arts and Crafts

Walford Mill Craft Centre
Quality craft shops, exhibitions and a
workshop area in an attractive riverside
setting.
Stone Lane, Wimborne
☎ 0202 841400
Off the B3078, north of the town centre
P 🍴 ♿ ♿

Gardens

Compton Acres Gardens
Fabulous gardens with rare plants, a
priceless collection of bronze and marble
statuary and a famous Japanese garden.
Canford Cliffs Road, Poole
☎ 0202 700778
P ✕ ♿ ♿

Cranborne Manor Gardens and Garden
Centre
Superb collection of spring bulbs, a knot
garden and an old fashioned rose collection.
Cranborne
☎ 07254 248
10 miles north of Wimborne Minster
P ✕ ♿

Historic Buildings

Brympton d'Evercy
A magnificent family home with extensive
gardens, a vineyard, Country Life Museum

113

WHAT TO DO AND SEE

in the Priest House specialises in cider-making. I Zingari cricket club collection.
Yeovil
☎ 0935 862 528
Off the A30 or the A3088, just west of Yeovil, signposted
P ✕

Corfe Castle
Impressive and atmospheric ruins of a mediaeval royal fortress standing in the Purbeck Hills.
Corfe
☎ 0929 480921
Off the A351 Wareham to Swanage road, 5 miles north-west of Swanage

Kingston Lacey House and Park
A beautiful 17th century house built by Sir Ralph Banks with a fine private picture collection and a 250 acre park. National Trust.
Wimborne
☎ 0202 883402
On the B3082, 1 mile west of Wimborne
P 🏠 ✕ 🚻 ♿

Sherborne Castle
A 16th century mansion built by Sir Walter Raleigh, the grounds around the lake were landscaped by Capability Brown.
Sherborne
☎ 0935 813182
1 mile east of Sherborne town centre

Smedmore House and Gardens
A 17th/18th century manor house with a fine collection of Dresden china, watercolours and dolls.
Kimmeridge
☎ 0929 480719
7 miles south of Wareham
P ♿

Museums

Christchurch Tricycle Museum
Victorian street scene and models.
Priory Car Park, Christchurch Quay
☎ 0202 479849
P ♿

Poole Museums
Three museums in the Old Town of Poole.
The Waterfront is a maritime museum;
Guildhall is a former Council Chamber and Court and Scaplens Court is a mediaeval merchant's house.
Poole Quay (Waterfront Museum), High Street (Scaplens Court), Market Street (Guildhall)
☎ 0202 675151

Natural History

Brownsea Island
A nature reserve with wading birds, migrants, red squirrels and Sika deer, it is the largest island in Poole Harbour.
Ferries from Poole harbour or Sandbanks
✕ 🚻 ♿

Merley Bird Gardens
Exotic birds set in a beautiful historic walled garden.
Merley, nr Wimborne
☎ 0202 883790
P 🏠 ✕ 🚻 ♿

Parks

Poole Park
100 acres of lakes and parkland on the edge of Poole Harbour with windsurfing, a mini-marina, crazy golf, putting, a zoo, a boating lake and a miniature railway.
☎ 0202 673322

OUTDOOR LEISURE/SPORTS

Fishing

Sea fishing

Sea Fishing Poole
Fisherman's Dock, The Quay, Poole
☎ 0202 679666

River fishing
The main rivers are the Avon, Stour, Frome and Piddle which are popular for salmon, trout and coarse fishing.
i Further information from the Tourist Information Centre.

WATERSPORTS

Sailing

Poole Bay, Poole and Christchurch Harbours offer sheltered areas for yachting. All types of watersports are available with sailing schools offering tuition and accompanied sailing or self-drive facilities.

Moonfleet Yachts
Cobbs Quay Marina, Hamworthy
☎ 0202 668410

Rockley Point School of Sailing
Rockley Sands, Hamworthy, Poole
☎ 0202 677272

Waterskiing

Ocean Bay Company
Also parascending, jet skiing.
2 Ulwell Road, Swanage
☎ 0929 422785

Windsurfing

Bournemouth Surfing Centre
127 Belle Vue Road, Southbourne
☎ 0202 433544

Bournemouth Windsurfing Centre
6 Falcon Drive, Bournemouth
☎ 0425 272509

WHAT TO DO AND SEE

i Berrow Road, Burnham-on-Sea,
Somerset
☎ 0278 787852
i The Market House, The Parade,
Minehead, Somerset
☎ 0643 702624
i Beach Lawns, Weston-super-Mare, Avon
☎ 0934 626838

AERIAL SPORTS

Ballooning

Taunton Hot Air Balloon Co Ltd
Pleasure flights, chartering, shows.
60 Bridge Street, Taunton
☎ 0823 333137

EQUESTRIAN

Riding and Pony Trekking

The Mendip Riding Centre
Riding school, also a ski centre with a
swimming pool and creche.
Lyncombe Lodge, Sandford, Avon
☎ 0934 852335

Quantock Riding Centre
Beech Hanger Farm, Kilve, nr Bridgwater
☎ 0278 74374

HEALTH

Leisure Centres

Hutton Moor Leisure Centre
Squash courts, a fitness gym, a multi-
purpose hall, a creche, and a cafeteria.
Hutton Moor Road, Weston-super-Mare
☎ 0934 635347

LOCAL FEATURES

Arts and Crafts

Old Cleeve Tannery
See sheepskins being converted into coats,
rugs and moccasins.
Old Cleeve, Minehead
☎ 0984 40291
Off the A39, signposted
🚌

Rambler Studio
An embroidery specialist, also watercolours,
miniatures, batik dyeing, lamps and
lampshades.
Oenone Cave, Holford, nr Bridgwater
☎ 0278 74315
➔A A39

Vellow Pottery and Silks
Stoneware pots by David Winkley; hand
painted silks by Sibylle Wex.
Lower Vellow, nr Williton
☎ 0984 56458
Off the A358, 2 miles south of Williton

Gardens

Hestercombe House Gardens
Designed by Sir Edwin Lutyens and
Gertrude Jekyll.
Cheddon Fitzpaine, Taunton
☎ 0823 337222
➔A A361
P 🏠 🚌

SOMERSET/AVON

Historic Buildings

Cleeve Abbey
A 12th century Cistercian Abbey with a 13th century dormitory and a 15th century refectory with a superb timber roof.
Washford, nr Watchet
☎ 0984 40377
→A A39
P 🕀

Combe Sydenham
Elizabethan house with gardens, a deer park, waymarked walks, trout ponds, fly fishing and a childrens playground.
Monksilver, nr Taunton
☎ 0984 56284
Off the B3188
P 🕀 🚌 ✗

Dunster Castle
A magnificent 13th century castle on the edge of Exmoor, the fortified home of the Luttrell family for 600 years, it rises dramatically above the village and the sea.
National Trust.
Nr Minehead
☎ 0643 821314
→A A39
P 🕀

Gaulden Manor
A Great Hall with a magnificent plaster ceiling and fine antique furniture; the grounds include a bog garden and a herb garden.
Tolland, Lydeard St Lawrence, Taunton
☎ 09847 213
Off the B3188
P 🕀 🚌 ✗

Museums

International Helicopter Museum
A unique collection of helicopters and autogyros with background displays on their history.
The Airport, Locking Moor Road, Weston-super-Mare
☎ 0934 635227
→A A368
P 🕀 🚌 ✗ ⛓ ⛓

Woodspring Museum
An Edwardian Gaslight Company workshop with a central courtyard, local Victorian seaside gallery, old chemist's shop, a dairy, costumes and an indoor nature trail.
Burlington Street, Weston-super-Mare
☎ 0934 621028
→A A370
P 🕀 🚌 ✗ ⛓ ⛓

Natural History

Ambleside Gardens and Aviaries
Over an acre of lake originally designed as a Japanese willow garden with aviaries of exotic birds.
Turnpike Road, Lower Weare, nr Axbridge
☎ 0934 732362
→A A38
P ✗ ⛓ ⛓

Brean Down Tropical Bird Garden
Over 170 different birds in a pleasant garden at the foot of Brean Down.
Nr Burnham-on-Sea
☎ 0278 75209
→A A370
P 🚌 ✗ ⛓

Railways

West Somerset Railway
Britain's longest preserved railway.
The Railway Station, Minehead
☎ 0643 704996
→A A39
P 🕀 ✗

Fishing

River fishing
Excellent in the Axe River.

Sea fishing
Sea angling is possible along the whole of Weston beach.

Trout fishing
The world famous Blagdon and Chew Valley lakes are open between April and October for trout fishing. Reservoirs are to be found at Cheddar and Barrow.

For further information:

Recreations and Conservation Officer
Bristol Waterworks Company, Woodford Lodge, Chew Stoke, Bristol
☎ 0272 332339

Wessex Water Authority
A choice of fisheries is offered in reservoirs at Durleigh (Bridgwater), Sutton Bingham (Yeovil), Clatworthy (Wiveliscombe), Hawkridge (Bridgwater) and Otterhead (Taunton).
King Square, Bridgwater
☎ 0278 457333

Walking

West Mendip Jubilee Way
A 30 mile walk from Uphill to Wells gives both serious hikers and casual strollers a chance to enjoy the magnificent scenery waymarked with distinctive oak posts.

Dinghy Sailing

South West Small Boat School
Instruction in sailing techniques available.
Uphill Boat Services, Uphill Wharf, Uphill
☎ 0934 627889

Windsurfing

Lanning Sports and Windsurfing Centre
66 Uphill Way, Uphill, Weston-super-Mare
☎ 0934 621078

AVON

i 8 Abbey Church Yard, Bath, Avon
☎ 0225 462831
i 14 Narrow Quay, Bristol, Avon
☎ 0272 260767

EQUESTRIAN

Riding
Mendip Riding Centre
Lyncombe Lodge, Churchill, nr Bristol
☎ 0934 852335

Midford Valley Riding Stables
Midford Road
☎ 0225 837613

Montpelier Riding Centre
Weston Farm Lane, Weston
☎ 0225 23665

LOCAL FEATURES

Art Galleries
Arnolfini Arts Centre
Modern art gallery with changing
exhibitions and performances of
contemporary music, dance, film and
theatre.
16 Narrow Quay, Bristol
☎ 0272 299191
→A A36
🚌 ✕ 🕭 🕭

Victoria Art Gallery
Collection includes European Old Masters
and 18th–20th century British paintings.
Bridge Street, Bath
☎ 0225 461111
🏛

Festivals and Fairs
May/June
Badminton Horse Trials, 3–6 May
Bath International Festival of Music and the
Arts, 25 May–10 June

Guided Tours
Car and Coach Tours
Private guided tours and open top bus tours
are run at frequent intervals.
i Details from the Bath Tourist
Information Centre.

Free guided walking tours
A detailed look at Bath's historic buildings,
they leave from outside the Pump Room
entrance in Abbey Church Yard. Mayor's
Honorary Guides are all volunteers.

Ghost walks
Start at the Garrick's Head near the Theatre
Royal.
☎ 0225 63618
☎ 0225 66541 for tickets

Historic Buildings
Bath Abbey
Late 15th century abbey built on the site of
an earlier Saxon and Norman building.
Magnificent example of the perpendicular
style of English Gothic architecture.

Dyrham Park
Richly furnished mansion built in Bath
stone set in beautiful parkland with views
across the Bristol Channel. Fallow deer
roam the park. National Trust.
☎ 027 582 2501
On the A46, 8 miles north of Bath
✕

Museums
American Museum in Britain
18 period furnished rooms and galleries all
illustrating American life between 17th and
19th centuries. Splendid views from the
gardens.
Claverton Manor, Bath
☎ 0225 60503
Off the A36 Warminster road
🚌 ✕

Bath Postal Museum
History of the Post and its Bath connections
– original letters from the 17th century,
postcards, uniforms, working machinery.
The building housed Bath's Post Office
when the world's first postage stamp was
used here on 2 May 1840.
Broad Street, Bath
☎ 0225 460333
→A A4/A36
🛍 🚌 ✕ 🕭

City of Bristol Museum and Art Gallery
Displays include ancient history, Bristol
ships, natural sciences, fine and applied
arts, Egyptology, ethnography, and glass.
Queen's Road, Bristol
☎ 0272 223571
🏛 ✕ 🕭 🕭

AVON

Roman Baths Museum
This Roman bathing establishment
flourished between the 1st and the 5th
centuries. The waters can be tasted in the
18th century Pump Room.
Bath
☎ 0225 462831
🚌 ♿ ♿

Theatres

Theatre Royal
One of Britain's oldest and most beautiful
theatres; a varied all-year programme;
backstage tours.
Sawclose, Bath
☎ 0225 448844 Box Office
🚌 ♿ ♿

Zoos

Longleat
The magnificent home of the Marquess of
Bath and his famous lions.
Warminster, Wiltshire
☎ 0985 3551
→A A362

Cycling

Cycle path
Easy going, winding path along the Avon
river valley using the flat, traffic-free route
of a disused railway, it offers safe and
peaceful cycling.

Fishing

Bath Trout Farm
Anglers' lake and fresh trout for sale.
Old Cleveland Baths, Hampton Row,
Bathwick, Bath
☎ 0225 60714

Crudgington I.M. Ltd.
Tackle shop.
37 Broad Street, Bath
☎ 0225 466325

Skiing

Avon Ski Centre
All equipment provided.
Lyncombe Lodge, Churchill, nr Bristol
☎ 0934 852828

Boat Hire

The Boathouse at Bath
Victorian boating station with wooden skiffs
and punts for hire.
Forester Road, Bath
☎ 0225 466407
Less than a mile from the city centre

Boat Trips

Bristol and Bath Cruises
Passenger boat cruises of Bristol Docks or
the River Avon.
☎ 0272 214307
♿

WHAT TO DO AND SEE

i New Forest Museum and Visitor Centre,
Lyndhurst, Hampshire
☎ 0703 282269

LOCAL FEATURES

Factory Visits

Eling Tide Mill
The only tide mill still producing
wholemeal flour.
The Toll Bridge, Eling, Totton,
nr Southampton
☎ 0703 869575

Falconry

New Forest Owl Sanctuary
Falconry displays, tours of aviaries, falconry
lessons.
Crow Lane, Crow, Ringwood
☎ 0425 476487
Off the B3347

Food and Drink

Lymington Vineyard
Award winning wines produced here.
Wainsford Road, Pennington, Lymington
☎ 0590 672112
✗

EQUESTRIAN

Riding and Pony Trekking

Forest Park Riding Stable
Rhinefield Road, Brockenhurst
☎ 0590 23429

Wagon Rides

New Forest Wagons
Balmer Lawn Road, Brockenhurst
☎ 0590 23633

HEALTH

Leisure Centres

The Pyramids Resort Centre
Clarence Esplanade, Southsea, Portsmouth
☎ 0705 294444

Rapids of Romsey
Activity and leisure pools with fitness
centre.
Southampton Road, Romsey
☎ 0794 830333

Gardens

Exbury Gardens
The de Rothschild family gardens; noted for
rhododendrons, azaleas, camellias and
magnolias.
Nr Southampton
☎ 0703 891203
3 miles from Beaulieu
P 🏠 ✗

HAMPSHIRE

Heritage

Rockbourne Roman Villa
Excavation of a large courtyard villa, over a 30-year period; a vast collection of interesting finds.
Rockbourne, nr Fordingbridge
☎ 07253 541

Historic Houses

Beaulieu
National Motor Museum, palace house and gardens, Abbey and exhibition; rides for the children on model cars.
Beaulieu
☎ 0590 612345
M3 and M27, easy access
P 🏠 ♿ ♿

Breamore House and Museums
Elizabethan Manor House in a tudor village.
Nr Fordingbridge
☎ 0725 22233
On the A338 between Salisbury and Bournemouth

Broadlands
Stately home of the late Lord Mountbatten; portraits, unique collections, riverside lawns and a Mountbatten exhibition.
Romsey
☎ 0794 516878
→A A31
P 🏠

Museums

New Forest Museum
Story of the New Forest, its traditions, wildlife and people.
High Street, Lyndhurst
☎ 0703 283914

The Sammy Miller Museum
Motor Cycle Museums; many unique cycles from 1900 onwards.
Gore Road, New Milton
☎ 0425 619696
🏠

Natural History

Dorset Heavy Horse Centre
Displays of horse-drawn farm machinery, working and show harness, pets corner; foals born every year.
Alderholt Road, nr Verwood
☎ 0202 824040
Off the B3081
P 🏠 ✗ ♿ ♿

Longdown Dairy Farm
A modern working farm that includes visitors.
Longdown, Ashurst, nr Southampton
☎ 0703 293326
→A A35
P 🏠 🚎 ♿ ♿

New Forest Butterfly Farm
Indoor tropical jungle, breeding butterflies and moths, insectarium with tarantulas, scorpions, praying mantis and other exotic creatures.
Longdown, Ashurst, nr Southampton
☎ 0703 292166
P 🏠 ♿ ♿

Parks

Paultons Park
Exotic wildlife; beautiful gardens; lake and working watermill; Kids Kingdom; minature railway; Land of Dinosaurs; Astroglide; Romany Village, museum and much more.
Ower, nr Romsey
☎ 0703 814442
A337/A31, 6 miles from Lyndhurst
P 🏠 ♿ ♿

Railways

Watercress Line
Steam locomotive rides.
Mid-Hants Railway, Alresford Station
☎ 0962 733810
Off the A31, 7 miles east of Winchester

Cycling

The New Forest is ideal cycling country.
i Cycle routes and cycle hire information available from the Tourist Information Centre.

Fishing

There is excellent freshwater angling in the River Avon, a waterway renowned for its salmon and coarse fishing. Forest waters and ponds can be fished with the permission of the Forestry Commission. There is trout fishing at a lake close to Lyndhurst and sea fishing in the Solent.

Leominstead Trout Fishery
Emery Down, Lyndhurst
☎ 0703 282610

Sea Angling Trips
From Keyhaven
☎ 0590 642923

Walking

Many waymarked walks exist in the New Forest. Contact the Forestry Commission for details.
☎ 0703 283141

Sailing

The Solent is a well known sailing area and both Lymington and Keyhaven are yachting harbours.

HAMPSHIRE/SUSSEX BORDERS

WHAT TO DO AND SEE

i St. Peter's Market, West Street,
   Chichester, West Sussex
☎ 0243 775888
i 1 Park Road South, Havant, Beachlands,
   Hampshire
☎ 0705 480024
i Sea Front, Hayling Island, Beachlands,
   Hampshire
☎ 0705 467111 summer only

AERIAL SPORTS

Ballooning

Golf Centres Balloons Ltd
Ballooning flights from a number of centres
in the area.
Balloon Booking Clerk, Cray Valley Golf
Club, Sandy Lane, St Paul's Cray, Orpington
☎ 0689 74388

Flying

Goodwood Flying School
Goodwood Airfield, nr. Chichester
☎ 0243 774656

Parachuting

Flying Tigers Skydiving Centre
Goodwood Airfield, nr Chichester
☎ 0243 780333

EQUESTRIAN

Riding and Pony Trekking

Escorted Rides
Lavant
☎ 0243 527035
☎ 0243 527431

HEALTH

Leisure Centres

Westgate
Wide range of activities: sports hall,
swimming pool, creche, squash courts, bar
and terrace, conditioning room, and a
keep-fit programme.
Avenue de Chartres, Chichester
☎ 0243 785651
🗑 ✗

LOCAL FEATURES

Festivals and Fairs

June
Petworth Festival
July
Chichester Festivities

Food and Drink

Chilsdown Vineyard
13-acre vineyard and winery based in a
unique Victorian station.
The Old Station House, Singleton,
Chichester
☎ 0243 63398
➔A A286
P 🗑 🚌 ✗

Gardens

Apuldram Roses
Specialist rose nursery and mature rose
garden.
Apuldram Lane, Dell Quay, Chichester
☎ 0243 785769
🗑

West Dean Gardens
35 acres of lawns, borders, specimen trees,
old roses, a wild garden and pergola all set
in a scenic downland valley.
West Dean, nr Chichester
☎ 0243 63303
P 🗑 ✗ 🦽 🦽

Guided Tours

Mary Godby
Town walks, coach tours and visits,
specialising in West Sussex.
Stable House, Amberley, Arundel
☎ 0798 831614

Heritage

Fishbourne Roman Palace and Museum
The remains of the north wing of a 1st
century Roman palace.
Salthill Road, Fishbourne, Chichester
☎ 0243 785859
➔A A27
P 🗑 🚌 🦽 🦽

Historic Buildings

Chichester Cathedral
Beautiful cathedral in the heart of the city;
the works of art range from Romanesque
stone carvings to famous modern paitings,
sculpture and tapestries.
The Royal Chantry, Cathedral Cloisters
☎ 0243 782595
➔A A27
🗑 🚌 ✗ 🦽 🦽

Goodwood House
Treasure house of the Dukes of Richmond
set in parkland with fine paintings
including some Canalettos, fine furniture
and Sevres porcelain.
☎ 0243 774107
✗ 🦽

WHAT TO DO AND SEE

Pallant House
An authentically restored Queen Anne town house with an art gallery and garden.
9 North Pallant, Chichester
☎ 0243 774557

Stansted Park
A neo-Wren house with an ancient chapel, walled gardens and a theatre museum set in an enchanting forest with the longest beech avenue in the south of England. Cricket is played on summer Sundays.
Rowlands Castle
☎ 0705 412265
Off the B2148
P

Museums

Chichester District Museum
Displays of geology, archaeology, social history and special exhibitions.
29 Little London, Chichester
☎ 0243 784683

Tangmere Military Aviation Museum
Museum sited on an historic airfield.
Chichester
☎ 0243 775223

OUTDOOR LEISURE/SPORTS

Cycling
i The Tourist Information Centre publishes a useful leaflet entitled *Cycling Round West Sussex*.

Daughtry's (Cycle Hire)
Also supplies fishing tackle and information.
44 The Hornet, Chichester
☎ 0243 783858

Walking
i The Tourist Information Centres supply leaflets of walks in the area.

WATERSPORTS

Boat Hire
Chichester Harbour Water Tours
Peter Adams, 9 Cawley Road, Chichester
☎ 0243 786418

Canoeing
Chichester Canoe Club
Secretary, 7 Redmoor, Main Road, Birdham
☎ 0243 512144

Windsurfing
Hayling Windsurfing
Northney Marina, Hayling Island
☎ 0705 467334

Southern Leisure Centre
Windsurfing, water-skiing and equipment hire.
Vinnetrow Road, Chichester
☎ 0243 774678

Yacht Charter
Chichester Sailing Centre Inc
Cruising courses, holidays, dinghy sailing and windsurfing.
Chichester Marina
☎ 0243 512557

WEST SUSSEX

WHAT TO DO AND SEE

i Marlborough House, 54 Old Steine,
    Brighton
☎ 0273 23755
i King Alfred Leisure Centre, Kingsway,
    Hove
☎ 0273 720371

AERIAL SPORTS

Hang Gliding

Freeflight Hang Gliding
274 New Church Road, Hove
☎ 0273 411239

EQUESTRIAN

Riding and Pony Trekking

Gatewood Farm
Robin Post Lane, Wilmington, Polegate
☎ 0323 483709

Three Greys Riding School
2 School Lane, Pyecombe
☎ 0273 843536

HEALTH

Leisure Centres

King Alfred Leisure Centre
Tropical leisure pool with beach, island and
waterchute; sauna, sunbeds, tenpin bowling
centre and table tennis.
Kingsway, Hove
☎ 0273 822228

LOCAL FEATURES

Aquariums

Brighton Sea Life Centre
Ocean life on a grand scale, more than 35
displays of marine creatures and a whale and
dolphin exhibition.

Marine Parade
☎ 0273 604234
 A23/M23 (town centre)
✕

Festivals and Fairs

November
London to Brighton Veteran Car Rally

Fun Parks

Pirates Deep
Indoor childrens adventure playground
featuring ball crawls, slides, ropes, childrens
cocktail bar, video room and adult seating
area.
Madeira Drive, Brighton
☎ 0273 674549
➔A A23 (town centre)
✕

Gardens

Sheffield Park Garden
Large 18th century garden designed by
Capability Brown with lakes and rare trees.
National Trust.
Danehill, nr Uckfield
☎ 0825 790655
P ✕ ♿

Historic Buildings

Lewes Castle
The shell keep of a Norman stronghold;
good views.
Lewes
☎ 0273 474379
➔A A277 (town centre)

Parham House and Gardens
Elizabethan House situated in a deer park
at the foot of the South Downs.
Pulborough
☎ 0903 742021
➔A A283
P ⌂ ♨ ✕ ♿

123

Preston Manor
Georgian manor house with an Edwardian home interior, servants' quarters, fine furnishings and pets' graves.
Preston Park, Brighton
☎ 0273 603005
→A A23 (town centre)
P ✕ ♿

Royal Pavilion
An eastern style palace built by Holland and Nash; original and contemporary interiors, Chinese porcelain and a magnificent music room.
Old Steine, Brighton
☎ 0273 603005
→A A23 (town centre)
🚌 ✕

Museums

Brighton Museum and Art Gallery
Fine collection of ceramics, art deco, art nouveau, archaeology, ethnography and fine art.
Church Street, Brighton
☎ 0273 603005
→A A23 (town centre)
🎭 ✕

Hove Museum and Art Gallery
English paintings, pottery, porcelain and silver.
19 New Church Road, Hove
☎ 0273 779410
→A A259 (town centre)
P 🎁 🚌 ✕ ♿

Natural History

Ashdown Forest Farm
Small farm with rare breeds of livestock and poultry; a spinning and weaving exhibition; a thatching demonstration; shearing and sheep dipping.
Wych Cross
☎ 0825 712040
→A A22
P ✕

Zoos

Drusilla's Park
New style zoo with generous enclosures, farmyard, railway, adventure playground, butterfly house, gardens and pottery.

Alfriston
☎ 0323 870234
→A A27
P 🚌 ✕ ♿

Cycling

Bicycle Hire
4 Temple Gardens, Brighton
☎ 0273 737979

Harman Hire
31 Davigdor Road, Brighton
☎ 0273 26090

Dry Slope Skiing

Stanley Deason Leisure Centre
Wilson Avenue, Brighton
☎ 0273 694281

Borowski Centre
New Road, Newhaven
☎ 0273 515402

Fishing

The Brighton Angler
Aquarium Colonnade, 1 Madeira Drive, Brighton
☎ 0273 671398

The Tackle Box
Brighton Marina
☎ 0273 696477

Sea Fishing

Blue Bird Speedboats
Charter boats available.
☎ 0323 29016

Brighton Marina Breakwaters
Charter boats available.
Brighton Marina
☎ 0273 693636

Ice Skating

Sussex Ice Rink
Queen's Square, Brighton
☎ 0273 24677

Sailing

Brighton Marina
Brighton Marina has 1700 berths; it also has bistros, bars, restaurants and speciality shopping. Yacht charter and fishing charter are available.
☎ 0273 693636
→A A259

Hove Lagoon
Dinghies and catamarans.
Kingsway, Hove
☎ 0273 430100

Sunsports
Dinghies and catamarans.
185 King's Road Arches, Brighton
☎ 0273 28584

EAST SUSSEX

i De La Warr Pavilion, Marina, Bexhill-on-Sea, East Sussex
☎ 0424 212023

i 3 Cornfield Road, Eastbourne, East Sussex
☎ 0323 411400

EQUESTRIAN

Riding and Pony Trekking

Cophall Farm Stables
Eastbourne Road, Polegate
☎ 0323 483975

HEALTH

Leisure Centres

Eastbourne Sovereign Centre
Four fabulous pools, a giant water skelter, bubble pools, water fountains, children's adventure and soft play areas.
Royal Parade, Langney Point, Eastbourne
☎ 0323 412444

LOCAL FEATURES

Art Galleries

Towner Art Gallery
Permanent collection of 19th and 20th century British art and craft.
High Street, Old Town, Eastbourne
☎ 0323 411688

Food and Drink

Merrydown Vintage Cider Making
Horam Manor is the home of Merrydown who have been cider makers since Norman times.
Horam Road, Heathfield
☎ 04353 2254
Off the A267 north of Eastbourne

Gardens

Leonardslee Gardens
Extensive landscaped garden in a marvellous setting; wallabies and Sika deer inhabit the gardens.
Lower Beeding, nr Horsham
☎ 0403 891212
→A A281/A279
P 🛈 ✗

Sheffield Park Garden
Large 18th century garden designed by Capability Brown with lakes and rare trees. National Trust.
Danehill, nr Uckfield
☎ 0825 790655
P ✗ &

Historic Buildings

Bodiam Castle
Bodiam is a National Trust castle that was built in 1385 to block the Rother Valley from incursions by the French.
Bodiam
☎ 0580 830436
Off the A229
P ✗

Great Dixter House and Gardens
A fine timber-framed hall house built in 1460 and restored by Sir Edwin Lutyens with fine furniture and needlework; informal gardens with yew hedges and original farm buildings.
Northiam
☎ 0797 253160
→A A28

Michelham Priory
Founded in 1229 for Augustinian Canons, the priory is surrounded by a moat and large gardens, it is approached through a magnificent gatehouse; a physic garden, working watermill, tudor barn, blacksmith and a rope museum.
Upper Dicker, Hailsham
☎ 0323 844224
Off the A22 and the A27
P 🛈

Museums

'How We Lived Then' Museum of Shops and Social History
Over 35,000 Victorian exhibits laid out in authentic shops.
Cornfield Terrace, Eastbourne
☎ 0323 37143

Local History Museum
The museum illustrates the history and development of the town from prehistory to the Edwardian era; it is on the lower floors of the Towner Art Gallery.
High Street, Old Town, Eastbourne
☎ 0323 411688

Wish Tower Invasion Museum
Housed in Martello Tower No 73, this museum concentrates on the defence of the south coast from Napoleonic times.
King Edward's Parade, Eastbourne
☎ 0323 410440

Natural History

Bentley Wildfowl and Motor Museum
Thousands of geese, ducks and swans; formal walled gardens, play areas for children, vintage cars and motorcycles.
Halland
☎ 0825 840573
Off the A22 and the A26, 7 miles north-east of Lewes, signposted
P 🛈

WHAT TO DO AND SEE

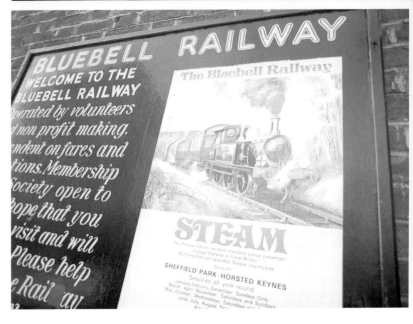

The Butterfly Centre
Tropical glasshouses with free flying
butterflies.
Royal Parade, Eastbourne
☎ 0323 645522

Parks

Princes Park
Opposite the beach, a popular family park
with a large boating lake, pedaloes and
rowing boats for hire.
Royal Parade, Eastbourne

Railways

The Bluebell Railway
Steam and vintage trains operate between
Sheffield Park and Horsted Keynes; a
collection of 30 historic locomotives.
Off the A275 between Lewes and East
Grinstead
☎ 082572 2370 timetable
☎ 082572 3777 enquiries

Kent and East Sussex Steam Railway
16 steam engines; rides.
Tenterden Town Station, Tenterden, Kent
☎ 05806 5155 enquiries

Zoos

Drusilla's Park
A notable small zoo; penguin bay, otter
valley and owls world.
Off the A27 west of Eastbourne
☎ 0323 870234
P ✕

OUTDOOR LEISURE/SPORTS

Cycling
Cuckmere Carriage Co. Ltd.
Berwick
☎ 0323 870598

Fishing
Fishing is good in the Cuckmere River,
Hampden Park, Lakelands Pond, Wallers
Haven, Langney Haven and Pevensey Haven.
Licences are available from local tackle
shops.

Tony's Tackle Shop
211 Seaside, Eastbourne
☎ 0323 31388

Compleat Angler Shop
22 Pevensey Road, Eastbourne
☎ 0323 24740
☎ 0323 24700

Walking
i A guide to local walks is available from
the Tourist Information Centres. It includes
town walks and rambles on the South
Downs Way.

WATERSPORTS

Boat Trips
Allchorn Brothers
Trips to Beachy Head Lighthouse and
circular tours to Birling Gap and Seven
Sisters.
Eastbourne
On the beach between the pier and the
bandstand
☎ 0323 34701

KENT

WHAT TO DO AND SEE

i Pierremont Hall, 67 High Street,
Broadstairs, Kent
☎ 0843 68399
i Fleur de Lis Heritage Centre,
13 Preston Street, Faversham, Kent
☎ 0795 534542
i Argyle Centre, Queen Street, Ramsgate,
Kent
☎ 0843 591086
i St. Peter's Church, Market Street,
Sandwich, Kent
☎ 0304 613565 summer only

AERIAL SPORTS

Parascending

Seawise Leisure
Western Undercliff, Ramsgate
☎ 0843 294144

EQUESTRIAN

Riding and Pony Trekking

Manston Riding Stables
15 Alland Grange Lane, Manston,
Nr Ramsgate
☎ 0843 823622

Plum Pudding Equestrian Centre
Plum Pudding Island, Minnis Bay,
Birchington
☎ 0843 47142

HEALTH

Leisure Centres

Hartsdown Park Sports and Leisure Centre
Swimming pool, trampolining, volleyball,
tennis, table tennis, roller skating, netball,
keep fit, gymnastics, approach golf, football,
basketball, badminton and aerobics.
Margate
☎ 0843 226221

Tides
Tropical indoor seaside with wild water
slides, waves, poolside spa, sun-suite, health
and fitness studio.
Victoria Park, Park Avenue, Deal
☎ 0304 373399

LOCAL FEATURES

Festivals and Fairs

June
Broadstairs Dickens Festival

August
Broadstairs Folk Week

Historic Buildings

Canterbury Cathedral
Mother Church of the Anglican
Communion, founded in 597, it was the
scene of Becket's martyrdom.
☎ 0227 762862
Off the A2, Canterbury city centre
🚌 ♿

Dover Castle and Hellfire Corner
An imposing mediaeval fortress and
underground war tunnels
☎ 0304 201628
→A A258
P 🚌 ✗

127

KENT

WHAT TO DO AND SEE

Museums

Dickens House Museum
Immortalised as Betsy Trotwood's house in
David Copperfield; many of Dickens
personal possessions are housed here.
2 Victoria Parade, Broadstairs
☎ 0843 62853
⇥A A255
🚌

Powell–Cotton Museum
Private collections from one man's lifetime
travels through Asia and Africa housed in a
beautiful Regency mansion set in parkland.
Quex Park, Birchington
☎ 0843 42168
⇥A B2048
P 🏠 🚌 ✕

Sarre Windmill
1820s wooden smock windmill, a traction
engine in the yard drives a steam saw,
milling machinery and a cider press. Bakery
products are available.
Sarre
☎ 0843 47573
⇥A A28/A253
P 🏠 🚌 ✕

**RAF Spitfire and Hurricane Memorial
Building**
A World War II Spitfire that saw active
service and a Hurricane restored to top
condition.
Manston
☎ 0843 823351

Natural History

Brambles English Wildlife
A large animal sanctuary set in natural
woodlands; an adventure playground, farm
animals and a nature trail.
Wealden Forest Park, Herne Common
☎ 0227 712379

Theme Parks

Dreamland White Knuckle Theme Park
The Marine Terrace, Margate
☎ 0843 227011

OUTDOOR LEISURE/SPORTS

Cycling

Ken's Bike Shop
26 Eaton Road, Margate
☎ 0843 221422

On Your Bike
20 Cutherbert Road, Westgate
☎ 0843 35577

Fishing

Coarse fishing
Freshwater fishing is popular in the River
Stour, River Wansum, Stonar Lakes and in
numerous dykes.

Sea fishing
The shoreline offers ample opportunity for
the experienced and inexperienced angler;
beaches, promenades, piers and rocks
produce good catches. For bigger fish,
charter boats are available from the harbour
at Ramsgate.

Fisherman's Corner
Boat charter is available.
6 Kent Place, Ramsgate
☎ 0843 582174
☎ 0843 67655

Kingfisheries
Sea and freshwater bait and day tickets for
Stonar Lake.
34 King Street, Margate
☎ 0843 223866
i A fishermans guide and tide tables are
available from the Tourist Information
Centres.

WATERSPORTS

Canoeing

Tidal Pool
Children's canoes are available for hire.
Main Sands, Margate

Thanet Canoe Club
Open to non-members.
Newgate Gap, Cliftonville
☎ 0843 225580

Jet Skiing

Water Sports International
Palm Bay, Cliftonville
☎ 0843 226079

Waterskiing and Windsurfing

Seawide Leisure
Waterskiing, windsurfing and wave riders.
Western Undercliff, Ramsgate and Main
Sands, Margate
☎ 0843 294144

SURREY

i Town Hall, New Zealand Avenue,
  Walton-on-Thames, Surrey
☎ 0932 228844
i The Civic Hall, London Road, Guildford,
  Surrey
☎ 0483 444007

AERIAL SPORTS

Ballooning
Flying Picture Balloons
Chobham
☎ 0276 855111 ext 125

Independent Balloon Co Ltd
74 North Street, Guildford
☎ 0483 300054

EQUESTRIAN

Riding and Pony Trekking
Bushy Park
The Green, Hampton Court
☎ 081 979 1748

LOCAL FEATURES

Art Galleries
Gomshall Mill and Gallery
An ancient watermill with an art gallery,
craft shops and antiques.
Gomshall
☎ 048641 2433
→A A25
♿

Gardens
Claremont Landscape Garden
The earliest surviving English landscape
garden, it was begun in the early 1700s.
Portsmouth Road, Esher
☎ 0372 469930
P 🏠 🚌 ✗ ♿ ♿

Painshill Park
An 18th century landscaped park.
Portsmouth Road, Cobham
☎ 0932 868113
P 🏠 🚌 ✗ ♿

Savill Garden
In Windsor Great Park.
Wick Lane, Englefield Green
P ♿

Wisley Gardens
Home of the Royal Horticultural Society.
Guildford
☎ 0483 224234
Off the A3 between Ripley and Cobham
P 🏠 ✗ ♿ ♿

Historic Buildings
Albury Park
Large Victorian mansion designed by Pugin
and famous for the ornate brickwork of the
chimneys.
Albury, nr Guildford
☎ 048641 2964
→A A248
P 🏠 🚌

Clandon Park
An outstanding 18th century country house
with a fine marble hall and Gubbay
collection of furniture, pictures and
porcelain.
West Clandon, nr Guildford
☎ 0483 222482
→A A3
P 🏠 🚌 ✗ ♿ ♿

Greated Manor
A fine Victorian Manor House.
Ford Manor Road, Dormansland, Lingfield
☎ 0342 832577
Off the B2028
P 🏠 🚌 ✗

Hatchlands
A handsome red brick house built in 1758
and notable for its interiors by Robert
Adam; a fine collection of keyboard
instruments and a garden.
East Clandon, nr Guildford
☎ 0483 222787
→A A246
P 🏠 ✗ ♿

SURREY

Polesden Lacey
A Regency villa remodelled after 1906 with fine paintings, tapestries, silver and extensive grounds.
Great Bookham, nr Dorking
☎ 0372 458203
→A A246
P 🏠 ✕ 🚻 ♿

Loseley Park
An Elizabethan country house with many works of art, a garden terrace and Moat Walk, a children's play area, farm trailer rides, a dairy farm and a rare breeds unit; the farm shop sells Loseley dairy and bakery products.
Guildford
☎ 0483 304440
→A A3100
P 🏠 🚌 ✕ 🚻 ♿

Hampton Court Palace
A magnificent Tudor Palace with later Baroque additions; famous for its Maze and gardens.
East Molesey
☎ 081 977 8441
P 🏠 ✕ 🚻 ♿

Natural History

Chapel Farm Animal Trail
Working farm set in magnificent countryside.
Westhumble, Dorking
☎ 0306 882865
🏠 ♿ ♿

Horton Park Farm
Children's farm with lots of young animals.
Horton Lane, Epsom
☎ 0372 743984
🏠 ✕ 🚻 ♿

Parks

Thorpe Park
Family leisure park with 400 acres of lakes and parkland; many attractions and rides.
Staines Road, Chertsey
☎ 0932 562633
🏠 ✕

Zoos

Chessington World of Adventures
Large zoo with a human circus, spectacular rides in a themed area, and a skyway monorail.
Leatherhead Road, Chessington
☎ 0372 727227
🏠 ✕ ♿

Birdwatching

Laporte Earths' Conservation Lake
Bird sanctuary and lake with paths and viewing platforms.
Nutfield Marsh Road, Nutfield
☎ 0737 765050
♿

Fishing

Weybridge Guns and Tackle Ltd
137 Oatlands Drive, Weybridge
☎ 0932 842675

Tillingbourne Trout
Anglers' lake, fly fishing, tackle shop and fresh trout.
Albury Mill, Albury
☎ 048641 2567

Walking

There are some lovely walks both in the Surrey countryside and in the many parks and commons.
𝑖 Self-guided walks booklets are available from Tourist Information Centres or at local libraries.

Surrey County Council
Walk leaders are available who lead fascinating rambles.
☎ 081 541 8800

Boat Hire

Guildford Boat House
River trips, holiday narrow boats, rowing boats and canoes for hire.
Millbrook
☎ 0483 504494

Maidboats Ltd
Cruiser hire on the Thames; holiday membership of rowing and sailing clubs and trips in passenger boats.
Ferry Yacht Station, Ferry Road, Thames Ditton
☎ 081 398 0271
☎ 081 398 0272

BUCKINGHAMSHIRE/HERTFORDSHIRE

i County Library, Kings Road,
Berkhamstead, Hertfordshire
☎ 0442 877638

EQUESTRIAN

Riding and Pony Trekking
Ashridge Farm Equestrian Centre
Ringshall, Little Gaddesden
☎ 0442 843443

Whippendell Riding School and Livery
Chipperfield Road, Kings Langley
☎ 0923 262396

HEALTH

Health Farms
Champneys
One of the oldest established health farms;
set in a country estate.
Wigginton, Tring
☎ 042 873155

LOCAL FEATURES

Historic Buildings
Ashridge Estate
A 4000-acre estate which includes Ashridge
Park, Aldury and Berkhamsted Commons,
Pitstone Windmill, woodlands, heathlands
and downlands rich in wildlife and fauna;
there are superb views from Ivinghoe
Beacon and the Bridgewater Monument.
Nr Berkhamsted
☎ 044 285227
Off the B4506, 3 miles north of the A41
P ⌘ ✗ ⅊ ⅊

Cliveden
On cliffs 200 feet above the Thames, it was
once the home of Nancy, Lady Astor, now it
is a hotel with gardens and woodlands,
including a magnificent parterre, water
garden and fine views.
Maidenhead, Berks
☎ 0628 605069
Off the B476, 2 miles north of Taplow
P ⌂ ⅊ ⅊

Hughenden Manor
Home of Benjamin Disraeli from 1847 until
he died in 1881; many of his pictures and
books are on display.
Nr High Wycombe
☎ 0494 32580
Off the A4128, north of High Wycombe
P ✗ ⅊ ⅊

West Wycombe Park
Fine Palladian mansion built in the mid
18th century and set in a landscaped park
which contains a swan-shaped lake and
statuary.
Nr High Wycombe
☎ 0494 24411
South of the A40, nr West Wycombe
P ⌂ ⅊

Museums
Zoological Museum
Nearly every kind of large mammal and
countless different birds, reptiles, fish,
insects plus a large selection of extinct
animals are represented.
Akeman Street, Tring
☎ 044 282 4181
➔A A41
⌂

Natural History
Chalfont Shire Horse Centre
Model farm, blacksmith shop, pets corner,
vintage lorries and daily demonstrations.
Gorlands Lane, Chalfont St Giles
☎ 02407 2304
Off the M25, jct 17
⌂ ✗

Parks
Gadebridge Park
Over 300 acres of open parkland with
nature trails, a paddling pool, bowls and
golf.
Hemel Hempstead
P

Zoos
Whipsnade Wild Animal Park
Set in 600 acres of parkland, you can walk
or drive around the wild animals at
Whipsnade.
Dunstable
☎ 0582 872171
Off the M1, jct 9, signposted
⌂ ✗

OUTDOOR LEISURE/SPORTS

Birdwatching and Wildlife
Tring Reservoirs
A haven for bird and wildlife.
On the B489 north of Tring

Fishing
Coarse fishing
Excellent for trout, carp, tench, bream,
roach, perch, pike and rudd.

National Rivers Authority
Public Relations Dept.
☎ 0734 593777

WATERSPORTS

Boat Hire
Bridgewater Boats
Castle Wharf, Berkhamsted
☎ 0442 863615

Cruises
Cruise into the Chilterns
Grebe Canal Cruises, Pitstone Wharf,
Pitstone, nr Leighton Buzzard
☎ 0296 661920
☎ 0628 472500 evenings
Off the B488

131

WHAT TO DO AND SEE

i St. Michael's Tower, The Cross,
Gloucester, Gloucestershire
☎ 0452 421188
i 20 Broad Street, Ross-on-Wye,
Herefordshire
☎ 0989 62768
i The Museum, 64 Barton Street,
Tewkesbury, Gloucestershire
☎ 0684 295027

AERIAL SPORTS

Ballooning
Ballooning in the Cotswolds
36 Cheltenham Road, Rendcomb,
nr Cirencester
☎ 028583 515

Jon Langley & Co.
Stroud
☎ 0453 825447

EQUESTRIAN

Riding and Pony Trekking
Badgworth Riding Centre
Cold Pool Lane, Up Hatherley, Cheltenham
☎ 0452 713818

HEALTH

Leisure Centres
Gloucester Leisure Centre
Bruton Way, Gloucester
☎ 0452 306498

LOCAL FEATURES

Art
Nature in Art
The International Centre for Wildlife Art is
located in a Georgian mansion which
houses a unique collection of wildlife
painting; outside sculptures and a nature
garden. Easels for hire.
Wallsworth Hall, Sandhurst, nr Gloucester
☎ 0452 731422
→A A38
P 🚌 ✕ &

Falconry
Birds of Prey Trust and Falconry Centre
Trained hawks, falcons, eagles and aviaries.
Newent
☎ 0531 820286
Off the B4215
P ✕

Gardens
Westbury Court Garden
Formal Dutch water garden.
Westbury-on-Severn
☎ 045276 461
Off the A48, 9 miles south-west of
Gloucester
🚌 & &

HEREFORD & WORCESTER/GLOUCESTERSHIRE

WHAT TO DO AND SEE

Historic Buildings

Berkeley Castle
A perfectly preserved castle over 800 years old; the scene of the murder of Edward II; ornamental gardens.
Berkeley, Gloucester
☎ 0453 810332
→A A38
P 🚍 ✕

Gloucester Docks
A collection of beautifully restored Victorian warehouses; attractions include the Waterways Museum, the Robert Opie Collection and an antique centre.
Southgate Street, Gloucester
→A A38

Sudeley Castle
The home and burial place of Katherine Parr, last wife of Henry VIII; art collection, craft centre, gardens, falconry displays, open-air theatre (late June) and adventure playground.
Winchcombe
☎ 0242 602308
On the A46, 6 miles north of Cheltenham
P ✕

Tewkesbury Abbey
Superb Norman abbey with 14th century vaulting and windows; a former Benedictine monastery, it has the tallest Norman towers in England and also the largest surviving Norman tower.
Church Street, Tewkesbury
☎ 0684 850959
→A A38
P 🚍 ♿

Museums

Cheltenham Museum and Art Gallery
Fine Dutch paintings, collections of ceramics and porcelain from China and the Far East, and a section devoted to Edward Wilson, who perished with Captain Scott on the ill-fated Antarctic Expedition of 1910.
Clarence Street, Cheltenham
☎ 0242 237431
→A A40
✕ ♿

Cotswold Countryside Collection
Collection of agricultural history housed in former house of correction.
Fosse Way, Northleach
☎ 0451 60715
Jct of the A40 and the Fosse Way, A429
P ✕ ♿

Natural History

Newent Butterfly and Natural World Centre
Tropical butterflies, snakes, insects and a pet animal zoo.
Birches Lane, Newent
☎ 0531 821800
Off the B4215

Zoos

Cotswold Farm Park
A collection of rare breeds of British farm animals; pets corner and picnic areas set high on the Cotswold Hills.
Guiting Power
☎ 0451 850307
Off the A46 north of Cheltenham
P 🚍 ✕ ♿

Cotswold Wildlife Park
200 acres of lawns and gardens, the animals range from the white rhino to reptiles; picnic areas and an adventure playground.
Burford outskirts
☎ 099382 3006

OUTDOOR LEISURE/SPORTS

Birdwatching

Slimbridge Wildfowl Trust
A trust set up by Sir Peter Scott; the world's largest and most varied collection of wildfowl; over 2300 birds of 180 different species; winter viewing of birds.
Slimbridge
☎ 0453 890065
Off the M5, jcts 13 and 14, signposted
🚍 ✕ ♿

Cycling

Crabtrees
50 Winchcombe Street, Cheltenham
☎ 0242 515291

Fishing

Coarse fishing
On the Gloucester and Sharpness Canal, the Rivers Severn and Avon; licenses and permits from Gloucester Angling Centre (see below).

Game fishing
On the Rivers Wye and Monnow and on stillwater lakes in the Cotswold Area. Salmon fishing on the Rivers Wye and Severn.

Allsports
126 Eastgate Street, Gloucester
☎ 0452 22756

Gloucester Angling Centre
45 Bristol Road, Gloucester
☎ 0452 20074

Skiing

Gloucester Ski Centre
2 slopes for beginners and accomplished enthusiasts.
Robinswood Hill, Gloucester
☎ 0452 414300
P ✕

WATERSPORTS

Boat Trips

Gloucester Docks
On the canal, from the quay by the Waterways Museum.

WHAT TO DO AND SEE

i 2 City Arcade, Birmingham, West
   Midlands
☎ 021 6432514
i Bayley Lane, Coventry, West Midlands
☎ 0203 832303
☎ 0564 794609

Sandwell Valley Riding Centre
Wigmore Farm, Wigmore Lane,
West Bromwich
☎ 021 588 2103

Umberslade Riding School
Blunts Green Farm, Blunts Green,
nr Henley-in-Arden
☎ 05642 4609

HEALTH

Health Clubs
Albany Hotel Club
Smallbrook Queensway, Birmingham
☎ 021 643 8171

LOCAL FEATURES

Art Galleries

Birmingham Museum and Art Gallery
A selection of British and European
paintings and sculptures from the 14th to
20th century; noted Pre-Raphaelite
collection.
Chamberlain Square, Birmingham
☎ 021 235 2834
City centre
🏛 ✗

Ikon Gallery
Regular exhibitions of contemporary art,
sculpture and photography.
58–72 Bright Street, Birmingham
☎ 021 643 0708
🏛

Herbert Art Gallery and Museum
Frederick Poke Collection of English 18th
century furniture and silver; Sutherland's
sketches of Coventry tapestry and natural
history section.
Jordan Well, Coventry
☎ 0203 832381

Arts and Crafts
Jewellery Quarter
Birmingham jewellery quarter and St. Paul's
Square once housed many of Birmingham's
silver and goldsmiths. It is now a
conservation area with many workshops and
jewellery retailers.

Festivals and Fairs
June
The Edgbaston Cup, Priory Tennis Club
The Ryder Cup, The Belfry Golf Club
Royal International Horse Show, National
Exhibition Centre

August
Super Prix Road Race, Birmingham City
Centre, August Bank Holiday

ADVENTURE

Multi-activity Centres
The Ackers Trust
Climbing and abseiling, mountain biking,
canoeing and kayaking, skiing and
development training on a large urban site.
Golden Hillock Road, Small Heath,
Birmingham
☎ 021 771 4448

EQUESTRIAN

Riding and Pony Trekking
Bournevale Riding Stables
Little Hardwick Road, Streetley
☎ 021 353 7174

WEST MIDLANDS

Gardens

Birmingham Botanical Gardens and Glasshouses
15 acres of gardens in central Birmingham with glasshouses containing many rare plants; exotic birds and waterfowl, a children's adventure playground and bands play on Sunday afternoons in the summer.
Westbourne Road, Edgbaston, Birmingham
☎ 021 4541860

Guided Tours

Middle of England Guided Tours and Travel
Walking and coach tours in Birmingham and throughout the region.
14 Sandhurst House, Icknield Street, Kings Norton, Birmingham
☎ 021 459 9290

Historic Buildings

Aston Hall
A fine Jacobean house noted for its grand balustraded staircase and panelled Long Gallery.
Trinity Road, Aston, Birmingham
☎ 021 327 0062
2½ miles from the city centre

Blakesley Hall
A timber-framed yeoman's farmhouse built around 1575 and carefully refurbished.
Blakesley Hall, Yardley, Birmingham
☎ 021 783 2193
3 miles from the city centre

Coventry Cathedral
The new cathedral, designed by Sir Basil Spence and opened in 1962, stands alongside the 14th century ruins. The interior houses outstanding examples of the finest works of modern art.
City Centre, Coventry
☎ 0203 224323
P &

Sarehole Mill
An 18th century water-powered mill in working order, the setting for J. R. Tolkien's *The Hobbit*.
Cole Bank Road, Hall Green, Birmingham
☎ 021 777 6612

Museums

Birmingham Museum of Science & Industry
All aspects of science, engineering and industry, including transport; world's oldest working steam engine.
Newhall Street, Birmingham
☎ 021 236 1022

Birmingham Railway Museum
12 steam locomotives.
670 Warwick Road, Tyseley, Birmingham
☎ 021 707 4696

National Motorcycle Museum
British-built motorcycles spanning the period 1898 to 1980; over 600 cycles on display.
Coventry Road, Bickenhill, Birmingham
☎ 021 755 3311

Music, Dance and Drama

Birmingham International Arena
A major venue attracting star performers from the music world and accommodating audiences of 3000 to 12,000. National Exhibition Centre, Birmingham
☎ 021 780 4133

City of Birmingham Symphony Orchestra
City centre, Birmingham
☎ 021 236 1555

Infoteline
Telephone information service to help you book tickets.
☎ 0839 333999

OUTDOOR LEISURE/SPORTS

Ice Skating

Solihull Ice Rink
Hobs Moat Road, Solihull
☎ 021 742 5561

WATERSPORTS

The Birmingham area has a notable canal system, ideal for cruising in narrow boats, canal walks and fishing.

Boat Hire

Brummagem Boats
Holiday hire fleet of 25 narrow boats; passenger trips and a restaurant boat.
Sherborne Street Wharf, Sherborne Street, Birmingham
☎ 021 455 6163

SHROPSHIRE

WHAT TO DO AND SEE

i Civic Centre, High Street, Whitchurch,
Shropshire
☎ 0948 4577

ADVENTURE

Clay Pigeon Shooting
Clay Target Club
Qualified instruction; shotguns available;
non-members welcome.
Llandegla
☎ 0978 88221

HEALTH

Leisure Centres
Plas Madoc Leisure Centre
Tropical plant and palms trees, leisure pool,
sun beds, sauna, gym, cabaret,

entertainments and major sports events.
Acrefair, Wrexham
☎ 0978 821600
On the A539 Llangollen road, 7 miles from
Wrexham

LOCAL FEATURES

Arts and Crafts
Johnsons Basket Centre
Specialists in all types of basketware and
pine furniture, custom made baskets.
Bangor-on-Dee
☎ 0978 780417
On the A525/B5069

Ludlow Castle, Shropshire

SHROPSHIRE

Alf Strange
Talks and demonstrations by practising blacksmith.
☎ 0691 622628
On the A495, 2 miles west of Ellesmere

The Rocking Horse Workshop
Traditional art of making wooden rocking horses, hand carved and painted in the Georgian and Victorian styles.
Ashfield House, The Foxholes, Wem
☎ 0939 32335

Gardens

Cholmondeley Castle Gardens
Hillside gardens and 19th century castle; water, rose and temple gardens; lakeside picnic areas.
Malpas
☎ 0829 720383
➔A A49
P 🏠 ✗ ♿

Dorothy Clive Gardens
A worked-out quarry reclaimed into a magnificent rhododendron garden; wonderful views.
Willoughbridge, nr Woore
☎ 063081 237
On the A51 between Nantwich and Stone
P 🏠 ✗ ♿ ♿

Hodnet Hall Gardens
Lovely gardens with superb trees, lawns, lakes and ancient buildings.
Hodnet, nr Weston-under-Redcastle
☎ 063084 202
➔A A53/A41
P 🏠 ✗

Historic Buildings

Dorfold Hall
Historic Jacobean house and garden.
Nantwich
☎ 0270 625245
➔A A534
P 🏠 🚌

Erddig House
Interesting late 17th century house with a formal walled garden, extensive woods, parkland and country walks. National Trust.
Nr Wrexham
☎ 0978 355314
Off the A525, 2 miles south of Wrexham
P 🏠 🚌 ✗ ♿ ♿

Hawkstone Hall and Gardens
A splendid Georgian mansion set in parkland.
Marchamley Village
☎ 063 084 242
Off the A442
🏠

Natural History

Bridgemere Wildlife and Heritage Centre
35-acre wildlife park with big cats, birds of prey, European mammals and a craft centre.
Nr Woore
☎ 09365 223
Off the A51, 5 miles south-east of Nantwich
P ✗ ♿

Stapeley Water Gardens and Palms Tropical Oasis
Exotic birds, rare plants, sharks, piranhas, tropical and cold water fish.
London Road, Stapeley, nr Nantwich
☎ 0270 623868
On the A51, 1 mile south of Nantwich
P ✗ ♿

Parks

Marbury Country Park
200 acres of woodland and open spaces; a bird hide and picnic areas.
Comberbach, nr Whitchurch
☎ 0606 77741
➔A A559
P ♿

Birdwatching

Ellesmere Visitor Centre
Large mere noted for its wildfowl; rowing boats, picnic area, fishing and playground.
The Mere
☎ 0691 622981
Off the A495 Whitchurch to Oswestry road
P ✗ ♿

Cycling

Wharf Motorcycle Shop
36 Green End, Whitchurch
☎ 0948 2151

Fishing

The River Dee is a noted salmon river, and there is also brown trout, sea trout and grayling. Permits for fishing on the Dee and the canal available from:

Warner's Fishing Tackle Shop
Deermoss Lane, Whitchurch
☎ 0948 5076

Walking

The Sandstone Trail
A 30-mile walk from Beacon Hill, Frodsham south to Grindley Brook locks.

The Shropshire Way
A 172-mile recreational footpath created by linking existing public rights of way on footpaths, bridleways and quiet lanes.

i Guides for these walks are available from the Tourist Information Centres.

DERBYSHIRE

i The Crescent, Buxton, Derbyshire
☎ 0298 25106

ADVENTURE

Caving and Rock Climbing
First Ascent
Courses in 'Cautious Caving' and
'Reassuring Rock Climbing'.
Far Cottage, Church Street, Longnor,
nr Buxton
☎ 0298 83545

Multi-activity Centres
High Ash Farm Field Studies Centre
Longnor, nr Buxton
☎ 0298 25727

Moorside Activity Centre
Hollingsclough, Longnor, nr Buxton
☎ 0298 83406

White Hall
Residential centre for open country
pursuits.
Long Hill, Buxton
☎ 0298 23260
Off the A5004, 3 miles north of Buxton

AERIAL SPORTS

Gliding
Derbyshire and Lancashire Gliding Club
Camphill, Great Hucklow, nr Tideswell,
Buxton
☎ 0298 871270

Hang Gliding
Peak School of Hang Gliding
2-day taster courses available.
The Elms, Wetton, nr Ashbourne
☎ 0335 27257

EQUESTRIAN

Riding and Pony Trekking
Northfield Farm Riding and Trekking
Centre
Northfield Farm Riding and Trekking Centre
Northfield Farm, Flash, nr Buxton
☎ 0298 22543
A53, 5 miles south of Buxton

HEALTH

Spas
Buxton Swimming Pool
Swim in Buxton's natural spa water;
solarium, indoor bowls and more.
Pavilion Gardens
☎ 0298 26548

LOCAL FEATURES

Arts and Crafts
Craft Centre
Old Stables Courtyard, Caudwell's Mill,
Rowsley
☎ 0629 733185
Off the A6, nr Bakewell

Rooke's Pottery
Original terracotta pots in production.
Hartington, nr Buxton
☎ 0298 84650
Nr the village centre
⌂

Gardens
Pavilion Gardens
23 acres of gardens and woodland walks; a
pavilion, erected in 1871 to a design by
Milner; a beautiful conservatory, opera
house, concert hall, children's play area,
miniature railway, putting and restaurant.
☎ 0298 23114
⌂

Guided Tours
Blue Badge Guides
Qualified tourist guides offer guided walks
around Buxton and Castleton as well as
organising full Peak District tours.
i Further information is available from
the Tourist Information Centre.
☎ 0298 25106

DERBYSHIRE

Historic Buildings

Chatsworth
The 'Palace of the Peak' with a fine collection of paintings, drawings and books; elaborate waterworks in the gardens.
Bakewell
☎ 0246 582204
On the A623, 4 miles east of Bakewell
P 🛈 ✕

Haddon Hall
A fine mediaeval House, seat of the Duke of Rutland, set in wooded hills overlooking the River Wye.
Bakewell
☎ 0629 812855
On the A6, 2 miles south of Bakewell
P 🛈 ✕

Hardwick Hall
Elizabethan home of Bess of Hardwick; notable needlework, tapestries and furniture.
Nr Chesterfield
☎ 0246 850430
On the M1, 2 miles south-east of jct 29
P 🛈 ✕

Museums

Buxton Micrarium
Special push-button projection microscopes to see the minutiae of the natural world.
The Crescent, Buxton
☎ 0298 78662
🛈 ♿

Buxton Museum and Art Gallery
'Wonders of the Peak' exhibition, displays of geology, discoveries from caves, prehistoric and Roman remains, monthly exhibitions of paintings, prints and photographs.
Terrace Road, Buxton
☎ 0298 24658
🛈

Glossop Heritage Centre
Authentic Victorian kitchen, changing exhibitions, art gallery showing local artists' work and a craft area.
Henry Street, Glossop
☎ 0457 869176
🛈

Natural History

Chestnut Centre Conservation Park, Otter Haven and Owl Sanctuary
Castleton Road, Chapel-en-le-Frith
☎ 0298 814099
Off the A625
🛈

Cycling

Peak Cycle Hire
Cycling from seven centres located in and around the Peak National Park. Explore beautiful and varied countryside along disused railway lines and quiet country lanes; suitable for all ages.

Peak National Park
Parsley Hay Cycle Hire, Buxton
☎ 0298 84493

Fishing

Waters in the National Park fall mainly within the Severn Trent Water Authority, Abelson House, 2297 Coventry Road, Sheldon, Birmingham.

Chatsworth Estate
Fly fishing on stretches of the River Derwent and Wye. Permits from the Estate office.
Nr Bakewell
☎ 0246 582204

Errwood Reservoir
Leased to Errwood Fly Fishing Club, day tickets available.
Goyt Valley, nr Buxton
☎ 0663 732212

Lightwood Reservoir
Fly fishing only. Permits from water bailiff.
Buxton
☎ 0298 23710

Stanley Moor Reservoir
Fly fishing only, permits from Peak Pets.
Axe Edge, nr Buxton

Peak Pets
Fairfield Road, Buxton
☎ 0298 71370

Walking

First Ascent
Easy walking holidays.
Far Cottage, Church Street, Longnor
☎ 0298 83545

Wanderlust
Walking and sightseeing holidays in the Peak District.
4 Boswell Court, Ashbourne
☎ 0335 46594

WHAT TO DO AND SEE

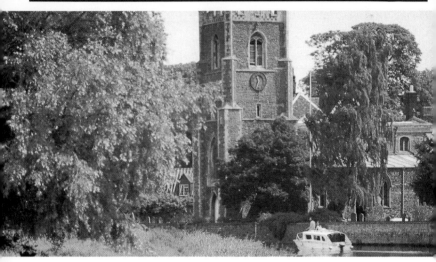

 Wheeler Street, Cambridge,
Cambridgeshire
☎ 0223 322640

EQUESTRIAN

The National Stud
Booking is essential for a tour of the stud.
☎ 0638 663464
Nr Newmarket July Race Course at the
jct of the A1303 and the A1304
P 🏠 🚌 ✗ ♿

Riding
Sawston Riding School
Common Lane Farm, Common Lane,
Sawston
☎ 0223 835198
6 miles south-east of Cambridge

LOCAL FEATURES

Gardens
The Swiss Garden
Romantic garden, 19th century, many
original buildings and ironwork, adjacent to
the Shuttleworth aircraft collection
Old Warden, nr Biggleswade
☎ 0234 63222
➤A A1
🏠 ✗ ♿ ♿

Historic Buildings
Anglesey Abbey
A 13th century Augustinian Priory; a private
house after 1591; 100 acres of world famous
gardens; outstanding collection of European
paintings, sculpture and objets d'art.
National Trust. Lode Water Mill nearby is
included in the price.
Lode
☎ 0223 811200
➤A A1134
🏠

Cambridge Colleges
The colleges are private places where people
live and work, but visitors are welcome to
walk through the courts and visit the
chapels and in some cases the halls and
libraries.

Hinchingbrooke House
The ancestral home of the Cromwells and
Earls of Sandwich.
Huntingdon
☎ 0480 51121
On the A604, ½ mile west of Huntingdon
🏠 🚌 ✗ ♿

Houghton Mill
The oldest remaining watermill on the
Ouse, 17th century, a massive timbered
structure with 19th century machinery.
National Trust.
Mill House, Mill Street, Houghton
☎ 0480 301494
Off the A1132, 3 miles from Huntingdon
P 🏠

Wimpole Hall, Park and Home Farm
Imposing house, extravagant decoration,
extensive gardens, walks, adventure
woodland, home farm and restored
Victorian stable block with working Suffolk
Punches, children's corner. National Trust.
Arrington, nr Royston
☎ 0223 207257
Off the A603
P 🏠 ✗ ♿ ♿

Museums in Cambridge
Fitzwilliam Museum
Outstanding collection of paintings,
antiquities, ceramics and armour.
Trumpington Street, Cambridge
☎ 0223 332900
🚌 ✗ ♿ ♿

WHAT TO DO AND SEE

Scott Polar Research Institute
Museum of polar life and exploration.
Lensfield Road, Cambridge
☎ 0223 337733
🏛

Sedgwick Museum
Extensive collection of geological specimens.
Downing Street, Cambridge
☎ 0223 333400
🏛 ♿

Museum of Zoology
Birds, insects, mammals and sea animals, stuffed and preserved.
Sidgwick Avenue, Cambridge
☎ 0223 336650
🏛 ♿

University Museum of Archaeology and Anthropology
Shrunken heads; totem poles; native dress; local finds.
Downing Street, Cambridge
☎ 0223 337733
🏛 ♿

Natural History

Wicken Fen
600 acres of wetland reserve, a remnant of the Great Fens, rich in plant, insect and bird life, nature trail, bird hides and exhibitions. National Trust.
Lode Lane, Wicken, Ely
☎ 0353 720274
➔A A1123
P 🏛 ♿ ♿ 🚌

Zoos

Linton Zoo
Beautiful gardens and wildlife in 10 acres of countryside.
Hadstock Road, Linton
☎ 0223 891308
Off the A604
P 🏛 🚌 ✕ ♿ ♿

Fishing

Information and licenses from:
Anglian Water
☎ 0223 61561

Grafham Water Reservoir
Trout fishing.
5 miles south-west of Huntingdon
☎ 0780 86 321

Thornton & Son
46 Burleigh Street, Cambridge
☎ 0223 358709

Skiing

Bassingbourn Ski Club
Hitchin
☎ 0462 34107

Walking

Devil's Dyke Walk
Early Saxon ditch embankment between Reach and Stetchworth built as a defensive fortification. Leaflet from Cambridgeshire Wildlife Trust.
☎ 0223 880788

Gog Magog Hills
Woods, grassland and iron-age fort at Wandlebury.
➔A A1307

Icknield Way Long Distance Footpath
Route of the oldest road in Britain along the chalk spine of Southern England. Walkers guide is available from the Icknield Way Association.
☎ 0279 505602

Ouse Valley Long Distance Footpath
Bluntisham along the River Great Ouse to Eaton Socon. Leaflets produced by Huntingdonshire District Council.
☎ 0480 561561

Wicken Walks
2 interlinked waymarked walks through the Fenlands. Leaflet from Cambridgeshire County Council Rural Management Division.
☎ 0223 317404

OUTDOOR LEISURE/SPORTS

Birdwatching

Little Paxton
Gravel pit lakes, migratory birds and walks.
Diddington
➔A A1

Cycling

Armada Cycles
47 Suez Road, Cambridge
☎ 0223 210421

I S Munro
Cambridge Street, Godmanchester
☎ 0480 452341

WATERSPORTS

Punting

Scudamore's
Granta Place, Cambridge
☎ 0223 359750

Windsurfing and Sailing

Grafham Water Reservoir
Grafham Water Sailing Club, West Perry, Huntingdon
☎ 0480 810478

Mepal Outdoor Centre
Sailing, playpark, canoeing, windsurfing.
Chatteris Road, Ely
☎ 0354 692251

SUFFOLK

i   The Cinema, High Street, Aldeburgh,
Suffolk
☎ 0728 453637 summer only
i   Town Hall, Princes Street, Ipswich,
Suffolk
☎ 0473 258070

AERIAL SPORTS

Parachuting

Ipswich Parachute Centre
Ipswich Airport, Nacton Road
☎ 0473 710044

EQUESTRIAN

Riding and Pony Trekking

Bentley Riding Centre
Bentley, Ipswich
☎ 0473 311715
→A A12

Newton Hall Equitation Centre
Swilland, nr Ipswich
☎ 0473 785616

HEALTH

Leisure Centres

Crown Pools
3-pool complex with a wave machine,
waterfall, fountains, skydiver shute, sauna
and solarium.
Town centre, Ipswich
☎ 0473 219231
✕

LOCAL FEATURES

Architecture

Leiston Abbey
14th century Abbey, remains include
transepts of church and range of cloisters.
Nr Saxmundham
☎ 0728 455532

Art Galleries

Wolsey Art Gallery
Collection of works by Thomas
Gainsborough and John Constable; fine art
collection by Suffolk artists.
Christchurch Park
🛏

Arts and Crafts

Snape Maltings
On the River Alde, craft shop, garden,
wholefood.
Snape, nr Saxmundham

Aldringham Craft Market
Pottery, wood, leather, glass, jewellery,
sculpture and toys.
Nr Leiston

Festivals and Fairs

June
Aldeburgh Festival

August
Snape Maltings Proms

Gardens

Blakenham Woodland Garden
5-acre bluebell wood, many rare trees
and shrubs.
Little Blakenham, Ipswich
☎ 0473 830344
4 miles north-west of Ipswich
P 🍴

Helmingham Hall Gardens
House; moat with drawbridges that are
raised each night; large park with herds of
deer and Highland cattle; gardens with
renowned herbaceous borders.
Helmington, Stowmarket
☎ 0473 890363
Off the B1077
P 🍴 ♿

Historic Buildings

Framlingham Castle
Massive walls, 13 towers built by the second
Earl of Norfolk.
Framlingham
☎ 072872 3330
Off the B1116
P 🍴

Orford Castle
Built by Henry II on the Suffolk coast in
1173, an important royal residence for over
100 years.
Orford
☎ 03944 50472
Off the B1084
P 🍴

Music, Dance and Drama

Snape Maltings
Old maltings now a world famous concert
hall.
Snape
☎ 0728 452935
→A A12
P 🚌 ♿

Parks

Easton Farm Park
Victorian farm setting for many animals,
rare breeds and Suffolk horses.
Easton, nr Wickham Market
☎ 0728 746475
→A A12
P 🍴 🚌 ✕ ♿ ♿

SUFFOLK

OUTDOOR LEISURE/SPORTS

Cycling

The Bicycle Doctor
18 Bartholomew Street, Ipswich
☎ 0473 259853

Fishing

Fishing on the Gipping and Orwell Rivers, and the Claydon and Barham Pits is controlled by:

Gipping Angling Preservation Society
19 Clover Close, Ipswich
☎ 0473 602828

Skiing

Suffolk Ski Slope
Bourne Hill
☎ 0473 602347

WATERSPORTS

Boat Trips

Orwell and Harwich Navigation Co Ltd
On the River Stour and Orwell
☎ 0255 502004

Lady Moira/Lady Florence
From Snape Maltings and Orford on the River Alde
☎ 0728 88303
☎ 0728 88305

Waldringfield Boat Yard
On the River Deben
☎ 0473 36260

Yacht Cruising

The Watersports Centre
A yacht cruising school; dinghy school; windsurfing, canoeing, adventure and instructional holidays or yacht and motor cruiser hire for continental holidays.
Oysterworld, Wherry Quay Marina
☎ 0473 230109

Sailing Holidays
Aboard the 90ft gaff ketch *Marjie*.
Ipswich
☎ 0379 898873

NORFOLK

i The Green, Hunstanton, Norfolk
☎ 0485 532610
i Station Approach, Sheringham, Norfolk
☎ 0623 824329 summer only

EQUESTRIAN

Riding and Pony Trekking

Stiffkey Valle Stables
Old Wells Road, Little Walsingham
☎ 0328 72377

LOCAL FEATURES

Antiques and Collecting

Fakenham Flea Market and Auctions
Thursday mornings in the old cattle
markets.
Hugh Beck Auctions, Fakenham
☎ 0328 51557

Architecture

Castle Acre Priory
Impressive ruins of a Cluniac Priory dated
about 1090.
Stocks Green, Castle Acre, Kings Lynn
☎ 0760 755394
On the A1065, nr Castle Acre village
P 🏠

Creake Abbey
Remains of an abbey church dating from
the 13th century.
Burnham Market
P 📷

Walsingham Abbey
Remains of an Augustinian Priory, including
a gate house, crypt and east window arch;
woodland and riverside walks.
Little Walsingham
☎ 0328 820259
On the B1105
P 🏠 🚌 ♿ ♿

Gardens

Glavenside Gardens
Picnic areas, water and rock gardens,
streams, ponds, boating and fishing by the
River Glaven.
Letheringsett, nr Holt
☎ 0263 713181
→A A148
P 🏠 ♿ ♿

Mannington Hall Gardens
Gardens with lake, moat, and woodland;
walks and country trails and a rose festival.
Mannington Hall, Saxthorpe
☎ 026387 4175
Off the B1149/B1354 jct.
P 🏠 🚌 ✕ ♿ ♿

Historic Buildings

Baconsthorpe Castle
A 15th century moated and semi-fortified
house; remains include the inner and outer
gatehouse and curtain wall.
Baconsthorpe, nr Holt
☎ 0223 455532 area custodian
→A A148
P 📷

Cley Mill
Well-preserved tower mill, used until 1918
as a flour mill.
Cley-next-the-Sea
☎ 0263 740209
→A A149
P 🏠 🚌

Holkham Hall
Beautiful 18th century Palladian manor by William Kent with fine paintings, tapestries, museum and wildfowl gardens.
Wells-next-the-Sea
☎ 0328 710733
➔A A149
P 🏠 ✕ ♿

Houghton Hall
Early 18th century house owned by the Marquess of Cholmondeley; superb state rooms, a collection of 20,000 model soldiers and stables with heavy horses.
Houghton
☎ 0485 528569
On the A148, 9 miles from Fakenham
P 🏠 🚐 ✕ ♿ ♿

Letheringsett Watermill
Historic working watermill with an iron waterwheel.
Riverside Road, Letheringsett, Holt
☎ 0263 713153
On the A148, 1 mile from Holt
P 🏠 🚐

Museums

Cockthorpe Hall Toy Museum
Over 2500 toys displayed in 7 rooms of a lovely 16th century manor house.
Cockthorpe, nr Stiffkey
☎ 0328 830293
➔A A149
P 🏠 🚐 ✕

Forge Museum
A working forge.
North Creake, nr Fakenham
On the B1355, 3 miles from Burnham Market
🏠

Glandford Shell Museum
Shells from all over the world, engraved and carved exhibits; a tapestry of the north Norfolk coast.
Glandford
☎ 0263 740081
On the B1156, 3 miles north west of Holt
🏠

Thursford Collection
Steam locomotives, showman's traction, mechanical organs, ploughing and traction engines, live concerts on the Wurlitzer.
☎ 032877 477
Off the A148, 6 miles north-east of Fakenham
P 🏠 ✕

Natural History

Kelly's Birds and Aviaries
Free flying macaws, toucans, cockatoos, parrots and parakeets; waterfowl and beautiful gardens.
Weybourne Road, Kelling, nr Holt
☎ 0263 711185
P

Birdwatching and Wildlife

Blakeney Point
Shingle spit, sand dunes with hides to see seals and birds. Shop and display in the Lifeboat House. National Trust.

Cley Marshes
Fresh water and salt marshes with a large number of rare migrants each year. Norfolk Naturalists' Trust. Cley Visitor Centre gives permits for the reserve.

Holkham
Sand and mud flats, salt marshes and sand dunes with Corsican Pines. Holkham Hall Lake has flocks of Canada Geese and wildfowl roosts. Nature Conservancy Council. For permits for birdwatching: Estate Office, Holkham Hall
☎ 0328 710227

Scolt Head Island
Island reserve with salt marshes and sand dunes. Access by boat from Brancaster Staithe. Nature Conservancy Council.

Titchwell
Reed beds, salt marshes and sandy shores, waders and wintering wildfowl. Royal Society for the Protection of Birds. Warden, Three Horseshoes Cottage, Titchwell. Access along sea wall footpath from car park to hides

Cycling

A1 Taxis
21 St. Peter Street, Sheringham
☎ 0263 822228

Engledow's Discount Cycle Warehouse
Creake Road, Sculthorpe, Fakenham
☎ 0328 4785

Fishing

Excellent coarse fishing, sea fishing and trout fishing in this area.
i A detailed leaflet is available from the local Tourist Information Centre.

Kingfisher Tackle
28 Beeston Road, Sheringham
☎ 0263 822098

Marine Sports
21 New Street, Cromer
☎ 0263 513676

Mr Bishop
32 Langham Road, Blakeney
☎ 0263 740200

Walking

Excellent local walks and coastal paths exist in this area including many with particular wildlife interest.
i The Tourist Information Centre has free leaflets with details of walks.

LINCOLNSHIRE

WHAT TO DO AND SEE

i Embassy Centre, Grand Parade, Skegness
☎ 0754 4821
i Cottage Museum, Iddesleigh Road,
  Woodhall Spa
☎ 0520 58775

ADVENTURE

Multi-activity Centres

Tattershall Park Country Club
Waterskiing, windsurfing school, jet skiing,
canoeing, rowing, pedalo, squash, snooker,
gymnasium, saunas, solarium, horse riding,
nature walks and lake swimming.
Tattershall
☎ 0526 43193
On the A153 Sleaford to Skegness road

AERIAL SPORTS

Flying

Ingoldmells
Skegness Aerodrome, Skegness
☎ 0754 2240

HEALTH

Leisure Centres

Seafront Complex
Indoor and outdoor pools with waterslides.
Grand Parade, Skegness
☎ 0754 610675

The Richmond Holiday Centre
Pool, sauna, sun beds and gymnasium.
Richmond Drive, Skegness
☎ 0754 69265

LOCAL FEATURES

Aquariums

Skegness Natureland Marine Zoo & Seal
Sanctuary
Performing seals, sealions, penguins,
aquarium, birds and butterfly house.
North Parade, Skegness
☎ 0754 4345

Arts and Crafts

Alford Craft Market
Demonstrations and street theatre.
→A A1104

Historic Buildings

Gunby Hall
Reynold's portraits. National Trust.
Nr Spilsby
☎ 0909 486411 NT regional office
→A A158
P 🏠 🚌 ♿

Sibsey Trader Mill
England's only remaining 6 sail, 6 storey
tower mill.
Sibsey
☎ 0205 750036
Off the A16, 5 miles north of Boston
P 🏠

Tattershall Castle
Spectacular 15th century grandee's tower
house, four great chambers with ancillary
rooms, fine brick vaulting and Gothic
fireplaces.
Tattershall
☎ 0526 42543
→A A153
🏠 ♿

Museums

Battle of Britain Memorial Flight
Spitfires, Hurricanes and Europe's only
flying Lancaster bomber.
RAF Coningsby
☎ 0526 44041
→A A153
P 🚌 ♿ ♿ ✕

Woodhall Spa Cottage Museum
Fine collection of photographs and town
history.
Iddesleigh Road, Woodhall Spa
☎ 0526 53775
🏠

Parks

Snipe Dales Country Park
200 acres, nature reserve, woods and
marked pathways.
Lusby and Winceby, nr Spilsby
☎ 0522 552222 (Recreation Officer)
→A A1115

Bottons Pleasure Beach
Modern pleasure park with rides, arcades
and bingo.
Skegness

Panda's Palace
Children's activity area.
Tower Esplanade, Skegness
☎ 0754 5494

Theatres

Embassy Centre
Concerts, cabarets; entertainment centre.
Grand Parade, Skegness
☎ 0754 68333

OUTDOOR LEISURE/SPORTS

Birdwatching and Wildlife

Gibraltar Point Nature Reserve
1500 acres of sandy dunes, saltmarsh, sandy
and muddy shores, dune slacks and
freshwater habitats for studying the flora
and fauna of the east coast. Guided walks.
☎ 0754 2677
→A A52
P 🚌 ♿ ♿

Tennis

North Shore Holiday Centre
Roman Drive, Skegness
☎ 0754 3815

WHAT TO DO AND SEE

i 16 Wheeler Gate, Nottingham,
Nottinghamshire
☎ 0602 470661

Newstead Abbey
800 year old priory, home of Lord Byron; it
was converted into a country mansion in
the 16th century; memorabilia and 300
acres of parkland.
Linby
☎ 0623 793557
➜A A60
P ✗ ♿

LOCAL FEATURES

Festivals and Fairs

August
Monsters of Rock Festival, Donington Park,
Castle Donington

October
Goose Fair, The Forest, Nottingham

Guided Tours

Mortimer's Hole Tour
300-ft long ancient passageway, a famous
cave.
i Information from the Tourist
Information Centre

The Nottingham Story
Entertaining audio-visual show, the story of
Nottingham.
i Information from the Tourist
Information Centre

Historic Buildings

Belvoir Castle
Home of the Duke and Duchess of Rutland,
superbly situated with staterooms,
furniture, tapestries and paintings and
regular displays of mediaeval jousting.
Nr Grantham
☎ 0476 870262
Off the A607 and the A52, signposted
P ✗

Nottingham Castle Museum
An art gallery and museum housed in the
17th century residence built by the Dukes
of Newcastle on the site of the royal
mediaeval castle; fine collections of
ceramics, silver, glass and paintings.
☎ 0602 483504
➜A A52 (city centre)
🚌 ✗

Museums

East Midlands Aeropark and Visitor Centre
12-acre park of exhibits, display and play
area.
East Midlands International Airport
☎ 0332 810621 ext 3361
Off the A453, nr Castle Donington
P 🏠 ♿

Brewhouse Yard Museums
Museum of daily life housed in converted
17th century town houses; period rooms
and displays.
Castle Boulevard, Nottingham
☎ 0602 483504
Foot of Castle Rock
🏠 ♿

NOTTINGHAMSHIRE

Canal Museum
A waterway museum in a former canal warehouse with loading areas and wharves.
Canal Street, Nottingham
☎ 0602 598835
🖾

Museum of Costume and Textiles
Elegant Georgian terrace houses, costume, lace and textile collections.
51 Castle Gate, Nottingham
☎ 0602 483504
➔A A52
🖾

Green's Windmill and Science Centre
Hands-on exhibits of light, magnetism and electricity, in a restored mill and adjoining science centre. The mill sells its own stone-ground flour.
Belvoir Hill, Sneinton
☎ 0602 503635
Off the A612, nr city centre
P ♿

The Story of Nottingham Lace
The story of Nottingham's lace industry, demonstrations of hand and machine lace-making.
Lace Hall, High Pavement, Nottingham
☎ 0602 484221
🚌 🖾 ✕

D H Lawrence's Birthplace Museum
Furnishings a facsimile of the Lawrence's; craft centre in renovated cottages nearby; *Sons and Lovers* Cottage is at 28 Garden Road, Eastwood.
8a Victoria Street, Eastwood
☎ 0773 763312
➔A A610
🚌 🖾 ✕

Wollaton Hall Natural History Museum
Elizabethan mansion houses the city's natural history and industrial museum, set in 500 acres of parkland; deer; and a beam engine.
Wollaton Hall, Wollaton Park
☎ 0602 281333
➔A A609
P 🚌 ✕ ♿

Tales of Robin Hood
The story of Robin Hood told in an award-winning form of mediaeval adventure and exhibition.
Maid Marian Way, Nottingham
☎ 0602 414414/483284
➔A A52 (city centre)
♿ 🖾

Natural History

White Post Modern Farm Centre
Working farm; farm animals and crops; llamas; quail; ostriches and egg incubator; lake picnic area and country walk.
White Post Farm, Farnsfield, nr Newark
☎ 0623 882977
On the A614, 12 miles north of Nottingham
P 🖾 🚌 ✕ ♿

Parks

Colwick Country Park
250-acre park adjacent to the Nottingham racecourse and river; dinghy hire, fishing areas, nature reserve, cycle and horse-riding trails.
Colwick Road, Nottingham
☎ 0602 870785
Off the B686
P ♿

Sherwood Forest Visitor Centre and Country Park
450 acres of ancient Sherwood Forest with the famous Major Oak; information centre and Robin Hood exhibition.
Edwinstowe
☎ 0623 823202
Off the B6034
P ✕ ♿

Birdwatching

Wetlands Waterfowl and Exotic Bird Park
Waterfowl reserve with many species; childrens farmyard and rare breeds.
Sutton-cum-Lound, nr Retford
☎ 0777 818099
➔A A638
P 🚌 ✕

Cycling

Olympic Cycles
43 Radford Road, Hyson Green, Nottingham
☎ 0602 702616

Dry-slope Skiing

Carlton Forum
Foxhill Road, Carlton, Nottingham
☎ 0602 872333

Ice Skating

Ice Stadium
Lower Parliament Street, Nottingham
☎ 0602 501938

Tenpin Bowling

Nottingham Bowl
Barker Gate, Nottingham
☎ 0602 505588

Holme Pierrepont National Water Sports Centre
Landscaped water parks offering sailing and board sailing instruction, picnic areas, nature reserves, walks and facilities for fishermen; regular rowing, canoeing and power boat events are held at Holme Pierrepont.
Adbolton Lane, Nottingham
☎ 0602 821212

SOUTH YORKSHIRE

i Town Hall Extension, Union Street,
    Sheffield, South Yorkshire
☎ 0742 734671
☎ 0742 734672

EQUESTRIAN

Riding and Pony Trekking

Massarella School of Riding
Thurcroft Hall, Brookhouse, Laughton
☎ 0909 566429
2 miles east of M1/M18 jct

Millview Riding School
Mark Lane, Fulwood, Sheffield
☎ 0742 305093
3 miles from Sheffield centre

LOCAL FEATURES

Art Galleries

Graves Art Gallery
Collection of British and European painting,
drawing, sculpture, Islamic pottery, Indian
and Japanese Art.
Surrey Street, Sheffield
☎ 0742 734781
✕ &

Mappin Art Gallery
Changing displays of 18th–20th century
British painting, sculpture; works by
Turner, Constable, Chantrey,
pre-Raphaelites and Moderns.
Weston Park, Sheffield
➔A A57
✻ 🚐 ✕ & &
☎ 0742 726281

149

SOUTH YORKSHIRE

Ruskin Gallery and Craft Gallery
Houses John Ruskin's 1819–1900 collection
of Guild of St. George, paintings,
watercolours, minerals, fine books and
illuminated manuscripts.
101 Norfolk Street, Sheffield
☎ 0742 735299
→A A57/A61
♿ ♿

Factory Visits

Abbeydale Industrial Hamlet
Turn of the century crucible steel and
scythe works, four water wheels, workers
cottages, managers house and museum.
Abbeydale Road South, Sheffield
☎ 0742 367731
→A A621
P 🏠 🚌 ✕ ♿

Shepherd Wheel
Water wheel driving grindstones in two
workshops, typical Sheffield cutlery grinder.
Whiteley Woods, Hangingwater Road,
Sheffield
☎ 0742 367731
→A A57/A625
🎫 ♿

Gardens

Sheffield Botanical Gardens
Aviary, aquarium, disabled persons garden,
extensive gardens with over 5500 plants.
Clarkehouse Road, Sheffield
☎ 0742 671115
→A A57
🎫 ♿ ♿

Historic Buildings

Sheffield Manor and Turret House
Mary Queen of Scots' prison for 14 years, a
special exhibition on the history of the
Manor.
Manor Lane, Sheffield
☎ 0742 734547
→A A616
🎫 🚌

Museums

City Museum
Major collection of local archaeology,
geology, wildlife, cutlery, Old Sheffield
Plate, clocks and ceramics.
Weston Park, Sheffield
☎ 0742 768588
→A A57
P 🎫 ✕ ♿ ♿

Industrial Museum
The story of Sheffield's industrial
development.
Kelham Island, off Alma Street, Sheffield
☎ 0742 722106
→A A61
P 🏠 ✕ ♿ ♿

Sheffield Bus Museum
Collection of 1926–1970 buses and coaches;
a locally built 1926 Sheffield tramcar.
Tinsley Tram Sheds, Sheffield Road,
Sheffield
☎ 0742 489166
→A A6178
P 🚌 ✕ ♿ ♿

Parks

Rother Valley Country Park
Country park with canoes, sailboards,
rowing boats, sailing dinghies, nature
reserve, visitor and craft centre, fishing,
walks and ski-slope.
Mansfield Road, Wales Bar, Sheffield
☎ 0742 471452
→A A618
P 🏠 ✕ 🚌 ♿ ♿

Railways

☎ **South Yorkshire Railway Co Ltd**
34 industrial locomotives including 5 steam
and 14 ex-British Rail engines.
Barrow Road, Meadow Hall, Sheffield
☎ 0709 556307

Theatres

Crucible Theatre
Norfolk Street, Sheffield
☎ 0742 769922

Cycling

Fairholmes Visitor Centre
Derwent Lane, Derwent
☎ 0433 50953

Fishing

Game fishing is offered in the Upper
Derwent Reservoirs: the Ladybower,
Derwent and Howden reservoirs, in the
season.
Derwent Lane, Derwent
☎ 0433 51254
10 miles west of Sheffield

Walking

The Peak District National Park
There is marvellous walking in the Peak
District near Sheffield. The Pennine Way
begins at Edale and walkers have access to
most of the Northern Moors. For further
details contact:
Aldern House, Baslow Road, Bakewell,
Derbyshire
☎ 062 981 4321

Waterskiing

Rother Valley Country Park
Jet skiing and waterskiing.
Mansfield Road, Wales Bar, Sheffield
☎ 0742 471453

MANCHESTER

i 9 Princes's Street, Stockport, Cheshire
☎ 061 474 3320
i Town Hall Extension, Lloyd Street,
Manchester, Lancashire
☎ 061 234 3157
☎ 061 234 3158

LOCAL FEATURES

Arts and Crafts

Paradise Silk Mill
Silk from cocoon to loom; guided trails of
mills and weavers houses.
Park Lane, Macclesfield
☎ 0625 618228
➔A A532
🏠 🚌 ✕

Factory Visits

Quarry Bank Mill
Water-driven textile mill, still spinning and
weaving after 200 years.
Styal
☎ 0625 527468
➔A A538
P 🏠 🚌 ♿

Historic Buildings

Adlington Hall
Manor House in quadrangle shape, once
surrounded by a moat; typical 'black and
white' Cheshire style, and handsome red
brick.
Macclesfield
☎ 0625 829206
On the A523, 5 miles north of Macclesfield
P 🏠 ✕

Arley Hall and Gardens
Victorian Jacobean style Hall with fine
plasterwork and wood panelling, large
private chapel, parklands, gardens, and a
Tithe barn with art gallery. Nearby Stockley
farm is a modern working farm open to the
public.
Near Great Budworth, Northwich, Cheshire
☎ 0565 777353
Off the A559
🏠 ✕

Astley Hall
Late Tudor English country house
surrounded by 105 acres of wooded
parkland, walks, lake, museum and art
gallery.
Astley Park, Chorley
☎ 02572 62166
Off the A581
P 🏠 🚌

MANCHESTER

Bramall Hall and Park
An outstanding black and white tudor style
Hall, set in 100 acres of parkland; activities
include tennis and bowls.
Stockport
☎ 061 485 3708
Off the A5102
P 🛏

Capesthorne Hall
Family home of the Bromley–Davenport
family and their ancestors since Domesday
times, adjoining Georgian chapel, park,
lakes, gardens and walks.
Macclesfield
☎ 0625 861221
➔A A34
P 🛏 ♿ ♿

Dunham Massey Hall and Park
Seat of the Earls of Stamford and
Warrington, richly furnished rooms,
gardens, stables, coachhouse, parkland and
deer sanctuary. National Trust.
Altrincham
☎ 061 9411025
Off the A56, nr Altrincham
P 🛏 ♿ ♿

Gawsworth Hall, Park and Gardens
Norman manor house. Open air theatre
and crafts.
Macclesfield
☎ 0260 223456
➔A A536
P 🛏 ✕

Lyme Park
1300-acre estate; deer park, wild moorland
scenery and beautiful formal gardens; an
outstanding collection of English clocks.
Disley, Stockport
☎ 0663 62023
On the A6, 6 miles from Stockport
P 🛏 ✕ ♿ ♿

Tatton Park
Magnificent mansion with glorious gardens,
deer park, meres, 1930s Home Farm and
Mediaeval Old Hall. Special events held here
include craft fairs and horse events.
Facilities for cycle hire, carriage rides,
fishing and sailing.
Knutsford, Cheshire
☎ 0565 654822
➔A A5034
P 🛏 ✕ ♿

Museums

Castlefield Urban Heritage Park
Britain's first urban heritage park includes
Museum of Science and Industry, a Roman
Fort, The Waterways, Castlefield Gallery,

Urban Studies Centre, Granada Studios
Tour, City Centre, G–Mex and the River
Irwell and Salford Quays; guides and guided
walks.
Information Centre, 330 Deansgate,
Manchester
☎ 061 832 4244

Jodrell Bank Science Centre
Telescopes, planetarium, video wall and
holograms, satellite TV, astronomy
exhibition and arboretum.
Macclesfield
☎ 0477 71339
➔A A535
P 🛏 ✕ ♿ ♿

Manchester Jewish Museum
190 Cheetham Hill Road, Manchester
☎ 061 834 9879
➔A A665
P 🛏 🚌

Silk Museum
The story of silk in Macclesfield.
Paradise Mill, Roe Street, Macclesfield
☎ 0625 618228
🛏 🚌 ♿

Parks

Etherow Country Park
Leisure pursuits include rambling,
birdwatching, sailing, model boating
and angling.
Compstall, Manchester
☎ 061 427 6937 warden
Off the B6104
♿

Mersey Valley
Leisure pursuits include walking, riding,
watersports and fishing. Further
information from the visitor centre.
Mersey Valley Wardens, Recreational
Services Dept, Altrincham Road, Sharston
☎ 061 905 1100

Birdwatching and Wildlife

Great Wood and Hurst Clough
A range of wildlife in partly wooded lands in
the Etherow Goyt Valley.
Information Centre, Lymefield,
Broadbottom
☎ 0457 65780

Walking

Middlewood Way
An 11-mile footpath and bridleway along an
old railway line.
For details contact:
Etherow Goyt Wardens
☎ 061 427 6937
Cheshire Ranger
☎ 0625 73998

MERSEYSIDE

i 29 Lime Street, Liverpool, Merseyside
☎ 051 708 8854

EQUESTRIAN

Riding and Pony Trekking

Croxteth Riding Centre
Croxteth Hall Lane, Liverpool
☎ 051 220 9177

Longacres Riding School
290 Southport Road, Lydiate
☎ 051 526 0327

HEALTH

Leisure Centres

Everton Park Sports Centre
Excellent amenities plus an international pool.
Great Homer Street, Liverpool
☎ 051 207 1921

LOCAL FEATURES

Art Galleries

Lady Lever Gallery
The first Lord Leverhulme's collection of English 18th century paintings, furniture, Wedgwood pottery, Oriental porcelains and pre-Raphaelite paintings.
Port Sunlight Village, Wirral
☎ 051 645 3623
→A A41
P 🏠 🚌 ✕ ৬ ৬

Sudley Art Gallery
Superb 19th century British paintings, artists including Turner; furniture by Bullock.
Mossley Hill Road, Liverpool
☎ 051 207 0001
P 🏠

Tate Gallery
Changing displays from the National Collection of Modern Art and exhibitions.
Albert Dock
☎ 051 709 3223
৬ ৬

Walker Art Gallery
A fine gallery, rich in early Italian and Flemish works, many European Art and Pre-Raphaelite items; a striking modern collection and a new sculpture gallery.
William Brown Street, Liverpool
☎ 051 207 0001
🏠 ✕ ৬

Williamson Art Gallery
British paintings and watercolours, English porcelain and maritime history exhibits.
Slatey Road, Birkenhead
☎ 051 652 4177
P 🏠 🚌 ৬

Arts and Crafts

Bluecoat Chambers
Listed Queen Anne building with gallery, craft shop, film theatre, concert hall and artists' studios.
Bluecoat Art Centre, School Lane, Liverpool
☎ 051 709 5297
→A A5047
🏠 🚌 ✕ ৬

Voirrey Embroidery
National embroidery centre; needlework supplies, courses and exhibitions.
Brimstage Hall, Wirral
☎ 051 342 3514
→A A5137
🏠

Gardens

Ness Gardens
Extensive displays of trees and shrubs, renowned heather, rock and herb gardens.
University of Liverpool Botanic Gardens.
Neston, Wirral
☎ 051 336 2135
🏠 ✕

Guided Tours

Sightseeing Tour/Beatle Tour
Merseyside Tourism Board
☎ 051 709 2444

Heritage

Birkenhead Priory
The oldest building on Merseyside, mid-12th century, now houses an interpretive display that traces the history of the site.
Priory Street, Birkenhead
☎ 051 666 1249
🏠

Historic Buildings

Croxteth Hall and Country Park
A 500-acre country park and hall with displays, furnished rooms, walled garden, rare breeds farm, miniature railway, gift shop and riding centre.
Muirhead Avenue East, Liverpool
☎ 051 228 5311
→A A580
P 🏠 🚌 ✕ ৬ ৬

MERSEYSIDE

Liverpool Cathedral
Largest cathedral in Britain with the biggest Gothic arches ever built; an excellent refectory.
St. James Road, Liverpool
☎ 051 709 6271
Nr City Centre

Metropolitan Cathedral of Christ the King
Circular modern cathedral, concrete and glass with fine stained glass windows and modern fabric wallhangings.
Mount Pleasant, Liverpool
☎ 051 709 9222
➔A A5038/A5047

Port Sunlight Heritage Centre
Model garden village built by William Hesketh Lever for his soap factory workers.
Greendale Road, Port Sunlight, Wirral
☎ 051 644 6466
➔A A41

Speke Hall
A Tudor manor house with rich Victorian interiors.
The Walk, Speke, Liverpool
☎ 051 427 9860
➔A A561

Museums

The Boat Museum
The largest floating collection of canal craft in the world.
Ellesmere Port, Cheshire
☎ 051 355 5017

Liverpool Museum and Planetarium
Collections from all over the world; from the wonders of the Amazonian rain forests to the mysteries of outer space.
William Brown Street
☎ 051 207 0001

Merseyside Maritime Museum
Floating exhibits, working displays and craft demonstrations, including a restored Victorian Dock.
Albert Dock, Liverpool
☎ 051 207 0001
➔A A565

Pilkington Glass Museum
The history and manufacture of glass.
Prescot Road, St Helens
☎ 0744 28882
➔A A58

Music, Dance and Drama

Philharmonic Hall
Home of the Royal Liverpool Philharmonic Orchestra.
Hope Street, Liverpool
☎ 051 709 3789

Parks

Wirral Country Park
Situated on the former West Kirby to Hooton railway line; a 12-mile footpath, with splendid views across the Dee Estuary.
Station Road, Thurstaston
☎ 051 648 4371
☎ 051 648 3884

Zoos

Knowsley Safari Park
A 5-mile drive through game reserves in 400 acres of parkland; children's amusement park.
Prescot, Merseyside
☎ 051 430 9009

Fishing

Richards Fishing Tackle
42 Brunswick Street, Liverpool
☎ 051 236 2925

Liverpool Angling Centre
492 Smithdown Road, Liverpool
☎ 051 733 2591

Walking

The Wirral Way
Wirral Country Park Rangers
☎ 051 648 4371

Liverpool Watersports Centre
Tuition for sailing, canoeing, windsurfing, etc. Narrowboat trips and canal walks are also organised.
☎ 051 207 4026

LANCASHIRE

i Wyre Borough Council, The Esplanade,
Fleetwood, Lancashire
☎ 03917 71141 summer only
i The Guildhall, Lancaster Road, Preston,
Lancashire
☎ 0772 53731
i 112 Lord Street, Southport, Merseyside
☎ 0704 33133

EQUESTRIAN

Riding and Pony Trekking
Crookland's Riding Establishment
Goosnargh Lane, nr Preston
☎ 0772 863017

HEALTH

Leisure Centres
West View Leisure Centre
2 large sports halls, fitness room, swimming
pools, squash courts, climbing wall and
creche facilities.
Ribbleton, Preston
☎ 0772 796788

LOCAL FEATURES

Art Galleries
Atkinson Art Gallery
19th and 20th century paintings,
watercolours, prints and drawings; modern
sculpture.
Lord Street, Southport
☎ 0704 33133
➔A A565
P ⛺ 🚌 ♿ ♿

Grundy Art Gallery
Lively monthly exhibition programme of
modern artists.
Queen Street, Blackpool
☎ 0253 75170

Haworth Art Gallery
Fine Edwardian building in 13 acres;
permanent Tiffany glass collection, English
and European watercolours; brass rubbing
centre; picnic areas and concerts in
grounds.
Haworth Park, Manchester Road, Accrington
☎ 0254 33782

Harris Museum and Art Gallery
Magnificent neo-classical building in Greek
revival style with an extensive collection of
fine art and exhibitions.
Market Square, Preston
☎ 0772 58248
Town centre
⛺ ✕ ♿ ♿

Gardens
Botanic Gardens and Museum
Gardens, aviary, childrens playground and
boating lake; museum display of Victoriana.
Churchtown, Southport
☎ 0704 27547
Off the B5244
P ⛺ ✕ ♿

Historic Buildings
Astley Hall
Elizabethan half-timbered Hall with a fine
collection of furniture, paintings and
pottery.
Astley Park, Chorley
☎ 02572 62166

Hoghton Tower
16th century hilltop mansion, with
banqueting hall, state apartments, historic
documents and dolls houses.
Nr Preston
☎ 025485 2986
➔A A675
🏠

Meols Hall
Ancestral home of the Fleetwood Hesketh
family with some very fine paintings, silver
and china. Game and Country Fayre held in
May.
Churchtown, Southport
☎ 0704 28171
➔A A565/A570
P 🏠 ♿

Rufford Old Hall
Late mediaeval half-timbered hall with an
ornate hammer-beam roof and screen; fine
collections of 17th century oak furniture,
16th century arms, armour and tapestries.
Rufford, nr Ormskirk
☎ 0704 821254
On the A59, 7 miles north of Ormskirk
🏠 ✕

Samlesbury Hall
14th century manor house. Sales of
antiques and collectors items, crafts and
other exhibitions are held here.
Preston
☎ 025481 2229
☎ 025481 2010
➔A A677
🏠 ✕

Museums
Ribchester Museum of Roman Antiquities
Independent museum and remains of the
fort of Bremetennacum.
Riverside, Ribchester
☎ 0254 878261
🏠 🚌

Natural History
Martin Mere Wildfowl Trust
Feed rare and exotic birds by hand.
Burscough, nr Southport
☎ 0704 895181

WHAT TO DO AND SEE

Parks

Beacon Fell Country Park
304 acres of open countryside with
recreational facilities and guided walks.
Nr Skelmersdale
☎ 0995 61693
On the A6, 8 miles north of Preston

Railways

Steamport Railway Museum
15 steam and 6 diesel locomotives.
Derby Road, Southport
☎ 0704 30693
➤A A565
P ✕ ♿

Zoos

Blackpool Zoo Park
Modern zoo set in landscaped gardens.
East Park Drive, Blackpool
☎ 0253 65027
🐾 ✕

Southport Zoo
Includes a breeding group of chimpanzees.
Princes Park, Southport
☎ 0704 38102
P 🐾 🚐 ✕ ♿ ♿

OUTDOOR LEISURE/SPORTS

Cycling

Lancashire cycleway provides an extensive
tour of the Lancashire countryside via 2
fully waymarked circular routes.
i Further information is available from
Tourist Information Centres.

Walking

Rossendale Way
A 45-mile circular route which explores
Rossendale's hills, valleys and towns.
i 8 leaflets are available from the Tourist
Information Centres with maps and
historical snippets.

Ribble Way
A 40-mile public footpath following the
course of the River Ribble.
i Further information is available from
Tourist Information Centres.

WATERSPORTS

Watersports are available in the major
seaside resorts along the coast, including
Blackpool, Fleetwood and Morecambe.

WHAT TO DO AND SEE

i Royal Bath's Assembly Rooms, Crescent Road, Harrogate, North Yorks
☎ 0423 525666

i 19 Wellington Street, Leeds, West Yorks
☎ 0532 478302

i De Grey Rooms, Exhibition Square, York, North Yorks
☎ 0904 621756

AERIAL SPORTS

Ballooning

Aire Valley Balloons
Underwood Cottage, Underwood Drive, Rawdon, Leeds
☎ 0532 506921

Gliding

York Gliding Centre
Rufforth Airfield, York
☎ 0904 83694
On the B1224, 5 miles west of York

EQUESTRIAN

Riding and Pony Trekking

Moor House Riding Centre
Sutton Road, Wigginton
☎ 0904 769029

Naburn Grange Riding Centre
Indoor school, cross-country course and pony trap driving available.
Naburn, nr York
☎ 090487 283
Off the A19, 4 miles south-west of York

LOCAL FEATURES

Art Galleries

York City Art Gallery
European and British painting spanning 7 centuries.
Exhibition Square
☎ 0904 623839
♿

Guided Tours

Free daily walking tours of York starting from Exhibition Square in the company of qualified guides.

Yorktour
Sightseeing guided tours both of the city and the surrounding area: Whitby and Castle Howard, Fountains Abbey, Yorkshire Dales and Herriot Country. Book through the Tourist Information Centre.
8 Tower Street
☎ 0904 641737

Historic Buildings

Beningbrough Hall
Fine Baroque house with a collection of paintings on loan from the National Portrait Gallery, Victorian kitchen and an adventure playground. National Trust.
Shipton-by-Beningbrough
☎ 0904 470666
Off the A19, 8 miles north-west of York
P 🍴 🚌 ✕ & &

Bramham Park
Queen Anne house with 66-acre French Baroque garden, Versailles on a smaller scale. International Horse Trials are held here.
Wetherby
☎ 0937 844265
→A A1
P 🍴 🚌

Castle Howard
Thousands of acres of parkland, a plant centre, rose gardens, nature walks and grounds.
York
☎ 065384 333
Off the A64, 15 miles north-east of York
P 🍴 🚌 ✕ & &

Fairfax House
Fine town house with 18th century furniture and clock collection.
Castlegate, York
☎ 0904 655543
York city centre
P 🍴 🚌 ✕ &

Harewood House
Family home of the Earl and Countess of
Harewood with fine Chippendale furniture,
works of art, magnificent grounds, an
adventure playground, garden centre, bird
garden and tropical rain forest exhibition.
Harewood, nr Leeds
☎ 0532 886225
On the A61, 7 miles north of Leeds
P 🕁 🚌 & &

Sutton Park
Georgian house with Chippendale, Sheraton
and French furniture, gardens designed by
Capability Brown and woodland walks.
Sutton-on-the-Forest
☎ 0347 810249
On the B1363, 8 miles north of York
P 🕁 🚌 ✕

York Minster
The largest mediaeval cathedral in northern
Europe.
York

Museums

City Art Gallery and Henry Moore Centre
Fine art collection including a notable
collection of English watercolours;
sculptures Jacob Epstein, Barbara Hepworth
and Henry Moore.
The Headrow, Leeds
☎ 0532 478248
➔A A660
🕱 🚌 & &

Jorvik Viking Centre
Visitors witness authentic sight, sound and
smell reconstructions of the city of Jorvik,
Viking name for York, 1000 years ago;
archaeological artefacts displayed.
Coppergate, York
☎ 0904 643211
➔A A19
P 🕁 🚌 & &

National Railway Museum
Display covering 150 years of British railway
history.
Leeman Road, York
☎ 0904 621261
➔A A19
P 🕁 &

Yorkshire Museum
Displays of Roman, Anglo Saxon, Viking and
mediaeval treasures of Britain. Wildlife
gardens.
Museum Gardens, York
☎ 0904 629745
➔A A59/A19
🕁 & &

Cycling
Auto Discount Cycling Tours
Ings Vie, Shipton Road, York
☎ 0904 30692

Cycle Scene
2 Ratcliffe Street, Burton Stone Lane, York
☎ 0904 653286

York Cycleworks
14–16 Lawrence Street
☎ 0904 626664

Fishing
Local fishing tackle shops can provide
information on fishing in the Ouse and
other rivers.

Skiing
Harrogate Ski Centre
Ski centre and dry-slope.
Yorkshire Showground, Hookstone Wood
Road, Harrogate
☎ 0423 505457
➔A A661
P ✕

Walking
Dramatic upland walking country stretches
40 miles across to the Yorkshire coast. For
information on the North Yorkshire Moors
contact:

National Park Visitor Centre
Town Hall, Market Place, Helmsley
☎ 0439 70173

Boat Hire and Trips
Round trip cruises and boat hire are
available from York city centre along
various stretches on the River Ouse.

Castle Line Cruises
Cruises to riverside inns for lunch or
supper stops.
Skeldergate Bridge
☎ 0836 739357

DURHAM AND CLEVELAND

WHAT TO DO AND SEE

i 43 Galgate, Barnard Castle, County
Durham
☎ 0833 690909
i Civic Centre, Victoria Road, Hartlepool,
Cleveland
☎ 0429 869706

ADVENTURE

Multi-activity Centres
Hudeway Centre
For families, groups and individuals:
canoeing, windsurfing, abseiling, riding,
caving and orienteering.
Hudegate Farm East, Middleton-in-Teesdale,
Barnard Castle
☎ 0833 40012

EQUESTRIAN

Riding and Pony Trekking
High Pennine Rides
Self-guided riding holidays for adults along
a choice of routes.
Brook Villa, The Green, Lanchester,
Durham
☎ 0207 521911

Hoppyland Trekking Centre
Pony trekking in Hamsterley Forest for
novice and experienced riders.
Hoppyland Farm, Hamsterley, Bishop
Auckland
☎ 0388 88617
☎ 0388 767419

LOCAL FEATURES

Art Galleries
Darlington Art Gallery
Exhibitions, loans and local artists.
Crown Street, Darlington
☎ 0325 462034
Town centre
🏛

Gardens
Durham College of Agriculture and
Horticulture
Gardens used as training grounds for
students so providing a fine display of
gardening styles. Gardening questions
answered at a gardening clinic.
Durham
☎ 091 3861351
On the A177, 1 mile south-east of Durham
city centre
P 🚌 ♿ ♿

Durham University Botanic Gardens
Set in mature woodland with exotic trees
from America and the Himalayas; display
house with tropical plants and cacti.
Hollingside Lane
☎ 091 3742671
→A A1050
P 🏛 🚌 ✕ ♿ ♿

Egglestone Hall Gardens
Informally laid out garden with winding
paths and streams; many rare plants
together with organically grown vegetables.
Eggleston village
☎ 0833 50378
South of Egglestone village
P 🏛 🚌 ✕ ♿

Heritage
Binchester Roman Fort
The house of the fort commander includes
the best example of a Roman military
bath-suite in Britain.
Bishop Auckland
☎ 0388 663089
1 mile north of Bishop Auckland
P 🏛 🚌

Historic Buildings
Auckland Castle
Principal country residence of the Bishops
of Durham since Norman times;
magnificent chapel built from the ruins of
the 12th century Banqueting Hall in 1665.
Public access to Bishop's Park.
Bishop Auckland
☎ 091 3864411 ext 2698
🚌 🏛 ♿

Barnard Castle
Imposing Norman stronghold overlooking
the River Tees, extensively renovated. Bowes
Museum has an art collection of national
importance.
☎ 0833 38212
🏛

DURHAM AND CLEVELAND

WHAT TO DO AND SEE

Bowes Castle
Massive 12th century stone keep
overlooking the valley of the River Greta on
the site of a Roman Fort that commanded
the approach to Stainmore Pass over the
Pennines.
On the A67, 4 miles west of Barnard Castle
🏛

Durham Castle
Norman castle of the Prince Bishops of
Durham founded in 1072; Norman chapel,
Great Hall and extensive kitchens.
Durham city
☎ 091 374 3800
P 🏛 🚌

Egglestone Abbey
Ruined 12th century abbey with a
picturesque setting above the River Tees; a
fine mediaeval pack-horse bridge nearby.
Nr the A67, 1 mile south-east of Barnard
Castle
🏛 ♿

Raby Castle
One of the largest 14th century castles in
Britain with fine pictures and furniture and
a collection of horse-drawn carriages and
fire engines.
Staindrop, Darlington
☎ 0833 60202
1 mile north of Staindrop on the Barnard
Castle/Bishop Auckland road
🏛 ✕ ♿ ♿

Rokeby Park
Palladian style country house with a unique
collection of 18th century needlework
pictures, period furniture and a print room.
Barnard Castle
☎ 0833 37334
On the A66 between the A1(M) and Bowes
P 🏛 🚌

Museums

**Beamish – North of England Open Air
Museum**
One of the top tourist attractions of the
region; vivid reconstruction of Northern life
in the early 1900's with tramway, shops,
pub and railway station.
☎ 0207 231811
Chester-le-Street
➜A A1(M) 4 miles west of Chester-le-Street
P 🏛 ✕ ♿ ♿

Parks

Hardwick Hall Country Park
18th century landscaped park with lake.
Sedgefield
➜A A177

Railways

Darlington Railway Centre and Museum
Historic engines "Locomotion" and
"Derwent" are displayed.
North Road Station, Darlington
☎ 0325 460532
On the A167 north of the town centre
P 🏛 🚌 ♿ ♿

OUTDOOR LEISURE/SPORTS

Fishing

Northumbrian Water own 11 reservoirs
operated as fisheries.
Recreation Dept, Northumbrian Water,
Abbey Road, Pity Me, Durham City
☎ 091 384 4222

Walking

The Durham Dales offer a wide range of
walks, from the long-distance Pennine Way
to walks suitable for families. Information
from the County Environment Department's
guided walk programme.
☎ 091 386 4411

SOUTH CUMBRIA

WHAT TO DO AND SEE

i   Glebe Road, Bowness-on-Windermere,
Cumbria
☎ 05394 42895 (summer only)
i   Coronation Hall, County Square,
Ulverston, Cumbria
☎ 0229 57120

ADVENTURE

Multi-activity Centres

Bigland Hall Sporting Estates
Fishing, riding, trekking, clay pigeon
shooting and archery.
Novices welcome.
Backbarrow, nr Ulverston
☎ 05395 31728

Summitreks
Outdoor activity courses and instruction
including canoeing, windsurfing, mountain
biking, abseiling/rock climbing and guided
mountain walks. Weekend or weekly basis.
14 Yewdale Road, Coniston
☎ 05394 41212

YMCA National Centre
Outdoor adventure and activity skills
training and nature discovery holidays
geared to the needs of families, youngsters,
teenagers and the over 50s.
Lakeside, Ulverston
☎ 05395 31758

EQUESTRIAN

Riding and Pony Trekking

Bigland Hall
Blackbarrow, Newby Bridge
☎ 05395 31728

Claife and Grizedale Riding Centre
Sawrey Knott's Estate, Hawkshead
☎ 05394 42105

LOCAL FEATURES

Falconry

Leighton Hall
Eagles fly (May–Sept) daily except Sat and
Mon at 3.30pm at this beautifully sited
country house. There are 1- and 4-day
courses in handling birds available.
Carnforth
☎ 0524 734474
Off the M6 at exit 35, signposted

Gardens

Graythwaite Hall Gardens
Garden laid out in the 1880s;
rhododendrons, azaleas and flowering
shrubs.
Newby Bridge
☎ 05395 31248
➔A A590

Historic Buildings

Dove Cottage
William Wordsworth's home during his
most creative years.
Grasmere
☎ 05394 35544
Off the A591, just south of Grasmere village
🚐

Holker Hall
Former home of the Dukes of Devonshire,
known for its fine wood carvings and
impressive gardens. Craft and Countryside
Museum and the Lakeland Motor Museum
are also situated here; adventure
playground; events throughout the year.
Cark-in-Cartmel
Flookburgh
☎ 05395 58328 ·
On the B5278 from Newby Bridge via
the A590
🚐 ✕ ♿

SOUTH CUMBRIA

Rydal Mount
Wordsworth's home at the time of his death in 1850 still owned by descendants of his family; magnificent views.
Ambleside
☎ 05394 33002
Off the A591, approx 1 mile from Ambleside and Grasmere
🚌

Sizergh Castle
In parts dating from the 14th century, fine collection of Elizabethan carvings and panelling, furniture and portraits; 18th century gardens. National Trust.
Nr Kendal
☎ 05395 60070
3 miles south of Kendal, north-west of the A6/A591 interchange
P 🚌 ✕

Museums

Museum of Lakeland Life and Industry
Reconstructions of workshops and farmhouse rooms; agricultural exhibits; Arthur Ransome and Postman Pat rooms; Lake District Art Gallery and Museum all housed in a Georgian town house by the riverside.
Abbot Hall, Kendal
☎ 0539 722464
Nr Kendal Parish Church, M6 exit 36
P 🏠 🚌

Parks

Fell Foot Country Park
18-acre lakeside park offering bathing, fishing, adventure playground, rowing boat hire and boat launching facilities. National Trust. Park open all year 10am–dusk. Shop and boat hire Easter–end Oct.
Newby Bridge
☎ 05395 31273
At the extreme south end of Windermere, on the east shore
P 🏠 ✕

Lake District National Park Visitor Centre
Exhibitions, "Living Lakeland", slide shows, films, shop, gardens, lakeshore walk and drystone walling area.
Brockhole, Windermere
☎ 05394 46601
➔A A591
P ✕ ♿

Railways

Lakeside and Haverthwaite Railway
Steam locomotive trips from Haverthwaite station through lake and river scenery of the Leven Valley. Connections are made at Lakeside with Windermere Cruises for Bowness and Ambleside.
Nr Newby Bridge
☎ 05395 31594
On the A590 to Haverthwaite

Birdwatching

South Walney Nature Reserve
Europe's largest gullery and big Eider colony with 4 hides.
Walney Island, Barrow-in-Furness
☎ 0229 41066
➔A A590
🚌

Cycling

Cumbria Cycle Way
Circular 280-mile (450km) waymarked route following quiet roads. Route available from Tourist Information Centres.

Lowick Mountain Bikes
Guided tours, itineraries and cycles for hire.
Red Lion Inn, Lowick, nr Ulverston
☎ 0229 85366

Fishing

Bosuns Locker
8-hour sea angling trips from Roa Island into Morecambe Bay on board *MFV Isla*. Passenger trips daily Easter–Oct 12 noon–6pm to Piel Island with its 12th century castle and South Walney Nature Reserve. Also available for private charter.
Roa Island, Barrow-in-Furness
☎ 0229 22520

Walking

Grizedale Forest Visitor Centre
Marked forest trails, picnic areas, cycle trails and fishing areas.
Grizedale, Ambleside
☎ 0229 860373

Guided walks
Throughout the area during the season (Easter–Oct) accompanied by experts.
i Enquire at the Kendal Tourist Information Centre.

Sailing

Lake Windermere Facilities
Permanent and holiday moorings, launching, recovery, boat registration, pump-out, winter storage and water supply.
Ferry Nab, Bowness-on-Windermere
☎ 05394 42753

NORTH CUMBRIA

WHAT TO DO AND SEE

i The Moot Hall, Brampton, Cumbria
☎ 06977 3433 (summer only)
i Carlisle Visitor Centre, Old Town Hall, Green Market, Carlisle, Cumbria
☎ 0228 512444
i The Green, Silloth-on-Solway, Cumbria
☎ 06973 31944 (summer only)

ADVENTURE

Clay Pigeon Shooting

Greenquarries Shooting Ground
Sporting clay pigeon shooting; gun hire, tuition. Open and practice shoots every Friday Apr–Aug.
Rosley, Wigton
☎ 06996 392
Off the B5299 9 miles south-west of Carlisle

Multi-activity Centre

Cumbria Outdoors
3 residential centres (2 near Keswick, 1 at Caldbeck), providing courses in sailing, windsurfing, canoeing, caving, climbing and general adventure, for families, individuals, the disabled and groups.
Cumbria Education Dept,
5 Portland Square, Carlisle
☎ 0228 23456 ext 2565

EQUESTRIAN

Riding and Pony Trekking

Blackdyke Farm
Tuition, hacking, show-jumping and cross-country.
Blackford, Carlisle
☎ 022874 633

Townhead Farm Stables
1-, 2- and 4-hour treks available.
Newbiggin, Heads Nook, Carlisle
☎ 076886 208

HEALTH

Leisure Centres

Sands Leisure Centre
A varied programme of opera, pop and choral music as well as comedy, ballet and childrens shows. Sports facilities include roller skating, squash, badminton and a climbing wall.
Carlisle
☎ 0228 25222

LOCAL FEATURES

Festivals and Fairs

July
Cumberland Show, Carlisle

August
Carlisle Great Fair

Guided Tours

Coach tours
To Hadrian's Wall: afternoons and evenings throughout the summer. To the Lake District: Sundays throughout the summer.
i Information from the Tourist Information Centre.

Walking tours
May–Sept daily 1.30pm at Cumbria and Border Heritage Guides, The Old Town Hall (Carlisle Visitor Centre)

Heritage

Hadrian's Wall
Built by the Romans between AD122 and AD128 to mark the northern boundary of the Roman Empire in Britain. Originally 15ft high and 40ft thick to keep out the marauding Picts, the wall is still well preserved particularly at Banks (east of Banks village) and Birdoswald (2 miles west of Greenhead off the B6318).

Historic Buildings

Carlisle Castle
Impressive remains of the mediaeval castle at a key point on the Anglo-Scottish border. English Heritage.
Carlisle
On the north side of the city, beyond the cathedral
☎ 0228 31777
🚌 ♿

Carlisle Cathedral
12th century cathedral featuring a 13th century stained glass east window, amongst the finest in Europe.
Castle Street, Carlisle
🚌

Lanercost Priory
Well preserved despite its violent history; Evensong services by candlelight. English Heritage.
☎ 06977 3030
2 miles north-east of Brampton, off a minor road south of Lanercost
P ♿

Naworth Castle
Home of the Earls of Carlisle set amidst the rugged Border countryside.
Brampton
☎ 06977 2692
On the A69, 2 miles from Brampton
P 🍴 🚌

Museums

Guildhall Museum
Carlisle's only mediaeval town house now displaying guild, civic and local history.
Greenmarket, Carlisle
☎ 0228 34781

Roman Army Museum
On the central sector of Hadrian's Wall next to Walltown Crags, providing an educational insight into the life of the Roman soldier.

163

NORTH CUMBRIA

Carvoran, Greenhead
☎ 06972 485
Off the B6318, 1 mile north-east of
Greenhead
P ✕ ♿

Parks

Talkin Tarn Country Park
Over 180 acres of farmland, woodland and
water with facilities for rowing, watersports,
coarse fishing and picnics.
Brampton
☎ 06977 3129

Railways

Leeds-Settle-Carlisle Line
Travel the 70 miles from Carlisle to Settle
through the Yorkshire Dales, over the
Pennines and on into the Eden valley.
B. R. Station, Carlisle
☎ 0228 44711

OUTDOOR LEISURE/SPORTS

Cricket

Edenside Cricket Ground
Carlisle
☎ 0228 61634

Walking

Fortify the Spirit
Guided walking holidays based at hotels,
led by experienced guides.
The Barn, Wellrash, Boltongate, Wigton
☎ 09657 522

Town and countryside walks
Programme of walks throughout the year
available from the Tourist Information
Centre.

NEWCASTLE/TYNE AND WEAR

WHAT TO DO AND SEE

i Central Station, Newcastle, Tyne &
Wear
☎ 091 230 0030
i City Information Service
☎ 091 261 0691 ext 231
i Unit 3, Crowtree Road, Sunderland, Tyne
& Wear
☎ 091 565 0960

EQUESTRIAN

Riding
Lincoln Riding Centre
High Pit Farm, East Cramlington
☎ 0632 815376

HEALTH

Leisure Centres
There are 25 leisure centres in Newcastle,
all with extensive facilities from roller
skating to pop mobility.
Contact the City Information Service (see
above).

LOCAL FEATURES

Archaeology
Arbeia Roman Fort
Remains of gateways, fort walls and
defences; site museum and excavations.
Baring Street, South Shields
☎ 091 456 1369
→A A183
⛐

Architecture
The Bridges over the River Tyne
Newcastle's skyline includes the Tyne
Bridge which has the largest arch span of
any bridge in Britain, at 531 feet and the
High Level Bridge designed by Robert
Stephenson.

Art Galleries
Bede Gallery
Small museum of Jarrow history and
monthly exhibitions.
Springwell Park, Butcherbridge Road,
Jarrow
☎ 091 489 1807
→A A194
P ✕ ⛐

Hatton Gallery
Collection of 15th century paintings and
drawings and exhibitions of contemporary
art.
The University, Newcastle
☎ 091 222 6000
→A A6127

Laing Art Gallery
British paintings and watercolours from the
17th century to the present. Works by John
Martin; textiles, ceramics, silver and glass.
Higham Place, Newcastle
☎ 091 232 7734
⛐ ⛐

Shipley Art Gallery
Victorian and Old Master paintings;
traditional and contemporary crafts and
temporary exhibitions.
Prince Consort Road, Gateshead
☎ 091 477 1495
→A A6127
⛐ ⛐

Heritage
The Roman Wall
The Roman Wall and the adjacent Military
Road (B6318) run east-west parallel to but
several miles north of the Tyne gap.
Further details from the City Information
Service (see above).

Historic Buildings
Aydon Castle
Built as a manor house at the end of the
13th century, converted to a farmhouse in
the 17th century; captured by the Scots and
English in turn.
On the B6321 or the A68, north-east of
Corbridge
☎ 0434 632450
🏠

Castle Keep
Norman Keep with panoramic views of the
city from the roof.
St. Nicholas Street, Newcastle
☎ 091 232 7938
→A A6125

Gibside Chapel
The Bowes family mausoleum, designed by
James Paine. National Trust.
Burnopfield
☎ 0207 542255
Off the B6314
P 🏠 ✕

Prudhoe Castle
Overlooking the River Tyne, Prudhoe Castle
commanded the principal north-south route
through Northumberland. Home of the
Dukes of Northumberland.
Prudhoe
Off the A695
☎ 0661 33459
🏠

Washington Old Hall
17th century manor house, home of George
Washington's direct ancestors.
Washington
☎ 091 4166879
→A A1
P 🏠 ⛐ ⛐

NEWCASTLE/TYNE AND WEAR

Museums

Hancock Museum
Zoo room, bird room, geology gallery and small side galleries.
Great North Road, Newcastle
☎ 091 232 2359
Off the A1 to the A6125
P

John George Joicey Museum
Almshouses from 17th century with period rooms and military collections.
City Road, Newcastle
☎ 091 232 4562
→A A6127
P ⛟ ✕ ♿

Military Vehicle Museum
World War II vehicles and others.
The Pavilion, Exhibition Park, Great North Road, Jesmond
☎ 091 281 7222
→A A6127
P ⛟ ✕ ♿

Museum of Science and Engineering
Blandford House, West Blandford Street, Newcastle
☎ 091 232 6789
→A A6115
✕ ♿ ♿

Natural History

St. Mary's Lighthouse
Lighthouse and bird watching centre.
Trinity Road, Whitley Bay
☎ 091 252 0853
→A A193
P ⛟ ♿ ♿

Railways

Bowes Railway
Standard gauge rope-hauled railway; 3 steam locos.
Springwell Village, Gateshead
☎ 091 416 1847
→A A1
P ⛟ ✕ ♿ ♿

Stephenson Museum
Railway engines and rolling stock.
Middle Engine Lane, North Shields
☎ 091 262 2627
→A A1
P ⛟

Tanfield Railway
Oldest existing railway in the world, opened 1725; steam-hauled passenger trains, vintage carriages, vintage workshop.
Marley Hill, Sunniside, Gateshead
P ⛟ ✕ ♿

Birdwatching and Wildlife

The Leas and Marsden Rock
Spectacular coastline famous for kittiwakes, cormorants etc; guided walks. National Trust.
South Shields
☎ 067074 691
→A A1300

Cycling

Glenbar Hire
217 Jesmond Road, Newcastle
☎ 091 281 5376

Walking

Derwent Walk Country Park
Disused railway walk served by 2 visitor centres.
Rowlands Gill, Gateshead
→A A694
P ⛟ ♿ ♿

The Heritage Way
Long distance footpath of some 68 miles (110 km) around Tyne & Wear. Numerous access points.
Mr J. C. Barford, Civic Centre, Regent Street, Gateshead
☎ 091 477 1011

WHAT TO DO AND SEE

i Belford Craft Gallery, 2-3 Market Place, Belford, Northumberland
☎ 0668 213888

ADVENTURE

Mountaineering and Rock Climbing

Bearsports
Wide range of adventure sports on offer including hill walking, rock climbing and abseiling.
Windy Gyle Outdoor Centre, West Street, Belford
☎ 0668 213289

Multi-activity Centres

Bearsports
Windsurfing, sailing, abseiling, hill walking, kayaking, canoeing, surf-skiing, rafting, camping and bivouacs, orienteering, riding, mountain biking, fitness-training and bird watching.
Windy Gyle Outdoor Centre, West Street, Belford
☎ 0668 213289

EQUESTRIAN

Riding and Pony Trekking

Bridgend Riding Stables
Bridge End Farm Cottage
Brewery Road, Wooler
☎ 0668 319

Slate Hall Riding Centre
174 Main Street, Seahouses
☎ 0665 720320

HEALTH

Leisure Centres

Alnwick Swimming Pool
Alnwick
☎ 0665 602933

LOCAL FEATURES

Arts and Crafts

Belford Craft Gallery
Local crafts, paintings, books, maps and cards for sale.
2–3 Market Place, Belford
☎ 0668 213888

Bondgate Gallery
Contemporary works by regional artists and craftsmen.
22 Narrowgate, Alnwick
☎ 0665 510771

The Brent Gallery
Watercolours of wildlife, farm life and Northumbrian landscapes by David Binns, ceramics by Stephen Binns.
Fenham Le Moor, nr Belford
☎ 0668 533

Festivals and fairs

June
Alnwick Fair

July
Belford Carnival Week

Historic Buildings

Bamburgh Castle
Restored mediaeval castle with collections of Central Asian armour, arms of 16th and 17th century, china and tapestries; includes Armstrong Museum.
Bamburgh
☎ 06684 208
From the A1 take the B1342 and the B1340
P 🏠 🚌 ✕ Ꮷ Ꮷ

NORTHUMBERLAND

Chillingham Castle
Mediaeval castle with Tudor additions and Georgian refinements set in magnificent grounds with views of the Cheviots; woodland walks, lake and formal topiary gardens.
Chillingham, Alnwick
☎ 06685 359
Off the A1 and the A697
P 🏠 🚌 ✕ ♿ 👶

Dunstanburgh Castle
14th century ruins in a dramatic coastal position. Reached by footpath from Craster.
Craster
☎ 0665 576231
On the B1339

Lindisfarne Castle
Tiny fort built in about 1550 and converted to a private house by Lutyens. National Trust.
Holy Island
☎ 0289 89244
→A A1
Island not accessible during high tide.
🏠

Lindisfarne Priory
Ruins of a monastery dated 1090, the cradle of Christianity in the North. English Heritage.
Holy Island
☎ 0289 89200
→A A1
Island not accessible during high tide.
P 🏠 👶 ♿

Preston Tower
14th century peel tower with displays of local history.
Chathill
☎ 066 589 227
→A A1
P

Museums

Grace Darling Museum
In honour of the heroine who rescued survivors from the wreck of the *Forfarshire*.
Bamburgh
☎ 0665 720037
On the B1340
🚌 ♿

Heatherslaw Mill
Restored working 19th century water-driven corn mill on the River Till.
Ford Forge, Cornhill-on-Tweed
☎ 089082 338
On the B6354
P 🚌 ✕ ♿ 👶

Natural History

Chillingham Wild Cattle Association Ltd
The purest surviving members of the wild white cattle which formerly roamed the forests of Northern Britain.
Estate House, Chillingham, Alnwick
☎ 06685 250
→A A697
P 🏠 🚌

Birdwatching

Farne Islands
Home for 18 different species of sea bird and the largest British colonies of grey seals. National Trust.
Warden/Naturalist, The Sheiling, 8 St Aidan's, Seahouses
☎ 0665 720651
National Trust Shop, 16 Main Street, Seahouses
☎ 0665 721099

Trips to the Farne Islands
On *MFV Glad Tidings*; landings and commentary.
Billy Shiel, 4 Southfield Avenue, Seahouses
☎ 0665 720308

Cycling

Game Fair
12 Marygate, Berwick–on–Tweed
☎ 0289 305119

Furnevels
Touring and adult bikes.
Bamburgh
☎ 06684 513
☎ 06684 574

Fishing

Excellent fishing on offer in Northumbria and the Borders. Further details from the Tourist Information Centre.

Shellacres
Salmon and sea trout fishing on the River Till.
Further details from: Edwin Thompson & Co, 44-48 Hide Hill, Berwick-on-Tweed
☎ 0289 304432

For permits and further information:
Northumbrian Water
Abbey Road, Pity Me, County Durham
☎ 091 383 2222

Walking

Northumberland Wildlife Trust
Guided and themed walks.
Hancock Museum, Barras Bridge, Newcastle-upon-Tyne
☎ 091 232 0038

LOTHIAN

i Waverley Market, Princes Street, Edinburgh
☎ 031 557 1700

EQUESTRIAN

Riding and Pony Trekking

Edinburgh and Lasswade Riding Centre
Kevock Road, Lasswade, Midlothian
☎ 031 663 7676

HEALTH

Leisure Centres

Ainslie Park Leisure Centre
International competition standard pool, flumes, spa pool, toddler's pool, fountain and water cannon as well as fitness room and indoor sports facilities.
92 Pilton Drive, Edinburgh
☎ 031 551 2400

LOCAL FEATURES

Art Galleries

National Gallery of Scotland
Works by Titian, Raphael, Rembrandt, Turner and Impressionists as well as the Scottish Masters; temporary exhibitions.
The Mound, Edinburgh
☎ 031 556 8921
♿ &

National Portrait Gallery
Great Scottish names from the 16th century to the present.
Queen Street, Edinburgh
☎ 031 556 8921
♿ &

Scottish National Gallery of Modern Art
20th century painting, sculpture and graphic art.
Belford Road, Edinburgh
☎ 031 556 8921
♿ &

Factory Visits

Edinburgh Crystal Visitor's Centre
Crystal glassmakers at work. Guided factory tours available.
Penicuik, nr Edinburgh
☎ 0968 75128
🏠 🚌 ✕

Festivals and Fairs

August
Edinburgh International Festival, including the Military Tattoo and the Fringe

Gardens

Royal Botanic Garden
Unique collection of unusual plants; rhododendron collection; rock gardens; plant houses and exhibition hall.
Inverleith Row, Edinburgh
☎ 031 552 7171 ext 260
♿ &

Guided Tours

Cadies Walking Tours of Edinburgh
Old Town/Graveyard Tour, Mr Clapperton's Ghosts and Gore, and more. Tours by day and night leave from the Witchery Restaurant.
Castle Hill, Royal Mile, Edinburgh
☎ 031 225 6745

Off the Beaten Track
Personally conducted tours through lowland Scotland. Half or one day tours.
Margaret Kinnear
☎ 031 667 4473

Heritage

Clan Tartan Centre
Where to track down your clan and tartan. Within the James Pringle Woollen Mill, 70—74 Bangor Road, Leith, Edinburgh
☎ 031 553 5100
☎ 031 553 5161
P ✕

Historic Buildings

Craigmillar Castle
Ruined mediaeval castle associated with Mary Queen of Scots.
Craigmillar, Edinburgh
☎ 031 661 4445
On the A68 Edinburgh to Dalkeith road
🏠

Dalmeny House
19th century mansion house with a notable art collection, French furniture, porcelain, tapestries and 18th century portraits. Walks in the grounds all year round.
South Queensferry
☎ 031 331 1888
Off the A90, 7 miles west of Edinburgh
🏠

LOTHIAN

Edinburgh Castle
Famous historic stronghold, home of the Scottish National War Memorial, the Scottish Crown Jewels, the Scottish United Services and the Royal Scots Regimental Museums.
Edinburgh
☎ 031 225 9846
P ⌂ 🚍

Hopetoun House
Adam mansion with 100 acres of parkland; state apartments and paintings by Rubens, Titian and Canaletto. Walled garden centre; nature trail and deer park.
South Queensferry
☎ 031 331 2451
⌂

Lauriston Castle
Mansion house with a fine furniture collection and a display of 'Blue John' ware.
2 Cramond Road South, Cramond
☎ 031 336 2060
⌂ 🚍

Palace of Holyroodhouse
Official residence of H.M. The Queen with outstanding picture gallery and state apartments.
Canongate, Edinburgh
☎ 031 556 1096
⌂

Museums

Huntly House
Historical exhibits.
Canongate, Edinburgh
☎ 031 225 2424 ext 6689
🖂

John Knox House
A picturesque 15th century house with connections with the Scottish reformer.
High Street, Edinburgh
☎ 031 556 9579
⌂

Lady Stair's House
A museum dedicated to the great Scottish writers Burns, Scott and Stevenson.
Lawnmarket
☎ 031 225 2424 ext 6593
🖂

Museum of Childhood
Historic toys, dolls and costumes.
High Street, Edinburgh
☎ 031 225 2424 ext 6645
🖂

Royal Museum of Scotland
Decorative art and sicence.
Chambers Street, Edinburgh
☎ 031 225 7534
🖂

Royal Museum of Scotland
Objects from Scotland's heritage.
Queen Street, Edinburgh
☎ 031 225 7534
🖂

Zoos

The Scottish National Zoological Park
Set in 80 acres of grounds.
Corstorphine Road, Edinburgh
☎ 031 334 9171
⌂

Birdwatching and Wildlife

Duddingston Loch
Bird sanctuary since 1923, with many rare birds.
The Scottish Wildlife Trust
☎ 031 226 4602 (for permission)

Cycling

Cycle touring routes available from Tourist Information Centres.

Central Cycle Hire
Mountain and touring bikes.
13 Lochrin Place, Tollcross, Edinburgh
☎ 031 228 6333

Fishing

Fishing in the Rivers Almond (Cramond), Esk (Musselburgh), Water of Leith and Union Canal (Edinburgh). Lochs and reservoirs nearby include the Bonaly Reservoir and Clubbiedean Reservoir (Edinburgh) and Duddingston Loch.

F. & D. Simpson (Tackle Shop)
28 West Preston Street, Edinburgh
☎ 031 667 3058

Ice Skating

Murrayfield Ice Rink
Riversdale Crescent, Edinburgh
☎ 031 337 6933

Skiing

Hillend Ski Centre
Artificial ski-slope.
Biggar Road, Pentland Hills, nr Edinburgh
☎ 031 445 4433

Walking

Mercat Walking Tours
Edinburgh
☎ 031 661 4541

Guided Walks
New Town, Edinburgh
☎ 031 557 5222

Guided Walks
Around Holyrood Park.
Scottish Wildlife Trust, Edinburgh
☎ 031 226 4602

Union Canal Guided Walks
Ratho, nr Edinburgh
☎ 0506 856624

FIFE

i South Street, Leven, Fife
☎ 0333 29464
i South Street, St Andrews, Fife
☎ 0334 72021

ADVENTURE

Multi-activity Centres

East Neuk Outdoors
Abseiling, archery, windsurfing, canoeing,
climbing, coastal walks, cycling,
birdwatching and historic tours.
Anstruther
☎ 0333 311929

EQUESTRIAN

Riding and Pony Trekking

Charleton Riding Centre
Colinsburgh
☎ 0333 34535
Off the A915 to Largoward, on the B941

Stravithie Riding Stables
Stravithie Estate, by St Andrews
☎ 0334 81251
On the B9131, 4 miles south of St Andrews

HEALTH

Leisure Centres

Cupar Sports Centre
Swimming pool, steambath, sunbeds and
fitness room.
Cupar
☎ 0334 54793

East Sands Leisure Complex
Leisure pool with giant water slide, jacuzzi,
steam bath, sunbeds, squash, snooker, bar
and restaurant.
St. Andrews
☎ 0334 76506

LOCAL FEATURES

Festivals and Fairs

February
St. Andrews Arts Festival

April
Golf Week, St Andrews

July
St. Andrews Highland Games

November
St. Andrew's Day Celebrations

Gardens

Botanic Garden
Won international acclaim for its design
and range of plants.
St. Andrews
🏠

Historic Buildings

Balcaskie
Sir William Bruce transformed a mediaeval
tower into one of the finest classical houses
in Scotland; beautiful gardens with view of
Bass Rock.
☎ 0333 730213
Nr Pittenweem
On the B942
🏠

Earlshall Castle and Gardens
Romantic castle home of the Baron and
Baroness of Earlshall built in 1546.
Collections of antique arms, furniture and
Jacobite relics.
Leuchars
☎ 0334 839205
On the A919, 1 mile east of Leuchars
P 🏠 ✕

The Royal Palace of Falkland
Country residence in the 15th and 16th
centuries for the Stuart kings and queens.
Falkland
☎ 033 757 397
➔A A912
🏠

171

FIFE

Kellie Castle
Fascinating 16th century castle with a beautiful Victorian walled garden. National Trust for Scotland.
Nr Pittenweem
☎ 033 38 271
On the B9171, 3 miles north-west of Pittenweem
🏠 ✕ ♿ ♿

Hill of Tarvit Mansion
Edwardian mansion provides a wonderful setting for fine furniture, paintings, tapestries, porcelain and bronzes. National Trust for Scotland.
Nr Cupar
☎ 0334 53127
On the A916, approximately 2 miles south-west of Cupar
🏠 ✕

Museums

British Golf Museum
The story of golf from its origins to the present day.
Golf Place, St. Andrews
☎ 0334 78880
Opposite the Royal and Ancient Golf Club

Crail Museum
The history and fishing heritage of Crail and the surrounding area.
☎ 0334 50869
Marketgate, Crail
🏠

Museum of the St. Andrews Preservation Trust
17th century building in North Street; photographs, paintings, grocers' and chemists' shops.
☎ 0334 72152
12 North Street, St. Andrews

Scottish Fisheries Museum
Record of Scotland's fishing trade.
☎ 0333 50869
Anstruther
🏠

Natural History

The Scottish Deer Centre
Ranger guided tours; nature walk; adventureland; craft shop.
Cupar
☎ 033781 391
➡A A91
🏠 🚌

Parks

Cambo Country Park
Farm machinery display; pets corner, nature trails and walks. Farm building converted to provide a restaurant.
☎ 0333 50810
On the A917 Crail road, 7 miles from St Andrews

Craigtoun Country Park
Dutch village, boating lake, woodland walks, picnic areas, miniature railway, putting, bowling and trampolines.
☎ 0334 73666
2 miles from St. Andrews

Fishing

Angling on Rivers and Lochs
Good trout fishing waters at Cameron Reservoir. Permits at hut near loch.
☎ 0334 76347
Approximately 4 miles south of St. Andrews

Clatto Loch
Fly fishing for brown trout.
Waterman's Cottage, Clatto Loch
☎ 0334 52595
Off the A916, 5 miles south of Cupar

River Eden and Ceres Burn
Brown trout and salmon. Permits from: J. Wilson & Sons, 169 South Street, St Andrews
☎ 0334 72477

Sea Angling
Sea angling trips run from several coastal villages and towns for cod, plaice, saithe, mackerel and wrasse.

Walking

i Details of many delightful local walks are available from Tourist Information Centres.

Guided Walks
North-east Fife Ranger Service organises summer walks.
☎ 0334 73666

Historical Guided Walks
St. Andrews and the University.
Tickets from the Tourist Information Centre.

Boat Trips

Anstruther Pleasure Trips
Boat trips to the Isle of May.
14 Dreelside, Anstruther
☎ 0333 310103

Diving

East Coast Divers
Facilities for sports divers including boat charter, compressed air and accommodation.
Anstruther
☎ 0333 310768

CLYDE COAST

WHAT TO DO AND SEE

i 39 Sandgate, Ayr, Ayrshire
☎ 0292 284196
i Municipal Buildings, South Beach,
Troon, Ayrshire
☎ 0292 317696 (summer only)

ADVENTURE

Shooting

Dalvennan Shooting Ground
Clay target shooting; practice lessons;
competitions.
Kirkmichael, Maybole
☎ 0292 531134
✗

Gamesport (Ayr) Ltd
Specialists in guns and fishing tackle. Local
shooting information freely given.
60 Sandgte, Ayr
☎ 0292 263822

EQUESTRIAN

Riding and Pony Trekking

High Mains Pony Trekking
Ian Loch, Wallacetown, Maybole
☎ 046581 504

LOCAL FEATURES

Factory Visits

John Walker & Sons Ltd
The world's largest Scotch whisky blending
and bottling plant. Free guided tours.
Hill Street, Kilmarnock, Ayrshire
☎ 0563 23401

Festivals and Fairs

April
Ayrshire Agricultural Show

June
Ayrshire Arts Festival
Burns Festival, Ayr
Ayr Golf Week

August
Ayr Flower Show

173

CLYDE COAST

WHAT TO DO AND SEE

Gardens

Belleisle Estate
Formal gardens, deer park, duck pond and
aviaries. South of Ayr.
✗

Rozelle Estate
Gardens, shrubbery, walks and sculpture
park.
Alloway town centre, south of Ayr

Historic Buildings

Bachelor's Club
A 17th century house where Burns, his
brother and 5 others formed themselves
into a debating society and Bachelors' Club
in 1780. National Trust.
Tarbolton, Strathclyde
☎ 0292 54190
🎁

Burns Cottage and Museum
Robert Burns was born in 1759 in this
two-roomed cottage which is kept furnished
as it would have been in his day; museum
contains manuscripts and his private
possessions.
Alloway, Strathclyde
☎ 0292 41215
🎁 ♿

Burns Monument and Gardens
Sculptures of characters from Burns' poems.
Alloway, Strathclyde
☎ 0292 41321

Culzean Castle
Designed by Robert Adam and beautifully
furnished, this 18th century castle is set in
560 acres of grounds.
9 miles north of Girvan
☎ 06556 274
🎁

Dunure Castle
Ruins of a prominent castle, the scene of
some horrific events. Now an attractive
picnic area.
On the coast south of Ayr
P

Souter Johnnie's Cottage
Home of the village cobbler, John Davidson,
the original Souter Johnnie of Burns' poem
'Tam O'Shanter'.
Kirkoswald, Strathclyde
🎁

Natural History

Enterkine Nature Trail
Natural woodland with badgers' setts, pond
and varied birdlife. Scottish Wildlife Trust
On the B744 nr Tarbolton

Parks

Craigie Park, Ayr
Riverside walks; gardens; pitch and putt.

OUTDOOR LEISURE/SPORTS

Cycling

The Cycle Shop
5 The Cross, Prestwick
☎ 0292 77360

Fishing

Game fishing
Game fishing on the Rivers Ayr, Doon and
Girvan for salmon, sea trout and brown
trout. Loch fishing nearby on lochs and
reservoirs. Contact the Tourist Information
Centre for a detailed leaflet. Tackle shops:
Gamesport (Ayr) Ltd
60 Sandgate, Ayr
☎ 0292 263822
Sea fishing
Good sea angling along Newton Shore, Ayr
harbour mouth and from the Heads of Ayr.
Boat fishing with good catches of cod,
haddock, thornback, ray and flatfish.

Ayr Sea Angling Centre
Tony Medina, 10 Britannia Place, Ayr
☎ 0292 285297

Ayr Marine Charters
59 Woodlands Crescent, Ayr
☎ 0292 281638

Brian Burns
Flat 2, 16 Bellevue Road, Ayr
☎ 0292 281648

Ice Skating

Ayr Ice Rink
With skate hire and disco music.
9 Limekiln Road, Ayr
☎ 0292 263024

Walking

Some local walks available from the Tourist
Information Centre.
Culzean Country Park
4 walks including a cliff walk.
The Park Centre
Off the A719, 12 miles south of Ayr
P 🚻 🚌

WATERSPORTS

Boat Trips

P.S.Waverley
The last sea-going paddle steamer in the
world sails from Ayr to ports on the Clyde
and to the islands during summer months.
☎ 041 221 8152

MACHRIHANISH

WHAT TO DO AND SEE

i Mackinnon House, The Pier,
Campbeltown, Argyll
☎ 0586 552056

EQUESTRIAN

Riding and Pony Trekking

Ardfern Riding Centre
Hacks or day rides. Appaloosas and
American Quarterhorses are bred and
trained on the estate.
Craobh Haven, by Lochgilphead, Argyll
☎ 08525 632
☎ 08525 270

Castle Riding Centre
Exciting trail rides, instruction and
holidays.
Brenfield, Ardrishaig, Argyll
☎ 0546 603274

LOCAL FEATURES

Arts and Crafts

Kintyre Crafts
Selection of Scottish gifts.
28 Long Row, Campeltown
☎ 0586 554491

Ronachan Silks
Scarves and stoles by Mary Pollok.
Telephone before calling.
Ronachan, Clachan, by Tarbert
☎ 08804 242

Meander in Machrihanish
Mill Cottage, Machrihanish
Handmade shirts and jackets
☎ 0586 81202

Wallis Hunter Design
Fabricators in gold and silver at work. Also
glass, leather, ceramics and woollens.
The Steading, Carradale
☎ 05833 683

Festivals and Fairs

May/June
Islay Festival

July/August
Rhinns of Islay Celtic Festival
Golf Festival, Machrihanish Golf Club
Highland Games and Agricultural Shows
Contact the Tourist Information Centre for
dates and venues.

Historic Buildings

Clan Macalister Centre
Glenbarr Abbey, 10 m NW of Campeltown on
A83
Recently refurbished medium sized family
home of the Macalisters of Glenbarr, now a
Clan Centre. Artefacts, furnishings and an
interesting look at family life in the 18th and
19th century.

Other Places of Interest

Davarr Island
Linked to the mainland by a bank of shingle
at low water. Picture of the Crucifixion,
secretly painted on the rock wall of a very
large cave 100 years ago.
Check tide times at Campbeltown TIC before
setting out.

Mull of Kintyre
The tip of the longest peninsula in Scotland.
Cliff scenery and views.

Gardens

Achamore House Gardens
Isle of Gigha
(Open end March – end October)

OUTDOOR LEISURE/SPORTS

Birdwatching and Wildlife

Mull of Kintyre Bird Tours
Minibus tours with a professional
ornithologist. Golden Eagle, Peregrine,
Buzzard, Gannet, Divers and many others to
be seen. Details available from the Tourist
Information Centre, Campbeltown

Cycling

Cycle hire from:

Campbeltown Bike Centre
Burnside Road, Campbeltown
☎ 0586 554480

Islay
☎ 0496 2042

Lochgilphead Caravan Site
Argyll
☎ 0546 602003

McAulay & Torrie
Islay
☎ 0496 2053

Fishing

Coarse fishing
Loch fishing on Loch Lussa,
Loch Auchalocy and Loch Ruan, Tangy
Loch and Crosshill reservoir. River fishing
on Coniglen Water, Glenbreckerie Water
and Lussa River.
Permits from:

Galbraith and Cochrane Paint Shop
Reform Square, Campbeltown

A P McGrory
Also fishing tackle and boat hire.
Main Street, Campbeltown

i Ask the Tourist Information Centre for
a detailed leaflet *Fishing Around
Campbeltown* produced by the Kintyre Fish
Protection and Angling Club.

OBAN

i Argyll Square, Oban, Argyll
☎ 0631 63122

ADVENTURE

Multi-activity Centres

Rua Fiola Island Exploration Centre
Adventure holidays for children on a
privately-owned island.
Cullipool, Luing, nr Oban
☎ 03873 72240

Shooting and Stalking

Fischer Scottish Touring Operator
Sporting organiser for stalking, shooting
and fishing.
Rudha Beg, Appin, Argyll
☎ 0631 73285

Scottish Sporting Agency
Agency for shooting, stalking, fishing and
sailing.
Dunstaffnage House, Connel, nr Oban
☎ 0631 71662

AERIAL SPORTS

Gliding

Argyll and West Highland Gliding Centre
Holiday courses and introductory flights.
Connel Airfield, North Connel, nr Oban
☎ 063171 243

Connel Gliding Club
D. Whitelaw, Creachann, Glenmore Road,
Oban
☎ 0631 66079
☎ 0631 63274

EQUESTRIAN

Riding and Pony Trekking

Achnalarig Farm and Stables
Glencruitten, Oban
☎ 0631 62745

Equi-Venture
Achinreir Farm, Barcaldine, nr Oban
☎ 0631 72320

LOCAL FEATURES

Art Galleries

Gallery and Rectory Design
Edna Whyte's paintings of horizon and west
coast seascapes exhibited in a beautifully
situated gallery.
Cullipool, Isle of Luing, nr Oban
☎ 08524 209
Cross by Cuan Ferry

McIan Gallery
19th and 20th century Scottish and
Continental paintings, including works by
the 'Glasgow School' of painters.
10 Argyll Square, Oban
☎ 0631 62303

Arts and Crafts

Argyll Pottery
See the potters at work.
Dalrannoch, Barcaldine, nr Oban
☎ 0631 72503
On the main A828

The Craft Shop
A co-operative shop for local crafts.
Craigard Road, Oban
☎ 0631 62479

Factory Visits

Oban Distillery
A working distillery, home of the Oban Malt
Whisky.
Stafford Street, Oban
☎ 0631 62110

Festivals and Fairs

May
Highland and Islands Music and Dance
Festival

July
West Highlands Yachting Week

August
Argyllshire Highland Gathering

Gardens

Ardchatten Gardens
Formal and wild garden surrounding the
historic Ardchattan Priory.
North Connel, nr Oban
☎ 0631 75274
5 miles east of Connel Bridge

Guided Tours

Macdougalls of Oban Tours
3 Mossfield Avenue, Oban
☎ 0631 62133

Historic Buildings

Dunollie Castle
13th century ruined tower-house and bailey,
on a rocky cliff on the Ganavan Road.
Oban
🏠

Dunstaffnage Castle
Mid 13th century castle in a good state of
repair.
Nr Oban
🏠

Inveraray Castle
18th century residence of the Duke of
Argyll, chief of the Clan Campbell;
collections of family portraits, silver,
tapestries, porcelain and armour.
Inveraray
☎ 0499 2203

OBAN

Museums

Inveraray Jail
A living 19th century prison. Gallows, courtroom and old prison with cells.
Inveraray
☎ 0499 2381

World in Miniature
Exhibition of miniature rooms and furniture; the work of 250 of Britain's finest miniaturists.
North Pier, Oban
☎ 08526 272

Natural History

Oban Rare Breeds Animal Park
Rare breeds of farm animals and deer.
Barranrioch farm, Oban
☎ 0631 77233
On the Glencruitten road
✕

Sea Life Centre
Live native marine exhibits including seals.
Barcaldine, Oban
☎ 0631 72386
On the A828, 10 miles north of Oban

OUTDOOR LEISURE/SPORTS

Fishing

The West Highlands are an angler's paradise. The rivers and lochs are well stocked with trout and salmon and there are also extensive opportunities for coarse fishing.
i The Tourist Information Centre will give detailed information on fishing.

Walking

Hebridean Ventures
Walking holidays, sailing and painting.
Brendan, Connel
☎ 0631 73285

WATERSPORTS

An important sailing centre with a wealth of opportunities for cruises, self-sail, fishing trips, bird watching trips etc.
i A complete list of companies is available from the Tourist Information Centre.

Boat Hire

Borro Boats
Small boats, sailing dinghies, motor boats and rowing boats for hire by the hour, day or week. Skippered sailing cruises.
Dungallan Parks, Gallanach Road, Oban
☎ 0631 63292

Diving

Argyll Boat Cruises
12 Breadalbane Street, Oban
☎ 0631 65687

Sailing

Alba Yacht Services Ltd.
Luxury self-sail charter yachts.
Dunstaffnage Yacht Haven, nr Oban
☎ 0631 65630
☎ 0631 64004

PERTHSHIRE

i High Street, Crieff, Perthshire
☎ 0764 2578
i 22 Atholl Road, Pitlochry, Perthshire
☎ 0796 47215
☎ 0796 47251

ADVENTURE

Multi-activity Centres

Croft-na-Caber Watersports and Activities Centre
Windsurfing, canoeing, sailing, waterskiing, parascending, rafting, jet bikes, climbing, shooting, fishing and cross-country skiing.
Kenmore
☎ 0887 830236
☎ 0887 830588

Highland Adventure
Riding and multi-activity holidays.
Glenisla, by Alyth
☎ 057582 238

EQUESTRIAN

Riding and Pony Trekking

Tullochville Trekking Centre
Tullochville Farm, Coshieville, nr Aberfeldy
☎ 08873 559

Strathearn Stables
Crieff Hydro Hotel, Crieff, Perthshire
☎ 0764 2401 ext 431

HEALTH

Leisure Centres

Perth Leisure Pool
Advanced leisure pool with flumes, wild water, outdoor lagoon, bubble beds, a 25-metre training pool, health suite, fitness room and children's pool.
Glasgow Road, Perth
☎ 0738 30535
✕

LOCAL FEATURES

Arts and Crafts

Crieff Visitor Centre
See Thistle Pottery and Perthshire Paperweights being made.
Muthill Road, Crieff
☎ 0764 4014
P 🚌

The Highland Horn and Deerskin Centre
Range of leather goods made from deerskin, leather and hornware for sale.
City Hall, Dunkeld
☎ 03502 569

Pitlochry Pottery
Workshop and showroom in 200 year old cottage.
East Haugh
☎ 0796 472790
2 miles south of Pitlochry
P

Stuart Crystal
Free tours of crystal factory.
Muthill Road, Crieff
☎ 0764 4004

Factory Visits

Edradour Distillery
Smallest distillery in Scotland.
By Moulin
☎ 0796 472095
2½ miles east of Pitlochry
🚌

Glenturret Distillery Ltd
Scotland's oldest distillery.
Crieff
☎ 0764 2424
Off the A85, 1 mile west of Crieff
🎁 🚌

Historic Buildings

Blair Castle
A white-turreted baronial castle, seat of the Duke of Atholl. Notable collections of furniture, pictures, embroidery, arms, porcelain and Jacobite relics; extensive grounds, nature trails, deerpark.
Pitlochry
☎ 079 681 207
Off A9, 6 miles north-west of Pitlochry
P 🎁

Museums

Atholl Country Collection
Display of local life including folklore and trades of the past. Includes: Blacksmiths Smiddy, Post Office, Crofter's Stable and Living Room.
Old School, Blair Atholl
☎ 079 681 232
🎁

Scottish Tartans Museum
Exhibition illustrating the development of tartan and highland dress; research and technical centre.
Drummond Street, Comrie
☎ 0764 70779

Music, Dance and Drama

Pitlochry Festival Theatre
The famous 'Theatre in the Hills', magnificently situated on the River Tummel. Popular plays, concerts and fringe events.
☎ 0796 2680

PERTHSHIRE

Natural History

Glengoulandie Deer Park
Deer and wildlife park. Visitors are able to walk or drive around the park.
☎ 08873 261
On the B846, 8 miles north-west of Aberfeldy

Pitlochry Power Station, Fish Ladder and Dam
Hydroelectric station where migrating salmon may be seen through windows in the fish ladder.
☎ 0796 473152
P

OUTDOOR LEISURE/SPORTS

Birdwatching and Wildlife

Loch of the Lowes
Osprey nest and wildlife may be watched from hides.
Scottish Wildlife Trust
☎ 0350 72337
Off the A923, 2 miles north-east of Dunkeld

Fishing

Perthshire contains a wealth of salmon, sea trout and brown trout waters and an increasing number of rainbow trout fisheries. There is also excellent grayling, pike, perch and roach fishing. The fishing is dominated by the mighty River Tay, one of the principal salmon rivers in Europe.
i For detailed information see *Fishing in Perthshire*, a comprehensive leaflet available from the Tourist Information Centre. Tackle shops:

A. Boyd
Tackle Dealers, King Street, Crieff
☎ 0764 3871

Highland Gathering
Guns & Tackle, 8 West Monlin Road, Pitlochry
☎ 0796 473047

Ice Skating

Atholl Curling Rink
Open and hotel competitions; visitor viewing.
Pitlochry
☎ 0796 473337

Walking

Detailed leaflets are available from the Tourist Information Centre.

Falls of Bruar
3 miles west of Blair Atholl. Spectacular forest walk by 3 grand cascades celebrated by Robert Burns.

Garry-Tummel Walks, Pitlochry
Network of marked paths beside rivers and lochs, through forest and woodland. Linked to walks to Killiecrankie.

Glen Lednock Circular Walk
Woodland walk with waterfalls.
Starts at Comrie village.

WATERSPORTS

Sailing

Lochearn Sailing & Watersports Centre
Sailing, windsurfing, canoeing and waterskiing: instruction and hire.
South Shore Road, St. Fillans
☎ 0764 2292
☎ 076485 257

FIRTH OF TAY

i The Library, High Street, Carnoustie, Angus
☎ 0241 52258 (summer only)
i 4 City Square, Dundee
☎ 0382 27723

ADVENTURE

Multi-activity Centres

Ancrum Outdoor Centre
Dry ski-slope.
10 Ancrum Road, Dundee
☎ 0382 644159

EQUESTRIAN

Riding and Pony Trekking

Camperdown Pony Trekking
Camperdown Park, Dundee
☎ 0382 623879

HEALTH

Leisure Centres

Dundee Swimming and Leisure Centre
Swimming pool, health suite, sauna, sunbed, steamroom, spa pool, keep-fit, pool tables and table tennis.
Earl Grey Place, Dundee
☎ 0382 203888

LOCAL FEATURES

Art Galleries

McManus Galleries
Fine Victorian Gothic building houses local history museum and art galleries with impressive collections of Victorian and Scottish paintings.
Albert Square, Dundee
☎ 0382 23141 ext 136

Seagate Gallery
Touring exhibitions of mainly modern art.
38–40 Seagate, Dundee
☎ 0382 26331

Arts and Crafts

Eduardo Alessandro Studios
Gifts, crafts, artwork and paintings by local artists and crafts people.
Gray Street, Broughty Ferry, Dundee
☎ 0382 737011

Peel Farm Craft Shop
Pottery, quilting, patchwork, dried flowers, basketwear and knitwear.
Lintrathen, by Kirriemuir
☎ 05756 205
Just off the B954
✗

Riverstone Domestic Stoneware
Workshop viewing and shop.
Oathlaw Pottery, Oathlaw, by Forfar
☎ 0307 85272
→A A94

Factory Visits

Shaws Dundee Sweet Factory
See how original toffees, fudges and boilings are made.
Fulton Road, Wester Gourdie Industrial Estate, Dundee
☎ 0382 610369
→A A972
✗ 🚌 ♿

Festivals and Fairs

June
Dundee City Festival (until August)
July
Dundee Highland Games
August
Dundee Water Festival

FIRTH OF TAY

Food and Drink

Cairn O'Mhor Winery
A unique range of country wines; tours of the winery.
East Inchmichael, Errol, Perth
☎ 0821 642214
☎ 0821 642781

Gardens

Branklyn Garden
Lovely 2-acre garden. National Trust for Scotland.
Dundee Road, Perth
☎ 0738 25535
On the A85, 1½ miles east of Perth
⌂

Historic Buildings

Earlshall Castle and Gardens
Built in 1546 by Sir William Bruce, an ancestor of the present owners. Renowned long gallery; famous topiary yews shaped as chessmen.
Leuchars, St. Andrews, Fife
☎ 0334 839205
On the A919, 8 miles from Dundee
🚌

Glamis Castle
Childhood home of the Queen Mother, a romantic castle set in a magnificent park and framed by the Grampian Mountains.
Angus
☎ 030784 242
☎ 030784 243
☎ 030784 274
P ⌂

Scone Palace
Crowning place of the Kings of the Scots on the Stone of Scone, this historic place is set in magnificent parkland. Highland cattle; adventure playground; veteran agricultural machinery display.
Perth
☎ 0738 52300
On the A93 Braemar road
P ⌂ 🚌

Museums

Broughty Castle Museum
Local history gallery which includes exhibits relating to Dundee's former whaling industry.
Broughty Ferry, Dundee
☎ 0382 76121

Natural History

The Scottish Deer Centre
Ranger-guided tours, nature trails, craft shop, adventureland.
By Cupar, Fife
☎ 033781 391
On the A91, 3 miles west of Cupar
P ⌂ 🚌 ✕ ♿ ♿

Parks

Camperdown Country Park
Wildlife park and adventure playground.
Dundee
☎ 0382 623555
➔A A923
⌂ ✕

Clatto Country Park
Canoeing, sailing, windsurfing and a programme of activities.
Dundee
☎ 0382 89076
➔A A923

Monikie Country Park
Sailing, canoeing and windsurfing.
Newbigging
☎ 082623 202
On the B962

Cycling

Cycle hire from:

Boddens Mountain Equipment
Mountain Bikes.
104 Annfield Road, Dundee
☎ 0382 645310

Mac Cycles
143c Nethergate, Dundee
☎ 0382 201471

Nicholson's Cycling Centre
2 Forfar Road, Dundee
☎ 0382 461212

Fishing

Fishing in the Tay Estuary for salmon, sea trout and flounder.
i Leaflet on fishing in local lochs is available from the Tourist Information Centre.
Tackle shops:

John R Gow & Sons Ltd
12 Union Street, Dundee
☎ 0382 25427

Shotcast Ltd
8 Whitehall Crescent, Dundee
☎ 0382 25621

Walking

Tayside is a walkers' paradise with low-level woodland walks, coastal paths, glen walks and higher-level hill walks; *Walks in Tayside* is available from the Tourist Information Centre.

Waterskiing

East Coast Watersports Ltd
Surf-skis, waterskiing, jet-skis and paragliding.
Esplanade, Broughty Ferry, Dundee
☎ 0382 79889

WHAT TO DO AND SEE

i Market Place, Arbroath, Angus
☎ 0241 72609

EQUESTRIAN

Riding and Pony Trekking

Glenmarkie Farm Riding Centre
Hacking and trekking through spectacular scenery.
Glenisla
☎ 057 582 341
3 miles north of Glenisla Post Office

HEALTH

Leisure Centres

Lochside Leisure Centre
Within the Forfar Country Park, this centre has sports halls, squash courts, a gym and drama studio. Also a cafeteria with views over Forfar Loch.
Forfar Country Park
☎ 0307 64201
Eastern shore of Forfar Loch

Montrose Swimming Pool
Pool with spring boards and family sessions with an inflatable chute.
The Mall, Montrose
☎ 0674 72026

LOCAL FEATURES

Architecture

Arbroath Abbey
Ruins of an abbey founded in 1178 by King William the Lion in memory of his friend Thomas à Becket. Eventual burial place of the King himself.
Arbroath

Pictish Stones
Aberlemno Sculptured Stones: cross slab in the churchyard and 3 other stones by the roadside.
On the B9134, 5 miles north-east of Forfar

Arts and Crafts

Peel Farm
Coffee and craft shop for home baking and local crafts.
Lintrathen Road
Just off the B954 Alyth to Glenisla road

Food and Drink

Forester's Seat Winery
View the whole wine-making process from the hand-squeezing of locally grown Angus fruit to the laying down of the year's vintage.
By Forfar
☎ 0307 81 304
On the A932 Forfar to Friockheim road
P ✗ ఈ ఈ

Gardens

Damside Garden
History of herbs and herb gardening plus traditional styles of gardening including Celtic, Knot, Roman, Monastic and Elizabethan.
By Johnshaven, Montrose
☎ 0561 61498
Off the A92 and the A94
P ⌂ ఈ ఈ

Historic Houses

Barrie's Birthplace
First home of novelist and playwright J. M. Barrie who wrote *Peter Pan*.
Kirriemuir, Tayside

Edzell Castle and Gardens
Beautiful walled garden created by Sir David Lindsay in 1604. The 'Pleasance' is a formal garden whose walls are decorated with sculptured stone panels. Historic Scotland.
☎ 031 244 3101
On the B966, 6 miles north of Brechin

House of Dun
Palladian House designed by William Adam. Fine views across Montrose Basin and woodland walks through the estate.
☎ 067 481 264
On the A935, 4 miles west of Montrose
✗

Museums

Signal Tower Museum
The signalling station for Bell Rock lighthouse now houses displays of local history.
Arbroath
☎ 0241 75598

Natural History

Mains of Dun Farm
Farm and wildlife estate with marvellous trees, woods and birdlife. 4 mile long railway between Bridge of Dun and Brechin has occasional steam service on Sundays.
Nr Montrose on the A935
☎ 067 481 332
☎ 0674 76336 (Countryside ranger)

WHAT TO DO AND SEE

Parks

Crombie Country Park
Loch and surrounding woodlands; walks and rambles with a ranger; mini highland games; orienteering course; tree trails; angling.
Carmylie, Broughty Ferry
☎ 02416 360
Off the B961
P & &

Monikie Country Park
Lochs, woodlands and parkland with a host of activities. Sailboards for hire, dinghy sailing on Toppers, canoeing, rowing and angling.
☎ 082 623 202 (Ranger)
On the B962 approx 1 mile beyond Newbigging
P &

OUTDOOR LEISURE/SPORTS

Birdwatching and Wildlife

Montrose Basin Nature Reserve
This 2000-acre tidal basin is a local nature reserve with a full-time ranger-naturalist. Large flocks of waders, wildfowl and seabirds use the Basin as a sanctuary. Hides are provided by the Scottish Wildlife Trust.

St. Cyrus National Nature Reserve
Lava cliffs and sand dunes, saltmarsh and sand flats.
St. Cyrus, Kincardine and Deeside
☎ 06748 3736

Fishing

Monikie Angling
Superb fishing on 2 ponds and at Crombie Loch is managed by Monikie Angling Club which has 18 boats.
Nr Newbigging
☎ 082 623 300 Club Bailiff

Walking

Tayside Hilltours
Guided walking holidays in the Tayside mountains to suit a wide range of abilities and interests.
26 North Loch Road, Forfar
☎ 0307 62045

CRUDEN BAY

WHAT TO DO AND SEE

i 54 Broad Street, Peterhead,
Aberdeenshire
☎ 0779 71904 (summer only)

ADVENTURE

Shooting
Game International Ltd
Driven and rough game shooting, stalking
and clay pigeon shooting.
The Firs, Mountblairy, Banff
☎ 0888 68618

EQUESTRIAN

Fourwinds Equestrian Centre
Lootingstone Croft, Rathen
☎ 03465 2326

Kirkton Riding Centre
Crudie
☎ 08885 610
Just off the A98, 7 miles east of Macduff

HEALTH

Leisure Centres
Peterhead Swimming Pool
A modern indoor pool with a sauna and
solarium.
Queen Street, Peterhead
☎ 0779 71757

CRUDEN BAY

LOCAL FEATURES

Art Galleries

Aberdeen Art Gallery
Impressionist, Victorian, Scottish and 20th century British painting, silver and glass collections.
Schoolhill, Aberdeen
☎ 0224 646333

Arbuthnot Museum and Art Gallery
Based on the collection of a local trader, Adam Arbuthnot, the museum depicts local history and boasts a fine coin collection.
St. Peter Street, Peterhead
☎ 0779 77778

Arts and Crafts

Portsoy Marble Workshop and Pottery
Marble polishing, pottery workshop and shop.
Shorehead, Portsoy
☎ 0261 42404

Scottish Sculpture Workshop and Sculpture Walk
Workshop and gallery open daily.
1 Main Street, Lumsden, by Huntly
☎ 04646 372

Factory Visits

Ugie Fish House
The oldest building in Peterhead and the oldest working fish house in Scotland. It still oak-smokes wild salmon and trout in the traditional manner.
Golf Road, Peterhead
☎ 0779 76209

Falconry

North East Falconry Centre
The only falconry centre in Northern Scotland. The birds are on display and there are hour-long flying displays twice daily.
Bruntbrae Farm
☎ 0466 87328
4 miles south of Banff

Gardens

Hatton Garden Centre
Large centre that specialises in growing heathers; gift packs available.
Northfield, Hatton
☎ 077984 490

Historic Buildings

Duff House
One of William Adam's finest buildings, built between 1725 and 1740. Now owned by Historic Scotland who are restoring it to its former glory.
Banff
☎ 0261 812872

Fyvie Castle
One of the most spectacular castles in Scotland it has long and chequered history during which many extensions and modifications have taken place. National Trust for Scotland.
Fyvie
☎ 0651 891266

Slains Castle
One of the most famous ruins in Scotland; inspiration to Bram Stoker when he wrote *Dracula*. Today it is an extensive cliff-top ruin reached by foot from the Main Street car park at Cruden Bay.

Natural History

Bullers of Buchan
Sea chasm some 200 feet deep where the ocean rushes in through a natural archway open to the sky. Cliff scenery is spectacular and seabirds of many varieties may be seen. Rough footpath leads from the car park to the edge of the chasm.
Off the A975, 3 miles north of Cruden Bay

Rattray Head
A true wilderness lying north of Peterhead where 70 foot sand dunes create a lunar landscape. Nearby is an RSPB reserve at Loch of Strathbeg.

OUTDOOR LEISURE/SPORTS

Birdwatching and Wildlife

Loch of Strathbeg Nature Reserve
A 2300-acre RSPB Reserve attracting geese, ducks and swans in the winter and many nesting birds in the summer. Over 180 species have been recorded.
☎ 0346 32017
6 miles south of Fraserburgh near Crimond village on the A952

Cycling

Robertson Sports, Cycle Hire
1–3 Kirk Street, Peterhead
☎ 0779 72584

Fishing

Trout, sea trout and salmon fishing on the River Ugie. There is a variety of fishing opportunities in and around Peterhead and Cruden Bay. For details contact the Tourist Information Centre.

Crimonmogate Fishery
6-acre lake well stocked with rainbow and brown trout; boat and jetty fishing. Permits issued on bank.
Lonmay, nr Fraserburgh
☎ 0346 32203

WATERSPORTS

Water skiing

Dolphin Watersports
Waterski tuition, power bikes, speed boats and wave riders for hire. Wet suits and equipment supplied.
Port Erroll Harbour, Cruden Bay
☎ 03302 3816

WHAT TO DO AND SEE

i 17 High Street, Elgin, Moray
☎ 0343 542666
☎ 0343 543388

AERIAL SPORTS

Gliding
Highland Gliding Club
Visitors welcome; flying tuition, trial flights.
Located at Dallachy airfield, near the mouth
of the River Spey.
☎ 0343 820568 (airfield)
☎ 05422 7785 (Chief Instructor)
On the B9104 Spey Bay Road

EQUESTRIAN

Riding and Pony Trekking
Aberlour Riding and Trekking Centre
Aberlour
☎ 03405 871467
Redmoss Riding Centre
Drybridge, by Buckie
☎ 0542 33140

LOCAL FEATURES

Antiques and Collecting
Cluny Auction Rooms
8–9a Cluny Terrace, Buckie
☎ 0542 33318
Elgin City Salerooms
Wards Road, Elgin
☎ 0343 547047/542475 (sales days)

Arts and Crafts
Baranoff Studio and Gallery
Paintings and plaques inspired by local
scenery.
6 Seafield Street, Cullen
☎ 0542 41410

Cairnty Weavers
Tuition in spinning and handweaving on
simple home-made equipment. Handspun
wool from own fleeces.
Cairnty Croft, Mulben, Keith
☎ 05426 261

The Mill Shop and Cashmere Visitor Centre
Johnstons of Elgin have 200 years
experience in spinning and weaving luxury
fabrics.
Newmill, Elgin
☎ 0343 549319
🚌 ✗

Factory Visits
Dallus Dhu
Highland distillery museum with traditional
tools of the trade.
1 mile south of Forres
☎ 0309 76548

Oldmills Working Watermill
Working mill with various craftspeople at
work, a collection of agricultural
implements and a lakeside trail.
Old Mills Road, Elgin
☎ 0343 540698
🚌 ✗

LOSSIEMOUTH

Gardens

Drummuir Castle Walled Kitchen Garden
A beautiful sheltered south-facing organic garden; plants for sale; gardening courses held.
☎ 05421 225
Off the B9014, midway between Keith and Drummuir
✕

Historic Buildings

Brodie Castle
Home of the Brodie family since 1160, it has a notable collection of furniture and paintings. National Trust for Scotland.
☎ 03094 371
5 miles west of Forres, off the A96
⌂ ✕ ♿ ♿

Elgin Cathedral
Known as 'the Lantern of the North' and regarded as one of the most beautiful Scottish cathedrals in its day, it is sadly now a ruin.
King Street, Elgin
☎ 0343 547171
♿

Museums

Elgin Museum
An independent museum with fascinating archaeological and mediaeval finds, militaria, costume, agriculture and local industry exhibits.
1 High Street, Elgin
☎ 0343 543675
⌂

Moray Motor Museum
Small but unique collection of cars and motor cycles housed in a converted mill.
Bridge Street, Elgin
☎ 0343 544933

Music, Dance and Drama

Brodie Castle Summer Season Events
Scottish Renaissance Music, Gaelic Singing, The Battlefield Band in Concert and Classical Concerts indoors and out.
Nr Forres
☎ 03094 371

Natural History

Darnaway Farm Visitor Centre
Estate tour of the Earl of Moray's Darnaway Castle and historic land, farm animals, milking herd; farm implements and woodland walks.
☎ 0309 4469
On the A96, 3 miles west of Forres
P ⌂ ✕ ♿ ♿

Birdwatching and Wildlife

Ornithology in Moray
Different habits in Moray make it an exciting place for birdwatching. Leaflet available from Tourist Information Centre.
☎ 0343 547029 Mr Lawrie
☎ 0343 543476 Mr Gervaise

Cycling

Flycycle Holidays
Mountain bikes for hire.
8 The Square, Cullen
☎ 0542 40638

Higher N Hire
Special rates for groups and families.
Craggonmore Cottage, Ballindalloch
☎ 08072 246

Fishing

Excellent game fishing, sea angling and loch fishing is available in this area. A detailed leaflet is produced by the Tourist Information Centre.

Tackle shops:
97d High Street Forres
Permits for River Findhorn, Muckle Burn, Loch of the Blairs and Lochindorb.
☎ 0309 72936

Fochabers Tackle and Guns
Permits for the River Spey.
91 High Street, Fochabers
☎ 0343 820327

North East Marine
For sea angling enquiries.
Mr A Trotman, The Wardens, Coularbank Road, Lossiemouth
☎ 034381 2580

Walking

The Speyside Way
Runs between Spey Bay and Ballindalloch (30 miles/48 km), with spurs from Craigellachie to Dufftown (4 miles/6 km) and from Ballindalloch to Tomintoul (15 miles/ 24 km). Detailed map and route description, accommodation and bus service timetables available from the Tourist Information Centre.

Sailing

Moray Watersports
Family run sailing school in the sheltered waters of Findhorn Bay. Dinghy sailing, windsurfing, canoes, rowing boats, fishing trips and activity holidays.
The Old Fisheries, Findhorn
☎ 0309 30239

BOAT OF GARTEN

i Grampian Road, Aviemore, Inverness
☎ 0479 810363

ADVENTURE

Multi-activity Centres

Highland Ventures Ltd
Fishing, shooting and off-road driving.
The Log Cabin, Aviemore Centre
☎ 0479 810 833

Loch Insh Watersports
Canoeing, sailing, windsurfing, cycling,
fishing and a dry ski-slope.
Hire and instruction.
Loch Insh, Kincraig
☎ 0540 651272

Shooting

Alvie Estate
Grouse, pheasant, duck, rabbit, roe and red
deer in the appropriate seasons. All types of
shooting can be arranged from rough
shooting to stalking and clay pigeons.
Alvie Estate Office, Kincraig
☎ 0540 651255
☎ 0540 651249

AERIAL SPORTS

Gliding

Cairngorm Gliding Club
Fly at Blackmill Air Field; training and
passenger flights available.
Feshie Bridge, Kincraig
☎ 0540 651317

EQUESTRIAN

Riding and Pony Trekking

Ballintean Riding Centre
Kincraig, Kingussie
☎ 0540 651352

Carrbridge Pony Trekking Centre
The Ellan, Station Road, Carrbridge
☎ 047984 602

HEALTH

Leisure Centres

The Aviemore Centre
All-weather leisure centre with swimming
pool, ice rink, theatre, cinema, sauna,
solarium, restaurants, discos and
amusements.
☎ 0479 810624

LOCAL FEATURES

Factory Tours

Dalwhinnie Highland Malt Whisky
Distillery tours.
Dalwhinnie
☎ 05282 208

The Malt Whisky Trail
Follow the signposted road tour which visits
8 malt whisky distilleries in the Grampian
Highlands. Leaflet from the Tourist
Information Centre.

BOAT OF GARTEN

WHAT TO DO AND SEE

Gardens

Speyside Heather Centre
Heather heritage centre with show garden displaying 200 varieties. Tea room with home baking.
Skye of Curr, Dulnain Bridge
☎ 047985 359
On the A95, 6 miles from Grantown

Musuems

Highland Folk Museum
Regional museum of country life.
Kingussie
☎ 0540 661307

Natural History

Cairngorm Reindeer Centre
Britain's only herd of reindeer.
Glenmore, Aviemore
☎ 047986 228

Highland Wildlife Park
Large drive-through reserve.
Kincraig
☎ 0540 651270
On the B9152 off the A9
P 🛈 ♿ ♿

Parks

Landmark Highland Heritage and Adventure Park
Pine forest nature centre, show and exhibitions, treetop trail, forest tower, adventure playground, steam powered sawmill and woodland maze.
Carrbridge
☎ 047984 613
Just off the A9 between Inverness and Aviemore
🛈

Rothiemurchus Estate
Forest and wildlife walks, farm tours and safaris, clay pigeon shooting school, fishing in well stocked lochs and birdwatching.
Rothiemurchus Visitor Centre, Aviemore
☎ 0479 810858
On the B970
P 🚌 ✕

Railways

Strathspey Railway Co. Ltd.
Steam railway between Aviemore and Boat of Garten. Special Osprey Tours.
Aviemore Speyside Station, Dalfaber Road, Aviemore
☎ 0479 810725

Theatres

Waltzing Waters
Aqua theatre with a 50-minute show.
Balavil Brae, Newtonmore
☎ 0540 673752

OUTDOOR LEISURE/SPORTS

Birdwatching

Loch Garten Ospreys
RSPB viewing hide and visitor centre. Open late April to late August.
Follow AA signs
☎ 0479 83694

Cycling

Inverdruie Mountain Bikes
Bikes with 18 gears, snow/mud bikes and road bikes; network of trails; maps and rucksacks provided.
Rothiemurchus Visitor Centre, Inverdruie
☎ 0479 810787

Sports Hire
Over 50 cycles for hire including mountain bikes and tandems.
Rear of Nethybridge Ski School
☎ 047982 333
☎ 047982 418

Fishing

Alvie Estate
Fishing on Rivers Spey, Feshie, Dulnain and Feithlinn. Boat fishing on Loch Insh and Loch Alvie. Ghillie assistance if required.
Estate Office, Kincraig
☎ 0540 651255
☎ 0540 651249

Grampian View
Fishing arranged on rivers or lochs. Ghillie available.
☎ 0540 651383

Osprey Fishing School
Fly fishing courses, fishing holidays and tackle hire.
Aviemore
☎ 0479 810132
☎ 0479 810911

Skiing

Cairngorm is the premier ski area in the country with a high standard of ski instruction.

Aviemore Ski School
Cairdsport, Aviemore Centre
☎ 0479 810310

Highland Guides
Nordic and cross-country skiing centre including guide service for wildlife, mountain climbing and historical tours.
Inverdruie, Aviemore
☎ 0479 810729

Walking

Ossian Guides
Professional trekking and tour guide.
Sanna, Newtonmore
☎ 0540 673402

DORNOCH

WHAT TO DO AND SEE

i The Square, Dornoch, Sutherland
☎ 0862 810400

EQUESTRIAN

Riding and Pony Trekking

East Sutherland Riding Centre
Culmaily Farm, Golspie
☎ 04084 254

East Sutherland Riding Centre
Skelbo Farm
By Dornoch
☎ 0408 633045

Invershin Trekking Centre
The Bungalow, Invershin
☎ 054982 296

HEALTH

Leisure Centres

Sutherland Swimming Pool
Golspie
☎ 0408 633437

LOCAL FEATURES

Architecture

Croick Church
Parliamentary church built by Thomas
Telford in 1827, associated with the
Highland Clearances.
12 miles from Ardgay

Dornoch Cathedral
Fine examples of 13th century ecclesiastical
architecture; former cathedral of the
Bishops of Caithness.

Art Galleries

Dorothy Dick Gallery
Exhibitions of sculpture, paintings and
prints.
47 The Village, Scourie
☎ 0971 2013

Arts and Crafts

Dornoch Craft Centre
Tartan manufacturers and craft retailers.
Old Town Jail, Dornoch
☎ 0862 810555
✗

Sutherland Wool Mills
Manufacturers of tweeds, rugs, scarves,
knitting and weaving yarns.
Brora
☎ 0408 21366

Factory Visits

Clynelish Highland Malt Whisky
Distillery Tours.
Brora
☎ 0408 21444
P 🚌

Historic Buildings

Dunrobin Castle and Gardens
The most northerly of Scotland's great
houses and one of the largest with 189
rooms. Opulent collection of furniture,
paintings, objets d'art and family
memorabilia.
Golspie
☎ 0408 633177
On the A9 just north of Golspie village
✗

Museums

Timespan
Highland heritage centre with scenes
recreated from the past; herb garden,
salmon leap, shops.
Helmsdale
☎ 04312 327
➔A A9
P 🗑

Natural History

Highland and Rare Breeds Farm
Traditional breeds of Scottish farm animals,
pets corner.
Knockan, Elphin
☎ 085 486 204
Between Inverpolly Nature Reserve and
Ledmore junction
🚌 🗑

OUTDOOR LEISURE/SPORTS

Birdwatching and Wildlife

Loch Fleet
Salt-water basin, the winter quarters of
countless migratory birds. Summer
breeding area for eider duck, shelduck,
waders, fulmars and petrels.
Scottish Wildlife Trust/Nature Conservancy
Reserve
4 miles north of Dornoch

Cycling

Inverhouse Sports
Road and mountain bikes for hire. Round
trip routes through stunning scenery.
Culrain, Ardgay
☎ 054982 213

Fishing

With over 2000 Lochs and lochans,
Caithness and Sutherland is the foremost
fishing area in the UK for freshwater
recreational fishing; brown trout, salmon,
sea trout and char.
  Coastal waters teem with cod, haddock,
whiting, conger eel, plaice, skate, turbot,
halibut and mackerel. Boats can be hired in
Embo and Golspie.
i Further information from the Tourist
Information Centre.

GWENT

i The Gatehouse, High Street, Chepstow, Gwent
☎ 02912 3772 summer only
i Newport Museum and Art Gallery, John Frost Square, Newport, Gwent
☎ 0633 842962
i Abbey Entrance, Tintern Abbey, Gwent
☎ 0291 689431 summer only

ADVENTURE

Mountaineering and Rock Climbing

Wyedean Adventure Days
Canoeing, caving, rock climbing, abseiling, orienteering and terrain biking on a daily basis for all ages.
11 The Barracks, Parkend, Lydney, Gloucs
☎ 0594 564154
→A A466

AERIAL SPORTS

Ballooning

Ynys Hywel Countryside Centre
Cwmfekinfach, Cross Keys, Gwent
☎ 0495 200113
→A A4048

EQUESTRIAN

Riding and Pony Trekking

Beacon Stables
Spring Vale, Pen-y-Fan, The Narth, Monmouth
☎ 0600 860404

HEALTH

Leisure Centres

Chepstow Leisure Centre
Pool, fitness room, sauna and solarium.
Crossways Green
☎ 0291 23832

LOCAL FEATURES

Arts and Crafts

Stuart Crystal Craft Centre
Bridge Street, Chepstow
☎ 0291 270135
Town centre
P ⅋

Festivals and Fairs

August
Chepstow Agricultural Show

Food and Drink

Caldicot Castle
Mediaeval banquets are held throughout the year in the candlelit Great Hall with traditional entertainment (book in advance). Set in a wooded country park there are picnic areas and an adventure playground.
Nr Newport
☎ 0291 421425
On the A48 Chepstow to Newport road signposted to Caldicot

Historic Buildings

Caldicot Castle and Country Park
Built during the 12th to 14th centuries, the fortress was restored in the 19th century and contains local history, craft and furniture displays.
Nr Newport
☎ 0291 421425
On the A48 Chepstow to Newport road signposted to Caldicot

Chepstow Castle
Overlooking the River Wye, the ruins dominate the town.
Chepstow town centre

Tredegar House and Country Park
A 17th century mansion set in magnificent parkland with craft workshops, carriage rides, boating, fishing and donkey rides.
Newport
☎ 0633 815880
Off the A48, signposted from the M4, jct 28
P ⅋ ⊞ ✕ ⅋ ⅋

Tintern Abbey
The abbey was built on a bend in the River Wye by the Cistercian order in 1311. It is one of the most beautiful and architecturally important ruins in Britain.
☎ 0291 689251
→A A466
P ⅋ ⅋

GWENT

Museums

Clearwell Caves Mining Museum
Guided tours of ancient iron mines and
caving trips available by appointment.
Coleford
☎ 0594 32535
East of Monmouth

Newport Museum and Art Gallery
Fine permanent displays, including over
300 teapots.
John Frost Square, Newport
☎ 0633 840064
Town centre

Railways

Dean Forest Railway
Static display, steam train rides in the
summer, riverside walk and picnic areas.
Norchard Steam Centre, Lydney
☎ 0594 843423
Off the A48 at Lydney
P

OUTDOOR LEISURE/SPORTS

Fishing

Good fishing is available in the Wye and
Usk rivers as well as in the Wentwood
Reservoir, Llandegfedd Reservoir and
Monmouthsire/Brecon Canal, information is
available from local fishing tackle shops.

Horse Racing

Chepstow Racecourse
Flat and national hunt racing are held
throughout the year, this course is the
home of the Welsh Grand National.
☎ 0291 622260
Between Chepstow and the village of St
Arvans

Skiing

Gwent Grass Ski Centre
Dry slope skiing on grass.
Usk
☎ 02913 2652

Walking

Offa's Dyke
Path along the Saxon Offa's Dyke, on the
English side of the River Wye. The path
(168 miles/270 km) follows the English
Welsh border from Chepstow to Prestatyn.

Wye Valley Walk
Another waymarked path, it begins at
Chepstow Castle and provides fine views of
the area.

Dean Heritage Museum Trust
Attractively located heritage information
centre, it includes many interesting
features: reconstructed cottage and mine;
archaeology and woodcraft exhibits; nature
trails; a waterwheel; a craft centre, barbecue
and picnic area and an adventure
playground.
Soudley, nr Cinderford
☎ 0594 22170
⇥A A48

The Forestry Commission
Marked trails in the woods above the River
Wye, in the Forest of Dean and the
Wentwood Forest. Superb scenic viewpoints
at the Wyndclyff, along the Wye Valley, at
the reservoir and Grey Hill, Wentwood and
at Symonds Yat further up the Wye.

GWYNEDD/DYFED

i The Wharf, Aberdovey, Gwynedd
☎ 0654 72321 (summer only)
i Terrace Road, Aberystwyth, Dyfed
☎ 0970 612125
☎ 0970 611955

EQUESTRIAN

Riding and Pony Trekking
Moelfryn Riding Centre
Bethania, nr Aberystwyth
☎ 09746 228

HEALTH

Leisure Centres
Borth Health Club
A five-station multi-gym, exercise bicycles, jogging machine, weights, sunbed, sauna, swimming pool, and jacuzzi.
Cliff Haven Hotel
☎ 0970 871 659

LOCAL FEATURES

Arts and Crafts
Aberystwyth Arts Centre
The main venue for the visual arts and crafts in Mid-Wales with live performances of music and theatre and a spectacular summer season.
☎ 0970 623232

Felin Crewi Working Watermill
Traditionally milled flour using water power, homebaked food served in the cafe.
Felin Crewi, Penegoes, Machynlleth, Powys
☎ 0654 3113
→A A489
P ✕

Tregaron Pottery
Hand thrown and decorated stoneware pottery.
Castell Flemish, Tregaron
☎ 097421 639
→A A485

Factory Visits
Llywernog Silver-Lead Mine
Follow the miner's trail in the only fully restored metal mine in Wales.
☎ 0970 85 620
On the A44, 11 miles from Aberystwyth
P 🗗 ✕

Museums
Centre for Alternative Technology
A village of the future with solar panels, windmills and waterwheels in use, insulation display, steam engines and crafts.
Machynlleth
☎ 0654 2400
Off the A487, 3 miles from Machynlleth

Ceredigion Museum
The story of Cardigan told in a restored Edwardian Theatre.
Terrace Road, Aberystwyth
☎ 0970 617911
🗗

The Great Aberystwyth Camera Obscura
A re-creation of a Victorian amusement on the summit of Constitution Hill, access by the Cliff Railway.
Aberystwyth
☎ 0970 617642
🗗

National Library of Wales
The main centre for research into the history, literature and life of Wales; it holds collections of valuable manuscripts and books.
Penglais Road, Aberystwyth
☎ 0970 623816
🗗

Railways
Aberystwyth Electric Cliff Railway
A conveyance for gentlefolk since 1896, it offers a sedate journey to the summit of Constitution Hill.
Cliff Railway House, Cliff Terrace, Aberystwyth
☎ 0970 617642
From the north end of the promenade

Tallylyn Railway
See the beautiful Welsh countryside from a steam locomotive.
Timetables available on request.
Wharf Station, Tywyn
☎ 0654 710472

Vale of Rheidol Narrow Gauge Steam Railway
It runs from Aberystwyth 12 miles to Devil's Bridge; explore the Rheidol Falls, climb Jacob's ladder and view the Devil's Punchbowl.
☎ 0685 4854 for the timetable

OUTDOOR LEISURE/SPORTS

Birdwatching and Wildlife
Ynys-Hir Reserve (RSPB)
A wide range of habitats, salt and freshwater marsh, reed bed, peat bog, woodland and open hillside on the south side of the Dyfi estuary; 67 species of bird and 26 species of butterfly breed here.
Eglwysfach village
☎ 0654 781265 Warden
On the A487, 6 miles south of Machynlleth
🗗 🚌

WHAT TO DO AND SEE

Fishing

This is a major fishing area.
i Pamphlets on freshwater angling with lists of clubs and associations and lists of boat operators for sea angling trips are available at Tourist Information Centres.
☎ 0970 612125

Walking

i Walk packs with maps and detailed guidance on the Rheidol Valley and the Teifi Valley are available at Tourist Information Centres and shops.

WATERSPORTS

Canoeing

Canoe excursions up the River Teifi depart daily from the foot of Cilgerran Castle.
☎ 0239 613966

Sailing

Aqua Sports
Andy Coghill, 17 Sea View Terrace, Aberdovey
☎ 0654 767754

Talyllyn Watersports
Tywyn
☎ 0654 710065

Smugglers Cove Sailing School
Cruiser and dinghy sailing.
Frongoch, Aberdovey
☎ 0654 767842

Sand Yachting

Borth Sand Yachting Club
Geth Evans, Geth's Boatshop, Borth
☎ 0970 871427

Surfing

Peter Hunt Watersports
High Street, Borth
☎ 0970 81617

Windsurfing

Splash Windsurfing
West Wales Marine, Penrhos
☎ 0654 767842

GWYNEDD/DYFED

i Conwy Castle Visitor Centre, Conwy,
   Gwynedd
☎ 0492 592248 summer only
i Marine Square, Salt Island Approach,
   Holyhead, Gwynedd
☎ 0407 2622
i Chapel Street, Llandudno, Gwynedd
☎ 0492 76413

ADVENTURE

Mountaineering and Rock Climbing

Franco Ferrero
High quality courses for small groups
including canoeing, mountain walking and
rock climbing.
3 Tan-y-Bwlch, Mynedd Llandegai, Bethesda
☎ 0248 602287

National Centre for Mountain Activities
Centre operated by the Sports Council to
provide mountain activities for beginners
and experts.
Plas-y-Brenin, Capel Curig
☎ 06904 214

Shooting

Plas Newydd Shoot
Driven or rough shooting on Anglesey's
famous estate.
c/o Liverpool Arms Hotel, Menai Bridge,
Isle of Anglesey
☎ 0248 713335

EQUESTRIAN

Riding and Pony Trekking

Bodysgallen Riding Holiday Centre
Bodysgallen Farm, Llandudno
☎ 0492 83537

Pinewood Riding Stables
Sychnant Pass Road, Conwy
☎ 0492 592256

Rhiwiau Riding Centre
Llanfairfechan, Gwynedd
☎ 0248 680094

LOCAL FEATURES

Aquariums

Anglesey Sea Zoo
Huge and varied collection of sea life
around the island displayed in natural
environments.
The Oyster Hatchery, Brynsiencyn, Anglesey
☎ 0248 430411
→A A5
& &

Arts and Crafts

Conwy Pottery
Hand decorated pottery in porcelain and
stoneware.
Tyn-y-Coed Farm, Glan Conwy, Colwyn Bay
→A A470

Gardens

Bodnant Garden
A fine garden with magnificent
rhododendrons, camellias, magnolias and
conifers.
Tal-y-Cafn
☎ 0492 650460
Off the A470, 8 miles south of Llandudno
P 🏠 &

Historic Buildings

Bodelwyddan Castle
A magnificent collection of portraits from
the National Portrait Gallery in a stately
home setting; a walled garden, a maze, an
adventure wood and an aviary.
Bodelwyddan, Clwyd
☎ 0745 584069
🏠

195

WHAT TO DO AND SEE

Conwy Castle
An impressive fortress built by Edward I
700 years ago.
Conwy

Penrhyn Castle
A majestic mock Norman castle in wooded
parkland overlooking the Menai Strait;
lavishly decorated inside with a collection of
dolls and steam engine museum. National
Trust.
Bangor
☎ 0248 353084
On the A5122, 3 miles east of Bangor
P 🏠 ✕ 🚻 ♿

Plas Newydd
The 18th century house of James Wyatt, it
occupies an unspoilt position adjacent to
the Menai Strait.
Isle of Anglesey
☎ 0248 714795
On the A4080, south of Llanfairpwll
P 🏠 ✕ 🚻 ♿

Natural History

Conwy Butterfly House
Butterflies flying free.
Bodlondeb Gardens, Conwy
☎ 0492 593149
Close to the quay and the town centre

Parks

Great Orme Country Park
Massive limestone headland that rises
679 feet to dominate Llandudno; guided
walks and field trips.
Country Park Warden
☎ 0492 74151

Padarn Country Park
Ride on a quaint little Lake Railway Steam
Train along the shores of Padarn Lake or

stop awhile and view Snowdon; visit the
Welsh Slate Museum, deserted village and
old slate quarry or explore the nature trails
and woodland walks.
Llanberis
➔A A4086

Zoos

Welsh Mountain Zoo and Gardens
Sea lion feeding, jungle adventureland and
chimpanzee world.
Old Highway, Colwyn Bay
☎ 0492 532938
🎁

OUTDOOR LEISURE/SPORTS

Fishing

Starida
Sea angler skipper of great experience will
arrange sea fishing trips of any duration or
cruises to Puffin Island aboard the *Starida*
which is based in Beaumaris.
☎ 0248 810251

Skiing

Ski Llandudno
The longest artificial ski slope in England
and Wales. At the end of the promenade,
through Happy Valley.
Llandudno
☎ 0492 74707

The Rhiw Goch Ski Centre
Skiing tuition and facilities.
Trawsfynydd Log Cabin Holiday Village,
Bronaber, Trawsfynydd
☎ 0766 87578

WATERSPORTS

Canoeing

Conwy Canoe Tours
Explore the Conwy Estuary by Canadian
canoe, no experience necessary.
36 Bryn Castell, Conwy
☎ 0492 596457

Diving

Anglesey Sea and Surf Centre
A new coastal centre offering courses in
canoeing, sailing and diving.
Porthdafarch, Trearddur Bay, Anglesey
☎ 0407 2525

Sailing

Plas Menai National Watersports Centre
Yacht cruising and dinghy sailing.
Caernarfon, Gwynedd
☎ 0248 670964

Windsurfing

Surfwind Rhosneigr
Beach Road, Rhosneigr, Anglesey
☎ 0407 720391

DYFED

i Old Bridge, Haverfordwest
☎ 0437 763110
i Drill Hall, Pembroke
☎ 0646 682148
i The Croft, Tenby
☎ 0834 2402

EQUESTRIAN

Riding

Haysford Stud Farm
Specialising in instruction of nervous riders.
Haycastle Road, Haverfordwest
☎ 0437 710512
Mainport Training
All forms of riding instruction.
The Mainport Centre, Ferry Lane, Pembroke
☎ 0646 684315

HEALTH

Leisure centres

Haverfordwest Sports Centre
Queensway, Haverfordwest
☎ 0437 710512
Pembroke Leisure Centre
Pembroke Road, Bush
☎ 0646 684434

LOCAL FEATURES

Art and crafts

Graham Sutherland Gallery
A unique collection of Sutherland's works.
Picton Castle, Rhos
☎ 0437 751296
P ☍ ▥ ✕ ♿ ⚤

Gardens

Manor House Wildlife and Leisure Park
Parkland with floral displays and varied
collection of animals and birds.
St. Florence
☎ 0646 651201
P ☍ ✕ ♿ ⚤

Picton Castle Grounds
Natural woodlands surrounding country
home owned by the same family for around
600 years.
Picton Castle, Rhos
☎ 0437 751326
P ☍ ✕ ♿

Historic Houses

Pembroke Castle
13th century castle dominating the town
Castle Terrace.
☎ 0646 681510
P ☍ ▥ ✕ ♿ ⚤

Tudor Merchant's House
National Trust
Preserved house showing how the rich
merchants lived in medieval times.
Quay Hill, Tenby
☎ 0834 2279
☍

Museums

Castle Museum and Art Gallery
Displays of Haverfordwest's history present
in the old Gaol alongside the ruins of the
Castle.
☎ 0437 763708
P ☍

Motor Museum and Leisure Park
Over 60 exhibits covering the history of
transport.
Keeston Hill, Haverfordwest
➜ A487 3 miles from Haverfordwest
☎ 0437 710175
P ☍ ✕ ♿

Museum of the Home
Dedicated to showing the minutia of
everyday home life over the last 300 years.
Westgate Hill, Pembroke
☎ 0646 681200
☍

Tenby Museum
The museum presents the story of Tenby
and the picture gallery includes works by
Augustus John, who was born in Tenby.
Castle Hill, Tenby
☎ 0834 2809
☍

Natural History

Sea Historic Gallery
Aquarium and geological display.
Westgate Hill, Pembroke
☎ 0646 682919
☍

Silent World Aquarium
A collection of the area's water creatures
with an emphasis on children.
Mayfield Drive, Narberth Road, Tenby
☎ 0834 449
☍ ♿ ⚤

OUTDOOR LEISURE/SPORTS

Cycling

The Skate and Bike Centre
South Parade, Tenby
☎ 0834 5134

Fishing

Excellent fishing, particularly sea fishing.
County Sports
3 Old Bridge Street, Haverfordwest
☎ 0437 763740
Penfro Fishing Tackle
31 Meyrick Street, Pembroke Dock
☎ 0646 682756
The Tackle Box
Willings Passage, Main Street, Pembroke
☎ 0646 621744

WEST GLAMORGAN

WHAT TO DO AND SEE

i Singleton Street, Swansea
☎ 0792 468321
i Oystermouth Square, Mumbles, Gower
Peninsular
☎ 0792 468321

ADVENTURE

Activity holidays

Clyne Farm Activity Centre
Residential activity holidays for the family.
Clyne Farm, Mayais
☎ 0792 403333

EQUESTRIAN

Horse riding

Clyne Farm Riding School
Tuition from novice to experienced.
Clyne Farm, Mayais
☎ 0792 403333

Forgemill Riding Academy
Cilonnen, Three Crosses, Gower
☎ 0792 873760

LOCAL FEATURES

Arts and craft

Castle Galleries
26 Walter Street
☎ 0792 648377
P ✍ ♿

Glynn Vivian Art Gallery
Painting and local crafts and china.
Alexandra Street
☎ 0792 651738
✍ ♿ ♿

Swansea Arts Workshop
Gloucester Place
☎ 0792 652016
✍

Gardens

Clyne Gardens
Famous for azaleas and rhododendrons
South of Swansea going towards Mumbles.
Blackpill
☎ 0792 401737
P ✍ 🚌

Ravenhill Park
Fforestfach
☎ 0792 586670
P 🚌

Historic buildings

Neath Abbey
Ruins of 12th century monastery.
Neath, 5 miles north east of Swansea
☎ 0792 812387
P ✍ 🚌 ✕ ♿

Museums

Maritime and Industrial Museum
Part of the new docks refurbishment this
museum tells the story of Swansea's long
association with the sea.
Maritime Quarter
☎ 0792 650351
✍ ♿

Swansea Museum
Wales's first museum with a broad range of
exhibits in beautiful surroundings.
Victoria Road
☎ 0792 653763
P 🍴

Natural history

Aberdulais Falls
National Trust
Waterfalls in colourful gorge; remains of
tinplate works powered by the falls.
➔A Off A456 just north east of Neath
☎ 0639 636674
🍴 ✕

Penscynor Wildlife Park
Wide range of animals and birds in parkland
setting.
➔A Off the A456 close to the Aberdulais Falls
☎ 0639 642189
P 🍴 🚌 ✕ ♿ ♿

Swansea Plantasia
Huge hothouse containing thousands of
plants from around the world.
Plantasia Parc, North Dock
☎ 0792 474555
P 🍴 🚌 ♿ ♿

Theatres

Dylan Thomas Theatre
Gloucester Place
☎ 0792 473238

OUTDOOR LEISURE/SPORT

Fishing

Coarse river fishing and sea fishing.
Capstan House
Beaufort Court, Beaufort Road
☎ 0792 310311

Linnard Sports
25 High Street
☎ 0792 655631

Skiing

Swansea Ski Centre
Morfa Statium, Upper Bank, Landore
☎ 0792 476578

WATERSPORTS

Boat Hire

Inshore Workboat Hire
Old Customs House, West Pier, Maritime
Quarter
☎ 0792 642608

Swansea Harbour Boatmen
Kings Dock
☎ 0792 653787

POWYS

i Vicarage Gardens Car Park, Welshpool
☎ 0938 552043

EQUESTRIAN

Riding

Penycoed Riding Stables
A complete range of riding instruction.
Llynclys Hill, Llanymynech
On the A483 10 miles north of Welshpool
☎ 0691 830608

HEALTH

Leisure centre

Armoury Leisure Centre
Brook Street, Welshpool
☎ 0938 554143

LOCAL FEATURES

Art and crafts

Oriel 31 Art Gallery
High Street, Welshpool
☎ 0938 552990
P 🏠🚌✕♿

Festivals and fairs

May
Montgomery County Agricultural Fair
P 🏠🚌✕♿

Gardens

Powis Castle Gardens
Parkland with formal gardens which were
created in the 17th century.
Immediately south west of Welshpool town
centre
☎ 0938 554336
P 🏠✕♿♿

Historic houses

Montgomery Castle
A ruined shell but still impressive.
Montgomery, on the A490 10 miles south of
Welshpool

Powis Castle
One of the most magnificent mansions in
the country with fine displays of furniture
and paintings.
A one mile walk through Powis Castle
Gardens from Welshpool town centre.
☎ 0938 554336
P 🏠✕♿♿

Welshpool Railway Station
Well worth a look, an ornate 19th century.
structure
P

Museums

Clive Museum
Museum within Powis Castle dedicated to
relics of Clive of India.
Powis Castle
☎ 0938 554336
P 🏠✕♿

Powysland Museum and Montgomery Canal
Centre
Local history and industrial archeology.
Canal Wharf, off Severn Street, Welshpool
☎ 0938 554656
P 🚲🚌♿

Natural History

Llanfyllin Bird and Butterfly World
Species from all over the world contained in
50 aviaries.
Domgay, Bachin Road, Llanfyllin
Off the A490 10 miles north west of
Welshpool
☎ 069 184 751
P 🏠✕

Moors Collection
Farm animals and rare breeds.
On the A438 Oswestry road 1 mile north of
Welshpool
☎ 0938 553395
P 🏠♿♿

Railway

Welshpool and Llanfair Light Railway
One of the 'Great Little Trains of Wales'
running 8 miles and linking Welshpool in
the Severn valley to Llanfair.
Caereinion in the Banwyn valley
☎ 0938 810441
P 🏠✕♿

OUTDOOR LEISURE/SPORT

Cycling

G.M. Brooks
9 Severn Street, Welshpool
☎ 0938 553582

Fishing

Local fishing is available including on the
Severn, for information on accessibility of
waters and for tackle go to:
Brians Angling Supplies
North Road, Llanymynech
On the A438 10 miles north of Welshpool
☎ 0691 830027

COUNTY DOWN/BELFAST

WHAT TO DO AND SEE

i 59 North Street, Belfast
☎ 0232 246609
i Down Leisure Centre, Market Street, Downpatrick, County Down
☎ 0396 613426
i Arts Centre, Bank Parade, Newry, County Down
☎ 0693 66232

Maysfield Leisure Centre
Swimming pool, sauna, solarium, squash courts, gym.
East Bridge Street, Belfast
☎ 0232 241633

Tropicana
Pools, giant inflatables, water slides, springing animals, elephant slide and deck chair patios.
Newcastle Centre, Central Promenade
☎ 039 67 22222

ADVENTURE

Mountaineering and Rock Climbing
Mountain Centre
Situated in Tollymore Forest Park; training in canoeing, mountaineering and adventure activities.
Bryansford, Newcastle
☎ 039 67 22158

EQUESTRIAN

Riding and Pony Trekking
Castlewellan Riding Centre
Drumee Road, Castlewellan
☎ 039 67 71497

Easthope Equestrian Centre
71 Killynure Road West, Carryduff, Belfast
☎ 0232 813186

Lagan Valley Equestrian Centre
Longhurst, 172 Upper Malone Road, Belfast
☎ 0232 614853

Mourne Trail Riding Centre
96 Castlewellan Road, Newcastle
☎ 039 67 24351

HEALTH

Leisure Centres
Down Leisure Centre
Swimming, sauna, squash courts, conditioning room, aerobics classes and keep-fit.
114 Market Street, Downpatrick
☎ 0396 613426
☎ 0396 613427

LOCAL FEATURES

Aquarium
Northern Ireland Aquarium
Featuring about 70 marine species found in Strangford Lough; models of seabed.
Rope Walk, Portaferry
☎ 024 77 28062
🐚 ✗

Archaeology
Nendrum Monastic Site
The remains of a pre-Norman monastery include 3 concentric enclosures and a ruined church round tower stump.
Mahee Island, Comber
Off the A22 and lough shore road
🐚

Architecture
Inch Abbey
Ruins of Cistercian monastery on an island in Quoile marshes, reached by a causeway.
Off the A7, 1 mile north-west of Downpatrick
🐚

Art Galleries
Arts Council Gallery
Contemporary art.
16 Bedford Street, Belfast
☎ 0232 321402

Bell Gallery
Irish artists.
13 Adelaide Park, Belfast
☎ 0232 662998

Tom Caldwell Gallery
Living Irish artists.
40–42 Bradbury Place, Belfast
☎ 0232 323226

WHAT TO DO AND SEE

Gardens

Botanic Gardens, Palm House and Tropical Ravine
Coffee, banana and cotton plants grow in this splendid curvilinear glass and cast-iron conservatory.
Belfast Botanic Gardens, Belfast
☎ 0232 324902

Dixon Park
Magnificent rose display all summer; host to the City of Belfast International Rose Trials.
Upper Malone Road, Belfast
☎ 0232 320202
P

Rowallane Gardens
Magnificent rhododendrons and azaleas, rare trees, shrubs and plants. National Trust.
Saintfield, Ballynahinch
On the A7, 1 mile south of Saintfield
☎ 0238 510131

Guided Tours

Belfast City Tours
3½ hour tours including the shipyards, Stormont and Belfast Castle.
Buses leave Castle Place
☎ 0232 246485

Around the Province
Ulsterbus runs day and ½ day tours to the Glens of Antrim, Antrim Coast, Giant's Causeway, Fermanagh Lakeland, Lough Neagh, Tyrone, Mournes, Ards Peninsula and Armagh.
☎ 0232 320011

Historic Buildings

Annalong Corn Mill
Powered by a waterwheel, the mill overlooks the harbour.
Marine Park, Annalong
☎ 039 67 68736

Castle Ward
Unique 18th century house with facades in different styles set in a 700-acre country estate with woodland, lake and seashore. Victorian laundry; formal and landscaped gardens; corn and saw mills, wildfowl.
Strangford, County Down
☎ 039 686 204
On the A25, 1 mile west of Strangford village
P

Dundonald Old Mill
18th century cornmill with a huge waterwheel.
231 Belfast Road, Quarry Corner, Dundonald, Belfast
☎ 0232 480117

Dundrum Castle
Built by John de Courcy in about 1177, later occupied by the Magennises.
Access from centre of Dundrum village.

Malone House
Early 19th century house set in beautiful parkland.
Barnett Park, Upper Malone Road, Belfast
☎ 0232 681246

Mount Stewart House and Gardens
The boyhood home of Lord Castlereagh, a fascinating 18th century house with one of the greatest gardens in Europe. The Temple of the Winds overlooks Strangford Lough. National Trust.
Newtownards
☎ 024 774 387
On the A20, 5 miles south-east of Newtownards
P

Museums

Down County Museum
Stone Age artefacts and Bronze Age gold found locally are displayed in this former jail.
The Mall, Downpatrick
☎ 0396 615218

Newry Museum
History of the 'Gap of the North'; archaeological items, touring exhibitions.
Arts Centre, Bank Parade, Newry
☎ 0693 66232

Transport Museum
Over 200 years of Irish transport; locomotives, street trams and road vehicles.
Witham Street, Belfast
☎ 0232 451519

Ulster Museum and Art Gallery
Noted for its Irish antiquities and art collection.
Botanic Gardens, Belfast
☎ 0232 381251

Natural History

Butterfly House
Over 30 species of butterfly.
Seaforde Nursery, Seaforde
☎ 039 687 225
On the A24

Streamvale Open Dairy Farm
Watch the milking from a viewing gallery or bottle feed a lamb. Pet's corner, nature trail, donkey rides.

WHAT TO DO AND SEE

38 Ballyhanwood Road, nr Dundonald Ice
Bowl, Belfast
☎ 0232 483244

Parks

Castlewellan Forest Park
The national arboretum, begun in 1740, is
an outstanding feature. Tropical birds in the
glasshouse; lake stocked with trout.
Off the A25 on Bannanstown Road
☎ 039 67 78664

Lagan Valley Regional Park
10 miles of towpath along the banks of the
Lagan River.
Starts near Belfast Boat Club on Loughview
Road, Stranmillis and ends upstream from
Moore's Bridge, Hillsborough Road, Lisburn
☎ 0232 491922

Tollymore Forest Park
Stone follies and bridges, Himalayan cedars
and a 100ft sequoia tree in the arboretum.
Wildlife and forestry exhibits; pony trekking;
fishing; walks in the foothills of the
Mournes. (see Mountain Centre)
☎ 039 67 22428
Off the B180 on Tullybrannigan Road

Theatres

Grand Opera House
Varied programme from opera to
pantomime.
Great Victoria Street, Belfast
☎ 0232 241919

Zoos

Belfast Zoo
In a picturesque mountain park overlooking
the city. See the spectacled bear, the only
one in the UK.
Antrim Road, Belfast
☎ 0232 776277
Off Antrim Road, 5 miles north of Belfast

OUTDOOR LEISURE/SPORTS

Birdwatching and Wildlife

Murlough National Nature Reserve
Sand dune system: heath and woodland
surrounded by estuary and sea; guided
walks.
On the A24, 2 miles south of Dundrum
☎ 039 675 467

Quoile Pondage National Nature Reserve
Guided walks, trails and lectures.
Off the A25 north of Downpatrick
☎ 0396 615520

Strangford Lough
The largest sea inlet in the British Isles
with 120 islands and a narrow sea channel
opening out to inner stretches of calm
water; one of the richest places for
estuarial wildlife in Europe. Leaflet and
map available from the Tourist Information
Centre.

Cycling

i Cycling routes are available from the
Tourist Information Centre, including a
51-mile route around the Ards Peninsula
and a route from Belfast to the Mournes.
Cycle hire from:

Bikeit
Mountain bikes.
4 Belmont Road, Belfast
☎ 0232 471141

McConvey Cycles
Mountain and touring bikes.
476 Ormeau Road, Belfast
and Unit 10, Pottinger's Entry, Belfast
☎ 0232 330322

Ross Cycles
44 Clarkhill Road, Castlewellan
☎ 039 67 78029

Fishing

The heart of Down is 'drumlin country',
with over 100 small lakes where, in addition
to a rod licence, you may only require the
farmer's or local angling club's permission
to fish. Game fishing in lakes and rivers is
controlled by the Dept of Agriculture. Game
fishing is good in Upper Bann River,
Shimna River in Tollymore Forest Park,
Castlewellan Lake, Ballykeel Lougherne,
Spelga Dam and Fofanny Dam.
  Sea fishing is good in Strangford Lough
and along the Mourne Coast.
  Good coarse fishing in the River Quoile
and many lakes. Detailed fishing leaflets are
available from the Tourist Information
Centre.

Walking

Mourne Countryside Centre
Guided walks.
91 Central Promenade, Newcastle
☎ 039 67 24059

The Ulster Way
A challenging long distance walking route
which encircles the province.
Walks include Lagan Valley walks, Belfast
and Cave Hill, the North Antrim coast and
the Mourne Trail.
i Route guides are available from the
local Tourist Information Centres.

COUNTY ARMAGH

i Town Hall, 6 Union Street, Lurgan,
County Armagh

ADVENTURE

Multi-activity Holiday Centres

Waterside House
Outdoor Recreation Officer, Civic Centre,
PO Box 66, Lakeview Road, Craigavon
☎ 0762 341199

EQUESTRIAN

Riding and Pony Trekking

Richhill Riding Centre
38 Annareagh Road, Richhill
☎ 0762 871258

HEALTH

Leisure Centres

Craigavon Leisure Centre
Sauna, sunbeds and a swimming pool.
Brownlow Road, Craigavon
☎ 0762 341333

LOCAL FEATURES

Historic Buildings

Ardress House
A 17th century house, farmyard, gardens
and a woodland walk. National Trust.
Annaghmore
☎ 0762 851236
On the B28, 7 miles west of Portadown

The Argory
Set in 300 acres of wooded countryside, a
neo-classical mansion with a stable yard and
sundial garden. National Trust.
☎ 086 87 84753
Off the B28, 7 miles west of Portadown

Armagh Friary
These are the ruins of the longest friary
church in Ireland (163 feet).
South-east of Armagh city

Killevy Churches
Famous 'back-to-back' churches. An
important early (late 5th century) nunnery.
Off the B113, south-west of Newry

Museums

Armagh County Museum
The Mall East, Armagh
☎ 0861 523070

Mullaghbawn Folk Museum
Small thatched roadside museum.
Mullaghbawn
☎ 0693 888278
On the B30

Natural History

Armagh Planetarium & Observatory
College Hill, Armagh
☎ 0861 523689
☎ 0861 522928

Parks

Gosford Forest Park
Gosford castle, walled garden and nature
trail.
☎ 0861 551277
On the B111 at Markethil

Slieve Gullion Forest Park
Thickly wooded mountain park, woodland
trail, walled garden, visitor centre.
☎ 069 37 38284
☎ 069 384 226
On the B113, 5 miles south-west of Newry

Peatlands Park
Narrow gauge railway, small lakes and peat
faces.
☎ 0762 851102
M1, exit 13, 7 miles east of Dungannon

OUTDOOR LEISURE/SPORTS

Birdwatching and Wildlife

Oxford Island National Nature Reserve
Walks; bird hides; picnic areas; boat trips.
☎ 0762 322205
M1, exit 10

Cycling

The Tourist Information Centre produces a
leaflet with cycle routes and cycle hire
shops.

Fishing

Coarse fishing in the River Bann, Lough
Neagh, Lugan Park Lake, and Clay Lake. The
Tourist Information Centre publish a leaflet.
Game fishing in Craigavon Lakes.

Skiing

Craigavon Ski Centre
Turmoyra Lane, Silverwood, Lurgan
☎ 0762 326606

Walking

Walk the Ulster Way (south section) from
Craigavon.

WATERSPORTS

Windsurfing

Craigavon Watersports Centre
Roundabout 1 off Craigavon centre
☎ 0762 342669
☎ 0762 341199

WHAT TO DO AND SEE

i Foyle Street, County Londonderry
☎ 0504 267284

ADVENTURE

Rock Climbing

Roe Valley Country Park
Canoeing, rock climbing and fishing in this country park.
Off the B192, 2 miles south of Limavady
☎ 050 47 22074

AERIAL SPORTS

Parachuting and Parascending

Wild Geese Centre
Train and jump in one day. Fantastic display team.
116 Carrowreagh Road, Garvagh
☎ 026 65 58609

EQUESTRIAN

Riding and Pony Trekking

City of Derry Riding Centre
189 Culmore Road, Londonderry
☎ 0504 351687

Hill Farm Riding and Trekking Centre
47 Altikeeragh Road, Castlerock
☎ 0265 848629

HEALTH

Leisure Centres

Lisnagelvin Leisure Centre
Tropical heat, crystal clear water, foam-topped waves, sauna, solarium and fitness centre.
Londonderry
☎ 0504 47695

Water World
Twin 85-metre covered slides, aquarium, giant frog slide, water cannons, pirate ship, jacuzzis, whirlpool, playpool, giant toadstool umbrella shower: a large fun-filled water leisure complex.
The Harbour, Portrush, County Antrim
☎ 0265 822001
♿

LOCAL FEATURES

Architecture

Banagher Old Church
An impressive ruin; the nave was built about 1100.
On the B74, 2 miles south-west of Dungiven

The Walls of Derry
These famous walls have withstood several sieges, the most celebrated lasted 105 days. Fine views from the top of the walls which encircle the old city.

COUNTY LONDONDERRY

WHAT TO DO AND SEE

Art Galleries

Gordon Gallery
Irish artists.
Ferryquay Street, Londonderry
☎ 0504 266261

Orchard Gallery
Centre for the visual arts.
Orchard Street, Londonderry
☎ 0504 269675

Arts and Crafts

Crafts Village
Shipquay Street, Londonderry
☎ 0504 268402

Festivals and Fairs

February
City of Derry Drama Festival
Londonderry Feis (runs into March)
Feis Cholmcille (Easter Week)

Oct/Nov
Foyle Film Festival

Gardens

Wilson Daffodil Garden
Rare collection of Irish-bred daffodils on the University campus.
☎ 0265 44141
On the A2 nr Coleraine Marina

Historic Buildings

Downhill Castle
Ruins of the home of the eccentric Earl–Bishop of Derry; the Mussenden Temple on the cliff top was built in 1783. 1-mile glen walk passes interesting architectural features. National Trust.
Mussenden Road, Castlerock
☎ 0265 848728
A A2

Hezlett House
17th century thatched cottage; the roof has an interesting cruck truss construction.
Liffock, Castlerock
☎ 0265 848567
On the A2 Coleraine to Downhill coast road

Springhill
A 17th century manor house with costume museum; family belongings have been preserved. National Trust.
Moneymore, Magherafelt
☎ 064 87 48210
On the B18, 1 mile from Moneymore
P ✕ ♿ ♿

St. Columb's Cathedral
Stained glass depicts heroic scenes from the great siege of 1688/9; locks and keys of the gates and some interesting relics.
Londonderry
☎ 0504 262746

Museums

Earhart Centre
Cottage exhibition on Amelia Earhart, first woman to fly the Atlantic solo; the famous aviator landed in a field here in 1932.
Ballyarnet Field, Londonderry
☎ 0504 353379
1½ miles from Foyle Bridge

Natural History

Portstewart Strand
Magnificent 2 mile strand and important dune system. National Trust.
West of Portstewart
♿ ♿

Parks

Ness Country Park
Broadleaved woodland walks; path passes the point where the Burntollet River plunges 10 metres over Ulster's highest waterfall. Nature trails.
Off the A6, 7 miles south-east of Londonderry
☎ 050 47 22074

Railways

Foyle Valley Railway Centre
The railway history of Derry; ride on a 1934 diesel railcar on a mile of track.
Foyle Road, Londonderry
☎ 0504 265234
Nr Craigavon Bridge

OUTDOOR LEISURE/SPORTS

Fishing

Sea fishing from boats and the shore is excellent along the north coast.

Some of the best game fishing waters are in the North West; the Finn, the Derg, the Mourne, the Dennet and the Glenelly run into the Foyle. Rod licenses and advice from:

The Foyle Fisheries Commission
8 Victoria Road, Londonderry
☎ 0504 42100

Walking

The Sperrin Mountains offer some fine walking opportunities.

WATERSPORTS

Sailing

Prehen Boathouse
River water sports centre offering sailing, waterskiing, rowing and canoeing.
☎ 0504 43405

FOR YOUR INFORMATION, WE'RE EVERYWHERE

Across the country over 600 Tourist Information Centres are waiting to help you on your quest for the great English holiday.

You've probably got an Information Centre in your local town. Make that your first stop and they'll be happy to help with all kinds of information wherever you're heading, many can even book accommodation in advance and offer free guides and maps.

When you arrive on holiday, check out the Tourist Information Centre there for up-to-date details of current events, nearby attractions and handy local hints on the best pubs, restaurants, shops and more.

Always friendly and ready to help, find your local Tourist Information Centre and be sure of a better English holiday.

Tourist Information *i*

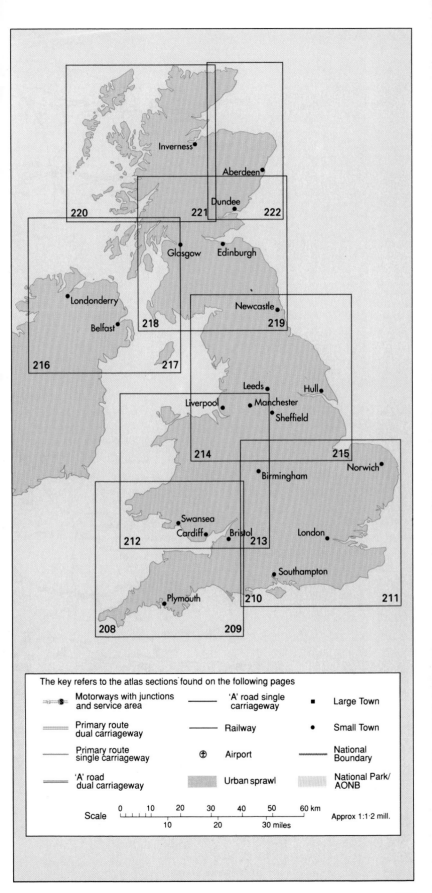

The key refers to the atlas sections found on the following pages

	Motorways with junctions and service area		'A' road single carriageway	■ Large Town
	Primary route dual carriageway		Railway	● Small Town
	Primary route single carriageway	⊕	Airport	National Boundary
	'A' road dual carriageway		Urban sprawl	National Park/ AONB

Scale   0   10   20   30   40   50   60 km
         0   10   20   30 miles

Approx 1:1·2 mill.

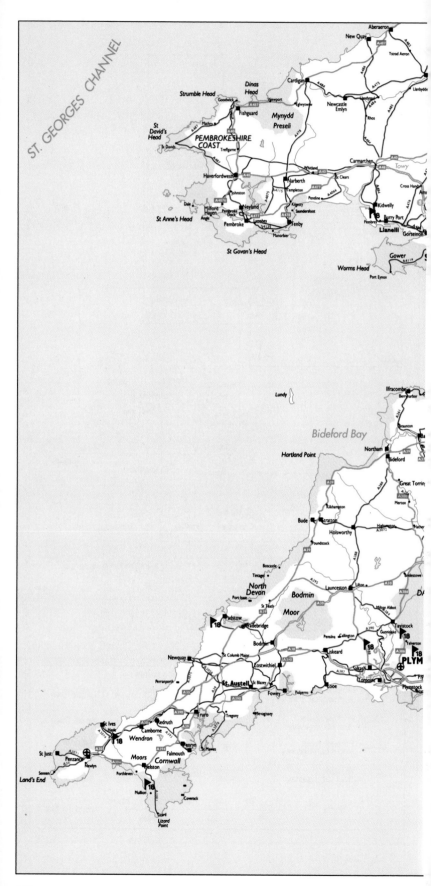

ST. GEORGES CHANNEL

Aberaeron
New Quay
A487
Ystrad Aeron
Llanbydde
A472
A475
Cardigan
Llandysul
Eglwyswrw
A478
Newcastle
Emlyn
Rhos
Strumble Head
Dinas
Head
Goodwick
Newport
Fishguard
St David's
Head
Mathry
PEMBROKESHIRE
COAST
Mynydd
Preseli
A40
Carmarthen
A40
Towy
St Davids
Trefgarne
Whitland
A40
A478
St Clears
Cross Hands
Haverfordwest
A40
Narberth
Templeton
A4066
Johnston
A4075
Kilgetty
Pendine
St Anne's Head
Dale
Milford
Haven
Angle
Pembroke
Dock
A477
Saundersfoot
A4139
Neyland
Lamphey
Tenby
Manorbier
Kidwelly
A484
Pembrey
Burry Port
Llanelli
Gorseinon
Pembroke
St Govan's Head
Gower
Worms Head
Port Eynon

Lundy
Ilfracombe
Berrynarbor
A361
Braunton
Ba
Bideford Bay
Northam
A39
Hartland Point
Bideford
A38
Great Torrin
A386
Merton
Kilkhampton
Bude
Stratton
Holsworthy
A3072
Hather
A39
Poundstock
A388
Boscastle
Highampton
Tintagel
Lilton
Boldestow
North Devon
St Teath
Launceston
A386
DA
Port Isaac
A395
Milton Abbot
Bodmin Moor
A30
Padstow 18
Tavistock 18
Wadebridge
Pensilva Callington
Gunnislake
Yelverton
Bodmin
A30
A390
Liskeard 18
A38
PLYM
Newquay
St Columb Major
A38
Saltash
St Blazey
A390
Lostwithiel
A387
Looe
Pi
Perranporth
A30
St Austell
A390
Fowey
Polperro
Torpoint
Plymstock
Tregony
Mevagissey
St Ives
Redruth
A390
Truro
Hayle
A30
Camborne 18
Wendron
Penryn
St Mawes
St Just
A30
Penzance
Cornwall
Falmouth
Newlyn
Moors
Helston
Sennen
Porthleven
Land's End
Mullion 18
Coverack
Lizard
Point

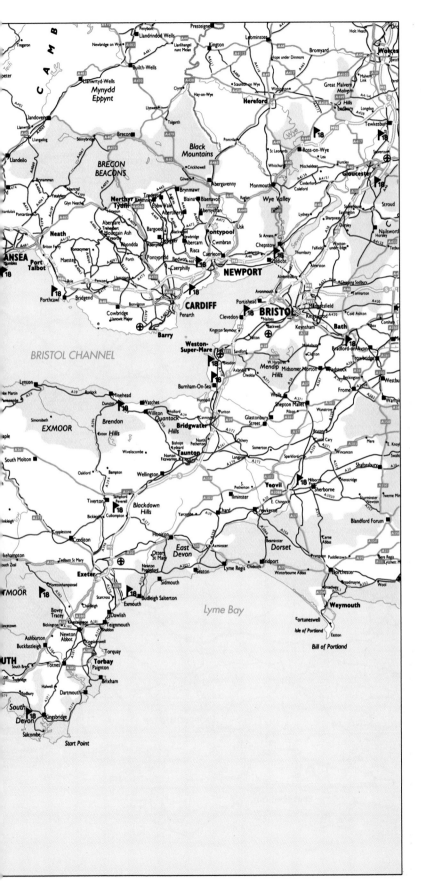

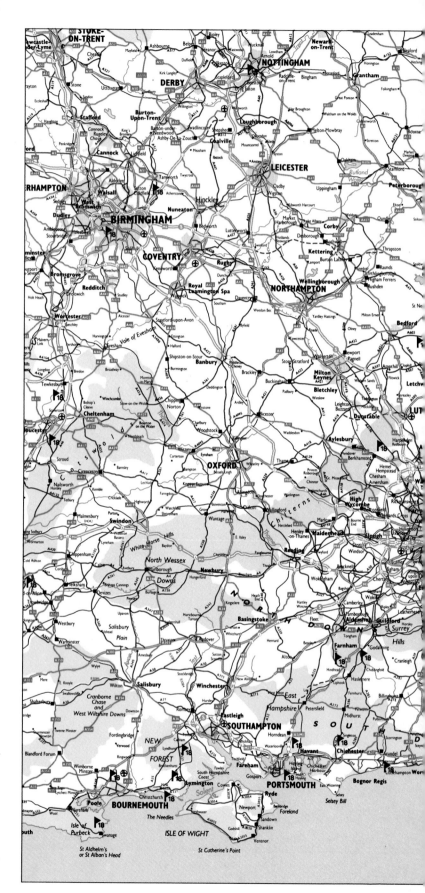

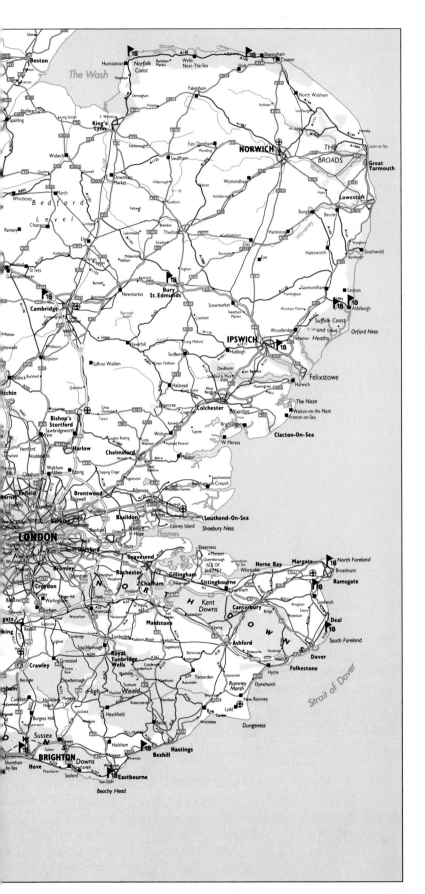

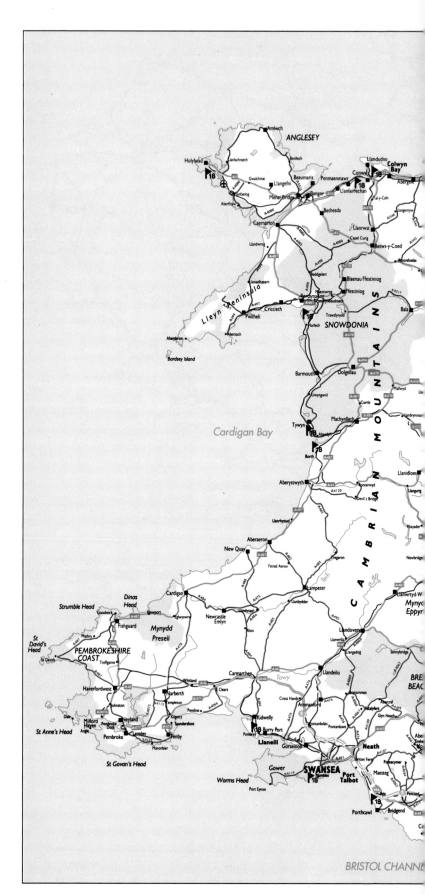

ANGLESEY

Amlwch

Llanfachraeth   Benllech

Holyhead   Llanfaelog

Gwalchmai   Llangefni   Beaumaris   Penmaenmawr

Aberffraw   Menai Bridge   Bangor   Llanfairfechan   Tal-y-Cafn

Caernarfon

Llandwrog

Llanaelhaearn

Lleyn Peninsula

Criccieth   Pwllheli

Penrhyndeudraeth   Porthmadog   Penrhyndeudraeth

Aberdaron   Abersoch   Harlech   SNOWDONIA

Bardsey Island

Barmouth   Dolgellau

Llwyngwril   Corris

Tywyn   Machynlleth

Aberdyfi

Borth

Cardigan Bay

Aberystwyth

Llanrhystud   Devil's Bridge

Aberaeron

New Quay   Ystrad Aeron   Tregaron

Lampeter

Cardigan   Llandysul   Llanybydder

Strumble Head   Dinas Head   Newport   Eglwyswrw   Newcastle Emlyn

Goodwick   Rhos

Fishguard   Mynydd Preseli   Llandovery

St David's Head   Mathry   Llanwrda   Llangadog

St David's   Treffgarne   Carmarthen   Llandeilo

PEMBROKESHIRE COAST   Towy

Haverfordwest   Whitland   Clears   Cross Hands   Ammanford

Johnston   Templeton   Pendine   Kidwelly

Dale   Narberth   Kilgetty   Burry Port   Gorseinon

Milford Haven   Neyland   Saundersfoot   Pembrey

St Anne's Head   Pembroke Dock   Tenby   Llanelli   Neath

Angle   Lamphey   SWANSEA   Port Talbot

Pembroke   Manorbier

St Govan's Head   Gower   Maesteg

Worms Head   Port Eynon   Porthcawl   Bridgend

CAMBRIAN MOUNTAINS

Blaenau Ffestiniog   Ffestiniog   Bala

Trawsfynydd

Llanidloes

Mallwyd   Llanbrynmair

Llandudno   Colwyn Bay   Abergele   Llangernyw

Conwy   Llanrwst   Betws-y-Coed   Pentrefoelas

Capel Curig

Beddgelert

BRISTOL CHANNEL

212

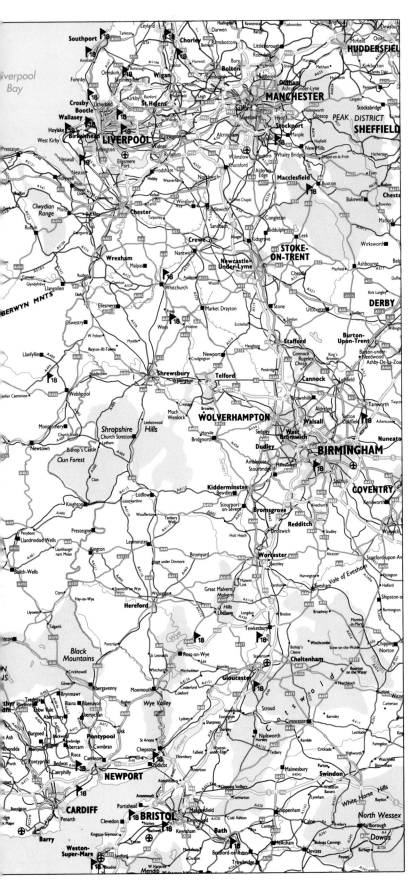

213

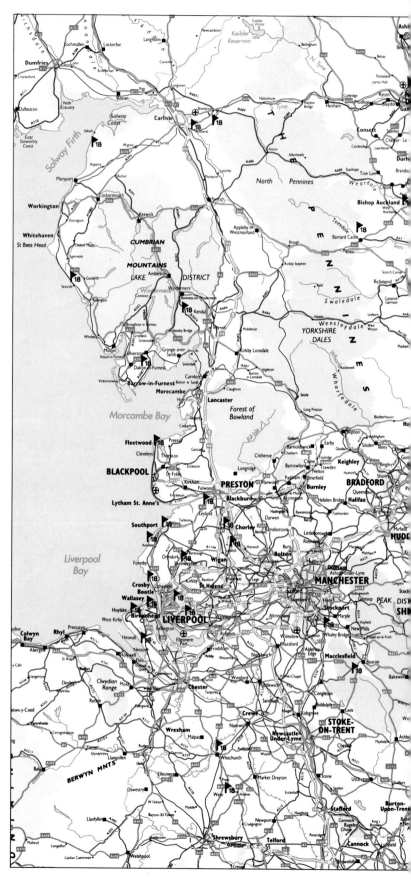

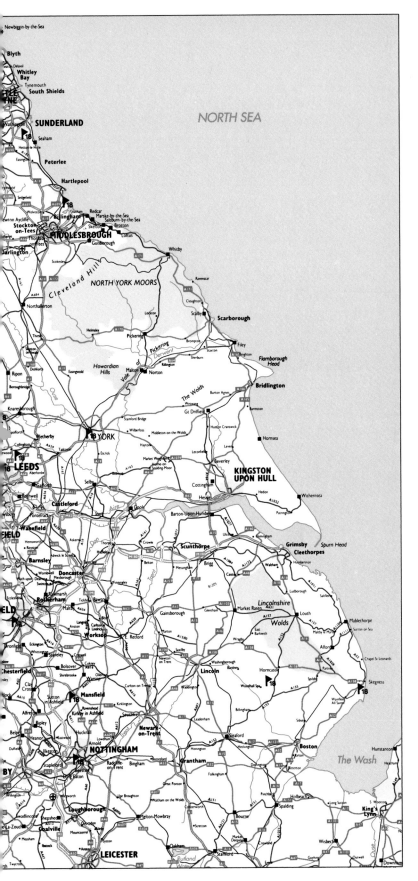

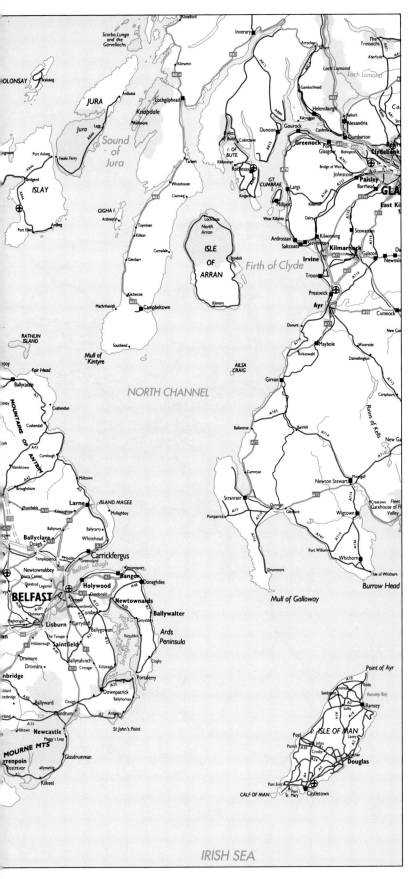

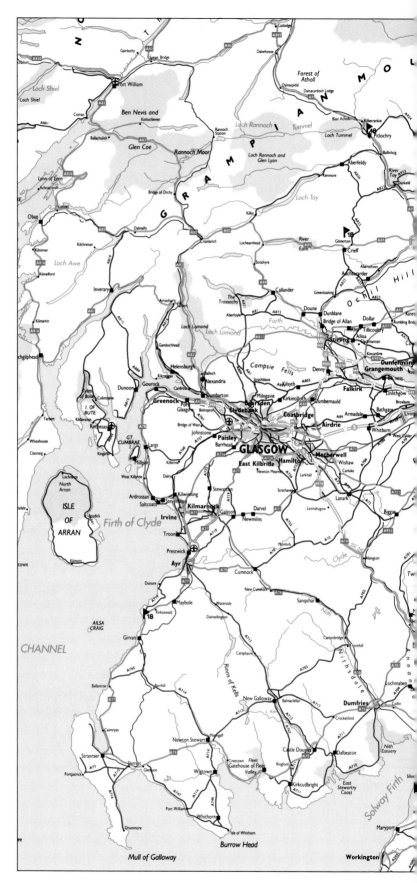

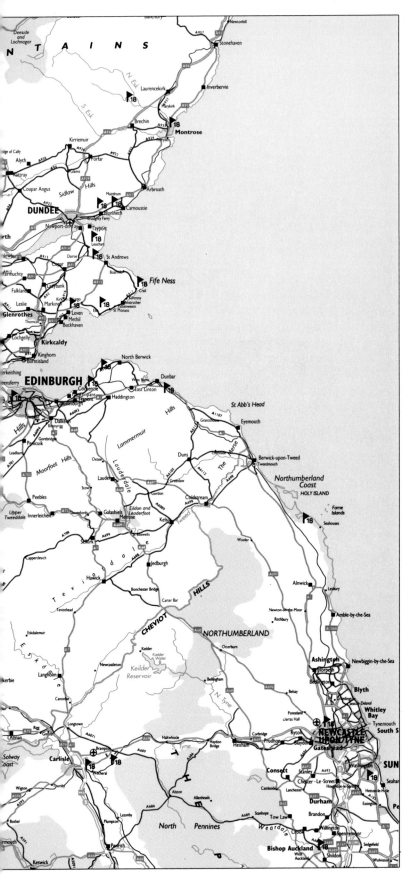

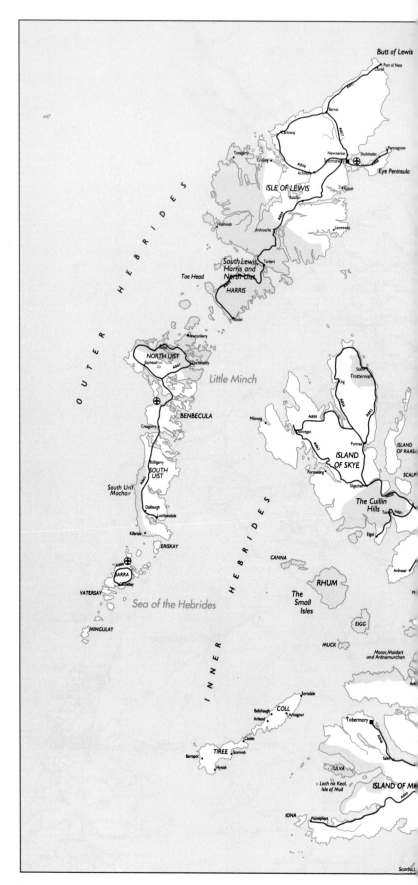

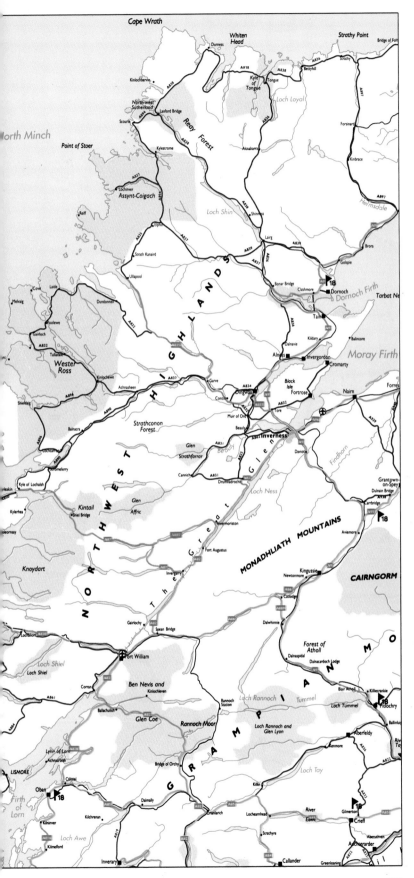

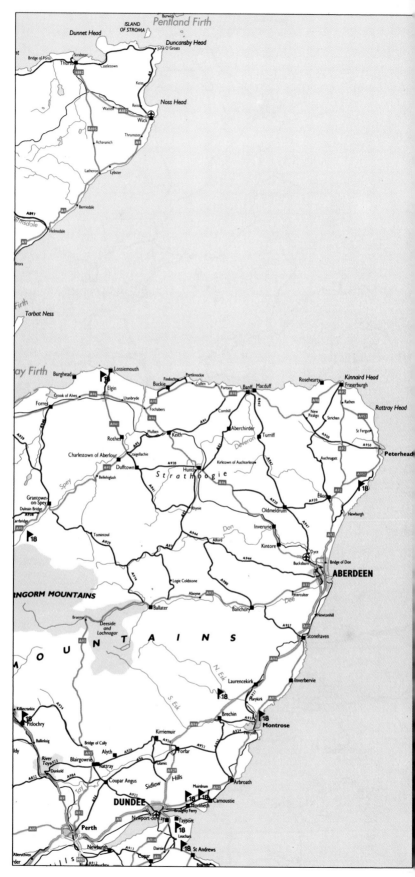

Pentland Firth

ISLAND OF STROMA
Burwick
Dunnet Head
Duncansby Head
John O'Groats
Bridge of Forss
Scrabster
Thurso
Castletown
Kerss
Watten
Reess
Noss Head
Achavanich
Thrumster
Wick

Latheron
Lybster

Berriedale
Helmsdale
Brora

Tarbat Ness

Moray Firth
Burghead
Lossiemouth
Findochty
Portknockie
Elgin
Buckie
Cullen
Portsoy
Banff
Macduff
Rosehearty
Kinnaird Head
Fraserburgh
Crook of Alves
Llanbryde
Fochabers
Cornhill
New Pitsligo
Rathen
Strichen
Rattray Head
Forres
Mulben
Keith
Aberchirder
Turriff
St Fergus
Rothes
Charlestown of Aberlour
Craigellachie
Dufftown
Huntly
Kirktown of Auchterless
Auchnagatt
Peterhead
Belliehiglash

Strathbogie

Deveron

Grantown-on-Spey
Dulnain Bridge
Carrbridge

Rhynie
Ellon
Newburgh

Tomintoul
Alford
Don
Inverurie
Kintore
Pyce
Bucksburn
Bridge of Don
ABERDEEN

CAIRNGORM MOUNTAINS
Braemar
Logie Coldstone
Aboyne
Ballater
Banchory
Dee
Peterculter
Newtonhill

Deeside and Lochnagar

M O U N T A I N S

Stonehaven

N Esk

Killiecrankie
Pitlochry
Laurencekirk
Inverbervie
Marykirk
Ballinluig
S Esk
Brechin
Trinity
Montrose

Bridge of Cally
Kirriemuir
Forfar

Alyth
Glamis

River Tay
Blairgowrie
Rattray
Dunkeld

Coupar Angus
Sidlaw Hills
Muirdrum
Arbroath

DUNDEE
Monifieth
Carnoustie
Newport-on-Tay
Broughty Ferry
Tayport
Perth
Leuchars

Newburgh
Darsie
St Andrews
Aberuthven
Cupar
Boarhills

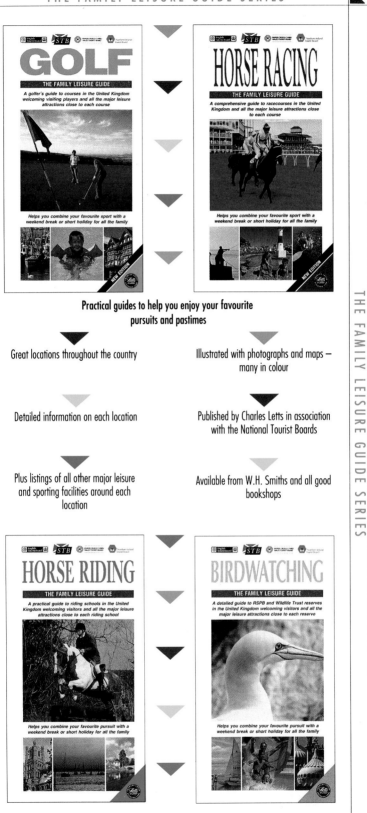

Practical guides to help you enjoy your favourite pursuits and pastimes

Great locations throughout the country

Detailed information on each location

Plus listings of all other major leisure and sporting facilities around each location

Illustrated with photographs and maps — many in colour

Published by Charles Letts in association with the National Tourist Boards

Available from W.H. Smiths and all good bookshops